# PERSON-CENTERED THERAPY: A REVOLUTIONARY PARADIGM

## JEROLD D. BOZARTH

**PCCS BOOKS**
Ross-on-Wye

First published in 1998
Reprinted 1999


PCCS BOOKS
Llangarron
Ross-on-Wye
Herefordshire
HR9 6PT
United Kingdom
Tel (01989) 77 07 07

**Person-Centered Therapy:
A Revolutionary Paradigm**

A CIP catalogue record for this book is available from the British Library

ISBN  1 898059 22 5




*Cover design by Denis Postle.*
*Printed by Redwood Books, Trowbridge, Wiltshire, United Kingdom*

# CONTENTS

# PREFACE

I have planned to write a book about the client-centered approach for over twenty years. However, the writings of Carl R. Rogers are so cogent and have been communicated so well that one more book has seemed presumptuous to this point. My belief is that Dr. Rogers' death in 1987 created a situation where distortions and misunderstandings of the approach have become exacerbated in the counseling and psychotherapy literature. Among other factors, the term of 'client-centered' versus the term of 'person-centered' has come to be viewed differently and conflictually by different authors and practitioners in the field. Some individuals view the person-centered approach as a catch-all term to identify therapies broadly compatible to client-centered therapy; such as, Person-Centered Gestalt, Gendlin's experiential therapy, and Human Relations Training.

Originally, Rogers used the term person-centered approach to identify the principles hypothesized in client-centered therapy as they might be implemented in other areas, such as education, business, groups and society. Texts that summarize counseling and psychotherapy now use the term, Person-Centered Therapy (Corey, 1990; Raskin and Rogers, 1989). This fact has practically made the argument about which term to use a moot point. I do not see much difference in the terms and agree with Rogers that there are no significant differences; i.e., that one does the same thing with a client in 'client-centered therapy' or in a group implementing the 'person-centered approach' (Rogers, 1987). Also, I tend to like the more egalitarian inference of the term, Person-Centered Therapy.

I concluded that Rogers never changed his theoretical stance as a therapist or his method of functioning (including response mode) as a therapist (Bozarth, 1990a; 1990b; 1991a). There was, nevertheless, more explicit attention given to the concept of therapist genuineness by Rogers after working with hospitalized 'psychotics' and after becoming involved in Basic Encounter Groups and large community groups. The principles and practice of Client-Centered Therapy are clarified by the term Person-Centered Therapy. The importance of the therapist's way of being is brought to the forefront by this term. Hence, I attempt to explicate the meaning of Person-Centered Therapy by examining some of the critical concepts associated with client-centered theory and with Rogers' contribution of the 'integration hypothesis' of the necessary and sufficient conditions.

This latter point concerning the integration hypothesis adds another complexity to Rogers' work. While re-examining Rogers' works, a colleague and I became acutely aware that the most prevalently considered statement of Rogers was not about client-centered therapy but about all therapies and all interpersonal relationships that have the intention of constructive personality change (Rogers, 1957). Most of Rogers' later work was focused on these core qualities of therapeutic effectiveness and not upon client-centered theory (Stubbs and Bozarth, 1996).

In addition, I have been frustrated with what I believe are gross misunderstandings and distortions of Rogers' ideas that seem to be based on the failure of well meaning individuals to understand or assimilate the concept that the client, not the therapist, knows what is best about his or her life. Students, particularly, are misled to view the person-centered approach from the stance of human relations training programs or are informed that the approach is only a pre-requisite to therapist interventions and strategies for the client. The overwhelming conclusion of over four decades of psychotherapy outcome research is virtually ignored by academicians, training supervisors and clinical practitioners (Duncan and Moynihan, 1994; Bohart and Tallman, 1996; Stubbs and Bozarth, 1994). This research clearly identifies the relationship between the therapist and client, and the resources of the client as accounting for seventy per cent of successful outcome.

I have practised the person-centered approach in therapy, small groups, large groups, administration, education and in life in general for over forty years. I learned the approach from clients while working with long term chronic 'psychotics' in state mental hospitals during the late nineteen-fifties and early nineteen-sixties. At the time, I had not learned the party line of many academicians and clinicians that this approach 'would not work' with individuals who were in 'psychotic' states of dysfunction. The professional hospital staff often assured me that nothing would help these 'psychotic' and 'institutionalized' individuals to function outside of the hospital. As it turned out, many of these individuals improved significantly to the point of reasonable self-sufficiency outside of the hospital. My observations of this improvement were buttressed by the hard evidence of reduced recidivism rates, functional employment, independent living, and self evaluations. It was this experience that encouraged me to gravitate towards studying and exploring the person-centered approach.

I associated as much as possible with those individuals who studied with Rogers at the University of Chicago; I was a participant and, later, presenter and facilitator at the La Jolla Program (which included client-centered community group experiences); I participated in encounter and community groups with Rogers and his various colleagues each summer since 1974 to his death in 1987; I worked on major research and developed training programs for the interpersonal skills training that was designed to investigate and develop therapists' embodiment of Rogers' hypothesized conditions for constructive therapeutic change. For most of my professional career, I taught graduate students of counseling and psychology at universities in several States. I was an educational administrator much of this time. My interest in Rogers' hypothesized conditions for constructive personality change ranged across my work as an administrator, therapist, group facilitator, instructor, rehabilitation counselor, researcher and investigator of societal change. These experiences have all added to my view of Person-Centered Therapy as a greater crystallization of the basic theory of Carl R. Rogers.

Jerold D. Bozarth
June 1998

**The Essence of Client-Centered Therapy
and the Philosophy of the Person Centered Approach**

J. D. Bozarth

## THE VALIDITY OF THE MOMENT

I know not what you will do or become
at this moment or beyond;
I know not what I will do except stay with you
at this moment
And be mother, father, sister, brother, friend, child, and lover
at this moment;
I exist for you and with you
at this moment;
I give you all of me
at this moment;
I am you
at this moment;
Take me and use me
at this moment
to be whatever you can become
at this moment and beyond.

# Acknowledgements

I would like to thank the publishers, book editors and co-authors for giving me their permission to use previously published articles. I appreciate David Cain's permission to use any of my articles published in the *Person-Centered Review*.

Co-authors of several of the articles used as chapters are Barbara Brodley, Ann Glauser (Shanks), Sam Mitchell, and Jeanne Stubbs (Laura Jeanne Maher) who supported me in many ways beyond being co-authors. I owe special appreciation to Dr. Jeanne P. Stubbs who encouraged me to compile some of my writings and ideas. She also started the writing process by obtaining permission from many of the publishers in order that I might use some of my previous publications in full or partial form. She, more than anyone, encouraged and engaged me to write this book. She reminded me that our 'castles in the sky' are the substance of our realities. My dream of writing this book became the reality that might otherwise never have occurred. The editorial attention and idea clarification provided by Cheryl Forkner and Ching Wah Lo was extremely valuable in helping me clarify difficult areas of understanding. Robert Oppenheimer helped me to identify and assimilate an inner truth; that is, that all shortcomings of acceptance are from within. The reflections and suggestions of Susan Pildes on several of the chapters and concerning many of my ideas provided important constructive input. Likewise, Elizabeth Strickler provided continuous encouragement and constructive review of particular chapters.

The intense constructive critical review by Sharon Mier helped me to put the book in the format which I felt would be worthwhile to publish. Sheila Haugh and Gill Wyatt helped me considerably in my deliberations concerning Rogers' concept of congruence. Gill Wyatt's editorial help and challenging questions resulted in additional clarification of many of the chapters. Majella McElwee's pragmatic sensitivity brought me to new understandings. David Spahn often stimulated and clarified many of my ideas and always offered new and refreshing ways to view complex phenomena. My daughter, Amy Bozarth Shenkel helped to format and put my poor grammar and punctuation into readable form. She was, also, an inspiration to many of my thoughts about therapy. My wife, Mary Lou, put up with me in my absorption of theory, ideas and sometimes strange behaviors. Moreover, she supported me in my quest in a different paradigm and often grounded me in the realities of the world and life.

There are also individuals who indirectly encouraged, inspired or challenged me to write this book. These individuals are the late Leonard A. Miller, Kevin M. Mitchell, Rudyard n. Propst (who initially introduced me to the client-centered approach), and Charles B. Truax. Others who influenced my thinking are Ralph Roberts, Guy Renzaglia, John Muthard, and C. H. Patterson. Richard Page often stimulated me with our discussions of therapy and interpersonal relationships. Several colleagues who were with Rogers at the University of Chicago often encouraged me to pursue my ideas concerning client-centered theory. Nat Raskin, John Shlien, Fred Zimring and Barbara Brodley were especially influential. I am indebted to the thinking and support given to me by Bruce Meador, Doug Land, and Bill Coulson when I attended and participated often in the La Jolla program. Bob Lee took me on the search to 'know' and to not be afraid. A binding thread was established with Jim Bowman and Chuck Stuart in a La Jolla program in 1975. Likewise, the La Jolla program was my connection with Reinhard Tausch who has always been an available consultant, facilitator and friend. John K. Wood lent me his sharp facilitative style with short phrases, paused silences and long dialogues that enabled me to get over blocks in my struggles. Carl Rogers genius and perceptions have greatly contributed to my perceptions of therapy and of life.

Many students provided me with support and constructive challenge over the years. Several previous students were the substance of the person-centered workshop started at Warm Springs Roosevelt Center in 1987. Paula Bickham, Dottie Coleman, Doug Bower, Jo Cohen, Ann Glauser, and Ed Glauser were a few of the students who now continue their professional contributions in person-centered ways.

In a different way, I acknowledge my late parents and grandparents who always treated me with unconditional positive regard. My grandmother, Freda Cose, was my greatest therapist. My sisters, Joyce and Karen, were also always supportive and there for me whenever I needed them. My seven month old granddaughter, Bridgett, represents the future and the inspiration for whatever contribution I might make to society. My greatest inspiration for this book has been Caitlin Bozarth, my seven year old granddaughter, who represents to me the youthful attitudinal quality of unconditional positive regard.

I thank the readers of this book for your patience with redundancy and repetition of some of the core concepts and basic material repeated in several chapters. Since most chapters correspond to previous articles or book chapters which I have written, core concepts and basic materials are repeated in various chapters. For example, Rogers' basic theory is summarized in different ways; and Rogers' necessary and sufficient conditions are summarized more than a couple of times. Some of this material was deleted or reduced in some chapters but left as it was in others. This was a dilemma to me because (1) I hoped to some extent for each chapter to stand by itself for those who would want to use the chapters as free standing papers and (2) I believe that the core of Rogers' message bears constant repetition because of its radical and revolutionary content.

At times, my frustrations and annoyance with the failure of scholars and practitioners in the profession of counseling and psychotherapy to understand or assimilate or accurately acknowledge Rogers' revolutionary ideas come to the forefront. I chose, for the most part, not to mellow these congruent expressions. Such expressions are not meant to denigrate individuals but rather to allow myself the freedom of being all of myself in this venture.

Finally, I offer special thanks to the publishers, Pete and Maggie Sanders and to Tony Merry for their support, editing, ideas and guidance. Tony Merry provided special support as an editorial reviewer for the publisher. I am pleased that he is the series editor of this book and of the upcoming books of other authors.

Jerold D. Bozarth

This book is dedicated to my daughter Amy, in whom I have observed the resilience of the actualizing tendency; to my seven year old granddaughter, Caitlin, who represents the youthful attitudinal embodiment of unconditional positive regard, and to my seven month old granddaughter, Bridgette Rose, in her search for self in being and becoming. And to my six month old grandson, Edward (Ned) Parker, who struggled to enter the world symbolizing the hope for human survival.

# THE THEORY AND PHILOSOPHY

# Overview of Person-Centered Therapy

1

This chapter provides an overview of person-centered therapy by focusing on the essence of this therapeutic approach. The emphasis of the chapter is upon the practicality of the therapist's 'being' as a therapist rather than upon what the therapist should 'do'. The therapist's actions emerge from the underlying attitudes of this way of being.

Five decades of psychotherapy outcome research now clearly identify the factors that contribute to successful client outcome. The factors of the client/therapist relationship and the client's internal and external resources (extratherapeutic variables) account for seventy-percent of success (Duncan, Hubble, and Miller, 1997). These are the variables that are the foundation of person-centered therapy. Further, there is, proposed in the literature, a treatment model based upon psychotherapy research that, in my view unrealized by the authors, is substantially the person-centered model (Duncan and Moynihan, 1994).

I predominately use the term person-centered therapy rather than client-centered therapy in order to emphasize the remarkable resiliency and self-resources of persons entering therapy. The term also suggests greater behavioral flexibility for the therapist than is often mistakenly associated with the term client-centered therapy. I maintain that the two labels are not different and that both terms refer to the theory proposed by Carl Rogers. Periodically, the terms are used interchangeably in this book. The term person-centered therapy represents to me a re-birth of Rogers' remarkable trust of each individual's potency for self-determination and self-authority.

### Lack of understanding and/or assimilation
Client-centered (or 'person-centered') therapy has not been understood or assimilated by most current scholars and practitioners of psychotherapy. The fundamental reason for this pervasive lack of understanding seems, at least in

Adapted with permission from:
Bozarth, J. D. (1990a). The Essence of Client-Centered Therapy. In Lietaer, G., Rombauts, J. and Van Balen, R. (eds.) *Client-Centered and Experiential Psychotherapy in the Nineties* , pp. 59-64. Leuven: Leuven University Press.

part, to be due to most therapists' perceptual stance that the therapist is the expert who appropriately intervenes to help the client resolve problems. Rogers' revolutionary stance that identifies the client as his or her best expert about his or her life is not well understood or assimilated by even the most brilliant scholars in the field of psychotherapy. For example, Arnold Lazarus believes that the 'necessary and sufficient conditions' for therapeutic personality change posited by Rogers is 'usually' the 'soil' for preparing appropriate intervention by the therapist (Lazarus, 1992). Another author suggests that there is no one set of necessary and sufficient conditions and that various interventions are needed at various times for various clients (Norcross, 1992). Others have consistently resounded the same theme; i.e., that the conditions may be necessary but are seldom sufficient (Fay and Lazarus, 1992; Norcross, 1992, Quinn, 1993). Authors exemplify the failures to understand Rogers' position when they refer to the attitudinal qualities as being preparatory for 'interventions' by the therapist.

### The revolutionary thrust

The revolutionary crux of Rogers' theory is that the therapist does not intervene and has no intention of intervening. The basic position is that the therapist trusts the actualizing tendency of the client and truly believes that the client who experiences the freedom of a fostering psychological climate will resolve his or her own problems. Person-centered therapy can not be adequately understood when viewing it from the framework of other theories, which have different basic assumptions. The potency of the approach can not be fully realized if the trust of the client by the therapist is short-circuited with interventions and with the therapist's ideas of what is 'really' best for the client. The therapy developed by Carl Rogers must be understood within the context of the theory he espoused.

Most critiques of Rogers' theory are indicative of a particular process and position taken by authors to criticize the theory and hypothesis (Bozarth, 1995). The process is, in essence, that of dismissing the fundamental assumptions of the approach (of the actualizing tendency and the self-authority of the client) as untenable or questionable and proceeding with criticism of the theory from other theoretical frames of reference. The position taken is embedded to varying degrees in the assumption that the therapist is the expert for the treatment and behavior change of the client. Hence, their theoretical argument is a shift in the meaning and understanding of Rogers' theory. Others exemplify the inaccuracy of viewing Rogers' theory from the perspective of different frameworks when they conclude that Rogers is suggesting a ' . . . unitary case formulation and universal treatment plan' and that Rogers ' . . . violates the principle of tailor-making the therapy to the needs of the patient' (Norcross, 1992, p. 8; Fay and Lazarus, 1992, p. abstract).

The perceptual stance of these authors that the clinician is an artful director of prescriptive matching for tailor-making treatment to the individual, is so radically different from Rogers' assumption of the client knowing what is best in his or her life that they have an ironic misunderstanding of person-centered therapy. They somehow do not understand that the practice of person-centered therapy is focused on individual differences and not predicated on ' . . . doing something to the client that is predetermined by an authoritative therapist who takes responsibility for the treatment and behavior of the client' (Bozarth, 1991a, p. 467). The experiencing of certain attitudes towards a person is not the same as prescribing ' . . . relationship stances and technical interventions for each situation . . .' (Norcross, 1992, p. 8). Fay and Lazarus are replete in their amazement of a different way of relating to people when they sarcastically state: ' . . . if Rogers were correct, there would be no point in bothering to learn any specific techniques - be warm, genuine, congruent and empathic and establish a good therapeutic alliance – period' (p. 3). Ironically, this is essentially correct. What one does, as a person-centered therapist, is what emerges in the relationship with the client. It is partly allowing the person the freedom to find his or her own ways of dealing with their problems by being in and accepting the client's perception of the world; hence, creating an atmosphere of unconditional positive regard. In the context of person-centered theory, it is creating an atmosphere of unconditional positive regard that enables the person to develop unconditional positive self-regard and, subsequently, to resolve his or her specific problems. The theory is not one that applies certain conditions the way one applies dosages of drugs to a person in an effort to finalize a treatment plan. The therapy is a human endeavour that trusts the growth of each individual, and wherein the therapist resonates in person-to-person ways.

Clinical research with 'impossible cases' and the conclusions of psychotherapy outcome research for the past five decades concur with the propositions of person-centered therapy (Duncan, Hubble and Miller, 1997; Duncan and Moynihan, 1994). The client/ therapist relationship and the resources of the client are the paramount concerns. Duncan, *et al.*, parallel the dedication of the person-to-person resonance of person-centered therapy as they summarized their work with 'impossible cases' along side the conclusions of psychotherapy outcome research. They state: 'Now we honor more simple but enduring acts: validating our clients' resources, courting their positive experience of therapy and honoring their theory of change . . .' (p. 33).

### Overview of person-centered therapy

This section offers an overview of the theory of client-centered therapy which I, along with Rogers, believe is the same as person-centered therapy (Rogers, 1987). I believe that the terms client-centered therapy and person-centered therapy are inter-changeable. The theories developed by Rogers are the same basic assumptions for either label. However, the term person-centered therapy implies that the therapist might be more flexible in what he or she does while being dedicated to the client's world. I contend that this is also the case for client-centered therapy. However, the label of client-centered therapy has become inaccurately associated with a particular response system. This response system is often referred to as 'reflection' or 'reflection of feelings'. The empathic understanding response style is grounded in Rogers' ideas but also too often results in a focus on the therapist's specific responses (Brodley, 1994). This is a response style that, in my opinion, was a natural idiosyncratic way of responding by Rogers and one that was promoted by the logical positivistic research of therapy interactions undertaken by Rogers and his colleagues at the University of Chicago in the 1950s.

### The foundation

The foundation block of person-centered therapy is the actualizing tendency. Rogers stated:

> Practice, theory and research make it clear that the person-centered approach is built on a basic trust in the person . . . (It) depends on the actualizing tendency present in every living organism's tendency to grow, to develop, to realize its full potential. This way of being trusts the constructive directional flow of the human being toward a more complex and complete development. It is this directional flow that we aim to release.
>
> (Rogers, 1986b, p. 198)

Rogers' construct of the actualizing tendency is an organismic theory wherein the fundamental qualities in human nature are viewed as those of growth, process and change. In Rogers' theory, 'Man is an actualizing process' (Van Belle, 1980, p. 70). Actualization is the motivational construct in organismic theory and, thus, is embedded in the organismic growth process and is the motive for change. The organism/person is the basic unit of inquiry in Rogers' conceptualizations. Although Rogers focused on the self-concept in earlier writings and brings in the concept of the formative tendency of the universe in later writings, the construct of the actualizing tendency for the human being is the clear foundation block in individual therapy.

The person-centered therapist operates on a number of assumptions associated with the actualizing tendency. These assumptions include the orientation that emphasizes the world of the whole person wherein the therapist eschews knowledge 'about' the client, relates as an equal to the client, and trusts and respects the client's perceptions as the authority about him/herself. The basic client/person-centered value is that the authority of the person rests in the person rather than in an outside expert. This value emphasizes the internal (i.e., the client's) rather than the external (i.e., the therapist's) view. Clients are viewed as going in their own ways, allowed to go at their own pace, and to pursue their growth in their unique ways. The external view is meaningless in the therapy process since the only function of the therapist is to facilitate the client's actualizing process. This process is a directional, growth directed process that includes movement towards realization, fulfilment and perfection of inherent capabilities and potentialities of the individual (Rogers, 1963). It is a selective process in that it is directional and constructive. It tends to enhance and maintain the whole organism/person. A summary of the theory can be stated as follows:

1) There is one motivating force in a client; i.e., the actualizing tendency.

2) There is one directive to the therapist; i.e. to embody the attitudinal quality Of genuineness and to experience empathic understanding from the client's internal frame of reference and to experience unconditional positive regard towards the client.
3) When the client perceives the therapist's empathic understanding and unconditional positive regard, the actualizing tendency of the client is promoted.

### Necessary and sufficient conditions

Person-centered theory posits the presence of a client who is incongruent, vulnerable and anxious but who is also in psychological contact with an attentive, empathic therapist. The therapist experiences and manifests three basic attitudes in the relationship. These attitudes are labeled as (1) congruence, (2) unconditional positive regard, and (3) empathic understanding of the client's internal frame of reference (Rogers, 1957; 1959). Rogers' most explicit statements about these attitudes were in his 1957 statement that hypothesized the necessary and sufficient conditions of therapeutic personality change in all therapies and constructive interpersonal relationships that have constructive personality change as a goal. These conditions are also presented with a slightly different slant in his 1959 theoretical statement on psychotherapy, personality theory and interpersonal relations from the client-centered frame of reference. In the integration statement of 1957, he stated:

1. Two persons are in psychological contact.
2. The first, whom we shall term the client, is in a state of incongruence, being vulnerable or anxious.
3. The second person, whom we shall term the therapist, is congruent or integrated in the relationship.
4. The therapist experiences unconditional positive regard for the client.
5. The therapist experiences an empathic understanding of the client's internal frame of reference and endeavours to communicate this experience to the client.
6. The communication to the client of the therapist's empathic understanding and unconditional positive regard is to a minimal degree achieved. (p. 96)

There are slight but perhaps important differences between the 1957 and 1959 statements. In the 1959 statement, Rogers did not mention that the therapist should '. . . endeavour to communicate . . .' the experiences of empathic understanding and unconditional positive regard to the client. He continued to emphasize the importance of the client perceiving these two attitudinal experiences of the therapist. Also, the 1959 theory statement refers to the first condition (the pre-condition) simply as 'contact' between the client and therapist rather than 'psychological' contact.

Rogers' (1957) definitions of the three attitudinal conditions are the following:

• Congruency (or genuineness): '. . .within the relationship (the therapist) is freely and deeply himself, with his actual experience accurately represented by his awareness of himself . . .' and '. . . he is what he actually is, in this moment of time . . .'
• Unconditional Positive Regard: '. . .the extent that the therapist finds himself experiencing a warm acceptance of each aspect of the client's experience as being a part of that client . . .'
• Empathic Understanding: 'To sense the client's private world as if it were your own, but without ever losing the 'as if' quality . . .'(pp. 95-103)

The particular manifestations or implementation of these attitudes are variable, within limits, depending upon the personal characteristics of both the therapist and the client.  Rogers, in his classic delineation of a theory of psychotherapy, personality and interpersonal relationships in 1959, hypothesized that in the psychotherapeutic relationship the more fully and consistently the therapeutic attitudes are provided by the therapist and perceived by the client, the greater the constructive movement that will occur in the client. Rogers' hypothesis can be generally stated in the following way:

When the therapist can consistently be a certain way (i.e., embodying the attitudinal qualities) towards the client while trusting the client's natural growth process, the forward growth tendency (the actualizing tendency) of the client will be promoted.

The natural growth process of the individual is promoted when the therapist can be a certain way by embodying certain attitudinal qualities. The therapist strives to be congruent, to experience unconditional positive regard and empathic understanding toward the client. It is interesting to note that Rogers' message is that the therapist experience empathic understanding of the client's frame of reference and experience unconditional positive regard towards the client. He adds that the client must perceive these two conditions, at least, to a minimal degree. In therapy, the foundation block of the theory is the actualizing tendency; i.e., the tendency of the organism to grow in a positive and constructive direction; for the person '. . . to become all of his/her potentialities' (Bozarth and Brodley, 1991). Put another way: when the therapist can be a certain way by embodying certain attitudinal qualities, then the client's actualizing tendency is promoted.  In addition, the self-actualizing tendency is promoted in a way that is harmonious with the experiencing of the actualizing organism.

### The essence of person-centered therapy

The essence (the basic nature and the basic core) of person-centered therapy is predicated upon the clients' authority of their own lives (Bozarth, 1990a). After examining the results of the Bower study, examining the evolution of Carl Rogers as a therapist and from an analysis of Rogers' writings, the essence of the approach is defined as follows (Bower and Bozarth, 1988):

The essence of person-centered therapy is the therapist's dedication to going with the client's direction, at the client's pace and in the client's unique way of being. (p.59)

And:

It is the full commitment '. . .to trust in the client's own way of going about dealing with his problems and his life.'

(Brodley, 1988a, p.15 )

The following points summarize findings that contribute to this conclusion: First, the Bower study which is a qualitative study of six notable person-centered therapists doing therapy. Three listeners independently reviewed an audiotape of each therapist's therapy sessions. The therapist and client participants responded to questions from the investigator. The emerging consensual data were the following:

1. Therapists had a wide repertoire of non-interfering responses. One therapist responded in a reflective way, with near intrusive reflective responses; another rarely commented, and then only in a way to clarify his uncertainties; another therapist was described as seductive by the listeners; another used a Gestalt-type metaphor that emerged from the client; and another therapist periodically 'moaned' throughout the session.
2. The clients perceived the therapists as being helpful; overall, the clients directed themselves in the process of inquiry. At times, they waited for the therapists to finish responses before continuing with their own explorations. In short, the therapists were experienced as being received by clients as permission-giving humans whose specific responses did not seem to interfere with the clients' directions.
3. The listeners perceived the therapists as disappearing in deference to their clients. They were experienced as being a 'shadow to the client'. Their presence appeared obvious but there was neither intervention nor intrusion of the personality of the therapist (Bower and Bozarth, 1988).

The overriding conclusion was that client-centered/person-centered therapists were experienced (by clients, listeners, and therapists) as non-interfering individuals who entered the world of the client in such a manner as to 'disappear' into the client's own process of development (Bower and Bozarth, 1988).

In brief, the study also suggested that: (1) The attitudinal qualities of empathy, unconditional positive regard, and congruence (described in various ways) were the consistent therapist attitudes that existed; (2) The therapists held a position of total trust in the client's own direction and way; (3) The therapists were active and involved with a total dedication towards understanding the client's world; (4) The therapists had a wide range of response repertoire and personality characteristics but were intent upon understanding and checking their understandings of their clients; and (5) The therapists did not attempt to intervene in the direction, process, or with the pace of the clients.

The therapists were actively involved and readily dialogued with their clients but 'disappeared' into the client's process.

## Analysis of the evolution of Carl Rogers as a therapist

My examination of Carl Rogers' evolution as a therapist is a qualitative inquiry to two questions (Bozarth, 1990b). These questions are: (1) Did Carl Rogers alter his fundamental views of client-centered therapy? and, (2) Did Carl Rogers change his operational functioning as a psychotherapist? It was my intent to further ask: What were these alterations? And, what changes occurred? My basic thought had been that there was significant alteration of some fundamental views; and that his functioning as a therapist had changed over the years.

My assessment of Rogers' comments in the literature, his demonstration films, and from previous personal communication led me to conclude that Carl Rogers did not alter his fundamental views of client-centered therapy. I noted that he was quite consistent in his fundamental views of the importance of the conditions of empathy and unconditional positive regard that congruent therapists needed to experience with their clients, and of his dedication to go with his clients in the direction that the client wanted to go and in the way the client wished to do it. He became more explicit about the importance of being 'genuine' in the relationship. The importance of genuineness (which Rogers periodically interchanged with congruence) as the primary condition to him was expressed in a dialogue with Wood and in an earlier statement when he commented that even when the conditions of unconditional positive regard and empathy were not experienced by the therapist that genuineness alone may be facilitative (Rogers and Sanford, 1984). His more explicit references to the importance of genuineness in the relationship did not represent any fundamental change in view. He was always dedicated to and intent on going with the client's direction, at the client's pace, and with the client's unique way of being (Bozarth, 1990b).

My assessment of Rogers' functioning as a therapist by reviewing demonstration films with Miss Mun, Gloria, and Kathy led me to conclude that Carl Rogers did not change his operational functioning as a psychotherapist (Rogers, 1980; Rogers and Segal, 1955; Shostrom, 1964). He did express a slightly wider range of responses over the twenty year period in the demonstration films; and had some spontaneous expressions that 'bubbled up', especially in the Gloria film. A qualitative evaluation of Rogers' response sets in the three films indicate Rogers' primary responses to be empathic understanding responses. The categories representing empathic understanding responses were identified as a 'continue frame' representing 'I am giving you my full attention, please continue'; and a check frame meaning, 'This is what I understand you to be saying. The analysis revealed: 100% of the responses in 1955 were check or continue responses (including empathic understanding responses); 90% of the responses in 1965 were continue or check responses (the few declarative responses were the notable responses often referred to in the Gloria film); 84% of the responses were continue or check responses in 1975 (Bozarth, 1990b).

Dr. Brodley's examination of eight of Rogers' interviews from the 1940s to late 1985 using a comparable evaluation scheme revealed that in seven of them 91% to 100% of Dr. Rogers' responses were empathic following responses (Brodley, 1988). The session consisting of 100% empathic following responses was the one in late 1985. Other research has confirmed this finding (Brodley, 1993).

Overall it seems accurate to say that Rogers increasingly referred to the importance of genuineness when working with clients and that 'realness' of the therapist was increasingly important in his thinking. He responded with slightly more varied comments over the twenty-year time span of the demonstration tapes but his preponderant response efforts were clearly geared to the understanding of his clients' worlds - whether in 1955, 1965, or 1985. Carl Rogers' fundamental views of person-centered therapy were not altered. He did not significantly change his operational functioning as a psychotherapist (Bozarth, 1990b).

A more holistic viewing of the films and tapes was interpreted as suggesting that Rogers allowed himself to be more expressive over the years. It also seems likely that his varied comments as a therapist over the time period were more client- and situation-specific. It became clearer to me that whatever Rogers said about person-centered therapy or did as a therapist was within the context of placing his trust in his clients without doing anything to them or 'being up to something' as a therapist.

These two examinations, firstly, of six notable person-centered therapists and secondly, of the evolution of Carl Rogers as a therapist, support Rogers' explicit statements about person-centered therapy; i.e., that the foundation block of the therapy is the actualizing tendency (Rogers, 1980); that '. . . it is the client who knows what hurts, what directions to go, what problems are crucial. It would do better to rely upon the client for the direction of movement in the process' (cited in Kirschenbaum, 1979, P. 89). He had a profound and unwavering dedication to trusting the client as his/her own best authority.

These reviews lead me to conclude with a functional theoretical premise: that the essence of person-centered therapy is the therapist's dedication to going with the client's direction, at the client's pace, and with the client's unique way of being.

## Implications of the essence of person-centered therapy

The implications of the essence of person-centered therapy are that it is a functional premise that precludes other therapist intentions. The therapist goes with the client, goes at the client's pace, goes with the client in his/her own ways of thinking, of experiencing, of processing. The therapist can not be up to other things, have other intentions without violating the essence of person-centered therapy. To be up to other things – whatever they might be – is a 'yes, but' reaction to the essence of the approach. It must mean that when the therapist has intentions of treatment plans, of treatment goals, of interventive strategies to get the client somewhere or for the client to do a certain thing, the therapist violates the essence of person-centered therapy. This holds true if the therapist is trying to move the client through a certain process, to encourage clients to experience themselves in a certain way, to teach clients to be empathic, or to impose other therapeutic methods on the client. It is a functional premise that includes wide therapist personality differences, unique ways of doing things, and idiosyncratic ways of responding as far as they are dedicated to the client's direction, the client's pace, and the client's unique way of being (Bozarth, 1984). It is a functional premise that begets therapists who ascribe to Rogers' principles to test the essence of the approach in a consistent way over time. It is thus that therapists can experience the potency of allowing individuals to engage in their own empowerment, in their own ways without being violated by the personal observations and theories of their therapists.

Implications of this theoretical stance are integrally related to the concept of the locus of control. The therapist is promoting a natural individual and general process in the client by being a certain way; that is, experiencing certain attitudes toward the client. The client is his/her own best expert about him/her self and his/her life. The therapist's intent is not to promote feelings or to help the client to become more independent or 'to get' the client anywhere. The goal is not self-actualization, actualization, independence or to help the client to become a 'fully functioning' person. The only therapist goal is to be a certain way and by being that way a natural growth process is promoted in the client. The foundation of person-centered therapy is consistent with the five decades of findings in psychotherapy outcome research and over ten years of clinical research with impossible clients. That is, the person of the client must be the master and director for successful outcome.

The remaining chapters in this book examine person-centered therapy from the perspective of this radically different paradigmatic approach to counseling and psychotherapy.

# Carl Rogers: Theoretical Evolution and Professional Contributions

2

Carl Rogers' life, contributions and theory have been extensively reviewed in several well written works (Evans, 1975; Kirschenbaum, 1979; Kirschenbaum and Henderson, 1989a, 1989b; Thorne, 1991; Van Belle, 1980). This chapter reviews the evolution of Rogers' professional contributions in relation to the expanding application of the principles of the approach.

Rogers identified a particular incident in therapy as the most prominent single event that symbolized the advent of client-centered therapy (Rogers, 1977). He described working with a young boy in a child and family guidance clinic. As part of the treatment, he tried desperately to help the mother understand her involvement in exacerbating the boy's psychological problems. Finally, Rogers noted that he simply did not think that he could further help the boy and told the mother that they needed to terminate therapy. As the woman reached the door, she turned saying to Rogers: 'Do you ever take adults for counseling here?' (Rogers, 1987, p. 48). Rogers' account was that the woman poured out her frustrations, problems and involvement with her son's problems. It was at this time that Rogers experienced with exceptional impact the therapeutic potency of understanding the other person's internal perception of the world.

Rogers' initial presentation of his theory apparently took place at the University of Minnesota on December 11, 1940, when he discussed a 'new' approach to psychotherapy (Kirschenbaum, 1979, p.112). It was controversial but captured the attention of both the clinical and academic communities. Later, Rogers acquired professional visibility by developing the theoretical foundations and completing a host of empirical investigations on psychotherapy process and outcome at the University of Chicago. It was here that he wrote the initial books on his theory, first focused upon as Nondirective Therapy and, later, as Client-Centered Therapy (Rogers, 1942; 1951). Nondirective Therapy emphasized the therapist's reliance on the clients' self resources and capacity to find their own solutions for personal change and upon the therapist as a midwife who followed the individual's direction. Misunderstandings of 'nondirectivity', however, equated the therapy as passive and the therapist as uninvolved. This led Rogers and his colleagues to coin the term, 'Client-Centered Therapy'. The term seemed less prone to attack but still cast the client as his or her own best resource; especially in contrast to the term, 'patient'.

The era of Rogers' association with the University of Chicago was when he received recognition for developing a new and revolutionary theory of psychotherapy. Several other major contributions came to the forefront during this time. These contributions include:

1. Rogers revolutionized the field of psychotherapy by being the catalyzing force for multiple professionals to practice psychotherapy (Kirschenbaum and Henderson, 1989, p. xi-xii) . Rogers professed that the only professionals who could do psychotherapy when Rogers first worked in therapy clinics were psychiatrists. Other practitioners were ancillary helpers to psychiatrists. Rogers developed his psychotherapeutic way of working with clients in the non-directive fashion. However, his 'non-directive' theory did not distinguish between the terms counseling and psychotherapy; even though, the practice of non-directive therapy was the same activity whether it was labeled counseling or psychotherapy. Hence, Rogers called his therapeutic work, 'Counseling'. By the time the medical profession discovered that his work was psychotherapy as well as counseling, it was too late for major confrontations. Other practitioners had already begun to practice psychotherapy. Other events, including increased professionalization of the various helping disciplines, greater education of psychological problems by the media, and previous emphasis of therapy as education by Alfred Adler blended with Rogers' explication of therapy. The work that increasingly obtained academic visibility at the University of Chicago thrust the psychotherapy treatment process into the realm of more therapy available from more sources. As such, it opened the way for expansion of clinical treatment opportunities.

2. Rogers was a major figure in demystifying psychotherapy, mainly through the use of audio recordings and films. Rogers and his colleagues were the first group to use audio recordings to examine therapy sessions and make them available to the professional community. In fact, they started with the use of 'wire' recorders and glass disks, which were cumbersome and awkward to use. Indeed, Rogers was one of the first individuals to make his own therapy sessions available for public scrutiny on both audiotape and films. Ms. Oak was one of the first films of a session of an on-going therapy relationship (Rogers, 1954). The film, 'Gloria' which involved demonstrations by Rogers, Fritz Perls (Gestalt Therapy) and Albert Ellis (Rational-Emotive Behaviour Therapy) of therapy sessions with the same client is still a classic film used in education programs (Shostrom, 1964).

3. Rogers was one of the first individuals to do scientific method, hypothesis-testing research on the work of the therapist. It is ironic that some individuals have cast Rogers as being 'soft-minded' when he and his colleagues were the first to apply scientific method research to their own work, testing hypotheses

about the theory while examining therapists' responses in relation to client process and outcome.

4. Rogers is one of the few theorists who has delineated their therapeutic approaches in a scientific method format that permits it to be tested through scientific inquiry (Rogers, 1959). Cast in linear scientific method hypotheses, Rogers states that if certain conditions exist in therapy, then certain processes are likely to occur in the client and, then, certain definable outcomes will take place.

5. Rogers' (1957) integration hypothesis concerning the necessary and sufficient conditions for therapeutic personality change was the impetus for research on psychotherapy for nearly four decades and is still a relevant and discussed topic (Bozarth, 1992b; Lazarus and Lazarus, 1991; Lazarus, 1993; Norcross, 1992; Stubbs and Bozarth, 1996). It was one of the first statements concerning integration of therapeutic approaches and, in view of recent research findings of the most effective variables in successful therapy (cited in Duncan and Moynihan, 1994; see also Chapter 19), Rogers' work is one of the most potent integrative statements in the field of psychotherapy.

6. The influence of Rogers' work permeates the work of therapists of all persuasions. In fact, a survey by Smith (1982) found that Rogers was rated as being the most influential psychologist before Freud, Skinner and others by the majority of American psychologists polled. His influence has been pervasive in the helping professions of counseling and psychotherapy. His emphasis upon the importance of the relationship has left its indelible mark on individual psychotherapy of all persuasions including, for example, pastoral counseling, career counseling, group counseling, education and conflict resolution.

In the early 1960s, Rogers began a project which has been described by some (e.g. Shlien, 1990, personal communication) as his watershed. He undertook a massive research project to examine the outcomes of working with chronic long-time hospitalized 'psychotics'. It was an experiment wrought with problems that went beyond the difficulty of maintaining a scientific research design. Kirschenbaum's account of this period of Rogers' life provides an especially clear and candid picture of the problems encountered (Kirschenbaum, 1979). Rogers went on a sabbatical to California early in the project and became interested in encounter groups. His interest and actual time with the Wisconsin project was severely restricted. In addition, the staff involved in the project had considerable conflict with each other and some of them were upset with the way Rogers handled the problems. Although there were encouraging results and some discoveries about making psychological contact with such clients, the overall results were equivocal. I personally believe that there was, along with the other problems, contamination of the project that resulted from the absence of actual belief in the foundation block (i.e., the actualizing tendency) of the client-centered approach by some of the therapists. At least three of the therapists did not identify themselves as necessarily being client-centered. They would 'do' client-centered communication or 'do' reflection but often had intentions to work with clients in ways that do not demonstrate the trust of clients to go at their own pace, in their own direction and in their own way. From my point of view, the expertise of the therapist very likely seeped into the therapy creating considerable contamination for investigating the viability of client-centered therapy with 'psychotics'. Indeed, the study was perhaps more of a study of Rogers' integration hypothesis of the necessary and sufficient conditions rather than client-centered therapy *per se*. Given the morass of problems, it is rather surprising to me that there were any indications of relationships of Rogers' hypotheses to success. Wisconsin was considered Rogers' watershed in several ways:

First, Rogers left the field of psychotherapy during the Wisconsin Project in order to focus on societal concerns. He hoped to investigate the principles of client-centered therapy in a broader domain. Although his early work reflected an interest in the relationship of the principles to such areas as group work, education and conflict resolution, he now took on a more concentrated effort to explore the societal impact of the principles that he delineated (Rogers, 1951, 1959).

Second, it turned out that Rogers and his new colleagues really did little empirical research and literally completed no widely known scientific method research after the Wisconsin Project.

During part of and immediately after the Wisconsin Project, Rogers' major activities were with encounter groups of eight to ten individuals. Rogers coined the term 'Basic Encounter Group' to designate an encounter group operating on client-centered principles and which might differentiate the client-centered approach from other directive and controlling groups which forced participants to deal with topics, issues and feelings. As part of this endeavour, he worked with several colleagues (e.g., William Coulson, Doug Land and Bruce Meador) in a training workshop identified as the La Jolla Program. This workshop was initially designed to be a two-week workshop to provide participants with a learning experience in the client-centered approach. With groups of 200 to 300 and sometimes more, they structured the program to allow all participants to meet together each morning for three hours, scheduled encounter groups each afternoon and a variety of other activities were scheduled by the participants during the first week. The community of participants generally developed their own activities during the second week often drawing on the expertise of the participants in the community workshop. One of the emerging findings, however, was the discovery that this many people could communicate and share in intimate ways in the large community group. I believe that this was a significant learning for Rogers and provided a significant context for his next venture.

In the early 1970s, Rogers' daughter, Natalie, suggested that she and her father do some work together. The result was what turned out to be an experiment with the large community group. Carl and Natalie Rogers with colleagues who included

Maria Bowen, Jared Kass, Maureen O'Hara and John K. Wood became 'convenors' (rather than facilitators) of groups of several hundred participants. The groups met in the large community meetings and developed the activities of the ensuing two weeks. The experience was chaotic but rewarding in that people did communicate with each other and share with each other in the large group and did develop community. As more and more people from a wide range of countries began to attend these groups, the groups were offered in countries other than the United States. Many variables not necessarily influencing individual psychotherapy converged on Rogerian principles when applied to societal activities.

One colleague of Rogers, Chuck Devonshire, developed ongoing training workshops in Europe using a model similar to the large community groups. Devonshire also initiated a number of cross-cultural workshops in Europe. Rogers was involved as a consultant and attended many of those workshops. Rogers also became part of a training group in New York that employed a similar model. His colleague and main collaborator in the development of this training program was Ruth Sanford, who later worked with him in extensions of the large community group.

Extensions of the above noted experiences were designated as Cross-Cultural Workshops and, later, as workshops designed to impact on international conflicts. It was during this time that Rogers wrote *On Personal Power*, and first used the term 'person-centered approach' (Rogers, 1977). He used the term initially to identify the application of client-centered principles beyond psychotherapy. The term applied to therapy has become somewhat controversial and viewed by some as a term that means something other than client-centered therapy. Although Rogers had been interested in such applications early in his career, he was now devoting most of his time and energy to such endeavours. Rogers' theory statement actually included a section on Interpersonal Relationships from a Client-Centered Framework. He viewed psychotherapy as one example of a good human interpersonal relationship (Rogers, 1959). His efforts to apply the philosophy of the approach to societal areas took him to an engagement in a small encounter group with participants from the Northern Ireland conflict and also with workshop participants in South Africa, Latin and Central America, Hungary and Russia. He was also successful in developing a workshop with leading dignitaries and influential world figures in Rust, Austria (Rogers and Ryback, 1984). A prestigious group of individuals nominated Rogers for the 1987 Nobel Peace Prize on the day of his death in February of that year.

In my view, Rogers' major life inquiry was his search for the common factors among therapies and relationships that induce 'therapeutic' and 'growth' effectiveness. Although Rogers is generally recognized for his contributions to psychotherapy and for the development of the theory of therapy identified as client-centered therapy, his major contributions had more to do with his search for common therapeutic variables in the helping professions and for finding and implementing impactful psychological atmospheres to promote personal and societal growth. Early in his career, Rogers asked the question, 'What, if anything, do all these therapeutic approaches have in common? (Kirschenbaum, 1979, p. 96; Rogers, 1939). At that time, Rogers identified four qualifications of the therapist for effective therapy as: (1) objectivity, (2) respect for the individual, (3) understanding of self and (4) psychological knowledge. He continued his search all of his life. His explications reached fruition in his classic paper on the necessary and sufficient conditions for therapeutic personality change as considered for all therapies and all helping relationships. A review of Rogers' writings after 1960 suggests that he focused on the core conditions for successful therapy and on the impact of experiences other than therapy as growth inducers in such areas as education, administration, conflict mediation, and universal peace rather than focusing upon client-centered theory.

Carl Rogers' wish to have impact was certainly achieved to a greater extent than most people realize. He influenced the very fiber of the study and practice of psychotherapy. He championed and practised a philosophy that impacted multiple areas. He hypothesized an integration statement concerning core attitudinal qualities of helping that is pervasive while ironically not well understood. He reminds even those who do not accept his growth hypothesis of the remarkable resiliency of human beings.

# Myths, Misunderstandings and Distortions

3

Over the years, client-centered therapy has endured numerous myths about the approach that are grounded upon unfounded assertions. These myths include such assertions as:

'The approach takes too much time.'
'The approach only works with neurotic middle class individuals.'
'The approach is most important early in the counseling relationship.'
'The client-therapist relationship cannot be equal.'
'The approach is culture-bound in the US.'

These and other such assertions, I believe, are primarily biases and misunderstandings that occur from other frames of reference. In addition, there are several fundamental distortions of the person-centered paradigm that are periodically fostered by some individuals who claim to be advocates of, or who are sympathetic to, the approach. This chapter reviews and responds to several of these myths and distortions. The major myths are the following:

## • Myth 1: The approach takes too much time.

This criticism apparently comes from the logic that since the therapist isn't 'doing' anything to hurry the client along, it must take a longer time for the therapy. The fact is that there is no evidence to support this rationale. One of the few studies on time-limited therapy found that client-centered and Adlerian time limited therapy were equally effective (Shlien, Mosak and Dreikhurs, 1959). Clinicians in private practice who are dedicated to the person-centered approach report wide ranges of time spent with their clients. Indeed, Rogers' demonstration with Gloria is a classic example of how just one forty-minute therapy session had a positive impact. Shlien (1998), who has met with Gloria's daughter, offers additional information that points to the resiliency of Gloria as a person who moved in a positive and

Adapted with permission from:
Bozarth, J. D. (1995a) Person-centered therapy: A misunderstood paradigmatic difference? *The Person-Centered Journal*, 2 (2), 12-17.

constructive direction. Gloria and Rogers developed a relationship in that space of time that led to periodic exchange of letters and phone calls throughout the years. Gloria showed considerable growth and progress handling difficult problems in her life. She acknowledged her relationship with Rogers as assisting her to this self-empowerment. As Rogers states: 'It is good to know that just one meeting where we meet as person to person can make a difference.'( Rogers, 1984 p. 425)

• *Myth 2: The approach only works with neurotic middle class individuals.*
The basis for this assertion seems to be from two inferences. The first is based upon the logic that since Rogers and his colleagues worked with clients in a university counseling center that the approach would not work with more severely disturbed clients. The second assumption seems to be that the approach does not deal with the pathology of individuals and is too simple to be effective with psychotics. Again, the experience of client-centered practitioners counters this statement. The University of Chicago Counseling Center staff did, in fact, work with more disturbed clients. Shlien (1971) and Rogers (Kirschenbaum, 1979) describe therapy sessions with 'psychotic' clients by the therapists at the Chicago Counseling Center. Rogers presented case examples of clients in the Wisconsin project. Truax developed a life long friendship with one of his clients in the Wisconsin project (Truax, 1969, personal communication). This person changed from a long-term immobilizing psychosis to high level functioning. There are reports of success working with long and short term hospitalized mentally ill clients (Brodley, 1988b; Prouty, 1994). I learned the person-centered approach working with long term hospitalized mentally ill clients who were irreconcilably doomed never to improve enough to be discharged from a state mental hospital. Yet, over eighty percent of the individuals I worked with over a two year evaluation were discharged and functioning outside of the hospital four years after placement. Also, the problem laden Wisconsin research project designed to examine the effectiveness of client-centered therapy with hospitalized 'psychotics' did provide enough evidence to indicate that, at least, the presence of Rogers' hypothesis of the necessary and sufficient conditions, had some positive impact with clients (Rogers, Gendlin, Kiesler, and Truax, 1967).

• *Myth 3: The approach is primarily important early in the counseling relationship.*
This criticism comes from the position taken from other frames of reference that view the conditions as the 'soil' for therapist interventions. It is, in part, cited from the perception that research has failed strongly to support the position that the conditions are necessary and sufficient (see chapter 19 on research). Apparently, the statement first occurred in behavioral research which took the position that the behaviorist would need to do more and that, for the behaviorist, the conditions were necessary but not sufficient (Krumboltz, 1967). This was generalized and carried forward by research reviewers as being scientifically supported.

• *Myth 4: The client-therapist relationship cannot be equal.*
Buber and Rogers had a dialogue that concerned this point as one of their disagreements (Kirschenbaum and Henderson, 1989). Buber refers to the state of therapy to Rogers:

> . . . you have necessarily another attitude to the situation than he (the client) has. You are able to do something that he is not able. You are not equals and cannot be. You have the great task, self-imposed – a great self-imposed task to supplement this need of his and to do rather more than in the normal situation . . . There is not only you, your mode of thinking, your mode of doing, there is also a certain situation – we are so and so – which may sometime be tragic. You cannot change this . . .There is some reality confronting us. (p. 50)

Rogers replied that:

> . . . But it has been my experience that is reality when it is viewed from the outside, and that really has nothing to do with the relationship that produces therapy. This is something immediate, equal, a meeting of two persons on an equal basis, even though, in the world of I – It, it could be seen as a very unequal relationship. (pp. 51-52)

The differences in understanding these two positions seem to me to be a different view of power. The person-centered position is from the view of power as from the Latin etymology, portiere, that essentially means to be all that you are capable of being. The counter position seems to focus on the definition of power as 'possession of control, authority or influence over others' (American Heritage Dictionary, 1995). The equality of the relationship is, in fact, in the attitude of the therapist's willingness to trust the client to go in his or her own direction, way and pace. It is the equality of two individuals in relationship.

• *Myth 5: The Person-Centered Approach is grounded in U. S. American culture and philosophy.*
There have been numerous critiques of Rogers' theory in relation to cultural values, frames of reference of various races, and even gender-perceptual stances (Holdstock, 1990; O'Hara, 1997). The position is often taken that Rogers' values were initially middle class American values and out of the U.S. culture of valuing independence, individual resourcefulness and materialistic accomplishments. I consider this a flawed argument that fails to consider the essence of the theory as an organismic, natural and universal theory. The theory applies to all human species and, indeed, to all living organisms (and even beyond: Rogers, 1980). When the theory is cast in a way that is considered inappropriate in particular instances, it is always cast in the format of the way individuals have learned to 'do' client-centered therapy. In chapter 11, I have argued that focusing on how to do person-centered therapy is one of the more inhibiting factors to the creation of the freeing environment for the individual. In addition, Rogers was consistent in his reference

to developing his theory from his observation of therapy clients who moved in positive directions when afforded the opportunity through a facilitative therapy atmosphere. Later, he held these same observations of individuals in encounter groups. His observations were the primary foundation of the theory; the growth hypothesis emerged from these observations. He observed this internal and natural process in individuals all over the world as he became involved in workshops and encounter groups over the years.

The more prominent distortions that also seem to exist with some person-centered therapists and others are the following:

1. The therapist has a systematic intention to help the client change in a certain way;
2. The therapist has objectives to help the client diminish or eradicate problems or particular issues;
3. The therapist is an expert at promoting a particular 'process' in the client;
4. The conditions cited by Rogers are necessary but are not sufficient.

There are other distortions but these seem to me to be the most prevalent among many individuals who align themselves with the principles of the person-centered approach as well as from those who hold different theoretical alliances. In a critique of criticisms of the person-centered approach by prominent authors, I noted the basic thrust of such criticisms as follows (Bozarth, 1995a):

> The process is, in essence, that of dismissing the fundamental assumption of the approach (that of the actualizing tendency and the self-authority of the client) as untenable or questionable and proceeding with criticism of the theory from other theoretical frames of reference. The position taken by these authors is embedded to varying degrees on the assumption of the therapist as the expert for the treatment and behavior change of the client. Hence, their theoretical argument is a *non sequitur* of the meaning and understanding of Rogers' theory. (p. 12)

To recapitulate the theory in still another way:

> It is when the therapist can embody the attitudinal qualities of congruency, unconditional regard, and empathic understanding in the therapeutic relationship with the client in a way that the client can perceive/experience these qualities with the locus of control belonging to the client that the actualizing process of the client is promoted.
>
> (Bozarth, 1987)

The general importance of the theoretical definition on each distortion of person-centeredness is that the crux of the theory is that of providing enabling conditions that promote a natural process in the client; that is, the actualizing process. This natural process that exists in humans is, at least partly, idiosyncratic in particular change ('to maximize one's potentialities') while also being universal at a more macro level; e.g., 'to maintain and enhance the organism'. Rogers and Sanford note that the fostering of the actualizing tendency through the embodiment of the therapeutic attitudes constitutes a continuing 'radical stance. . .which advocates complete trust in individual growth and development under stated conditions' (Rogers and Sanford 1984, p. 1388). Rogers' position on the locus of control essential to facilitate the actualizing tendency is aptly stated (Rogers, 1977):

> The politics of the client-centered approach is a conscious renunciation and avoidance by the therapist of all control over, or decision-making for, the client. It is the facilitation of self-ownership by the client and the strategies by which this can be achieved; the placing of the locus of decision-making and the responsibility for the effects of these decisions. It is politically centered in the client. (p. 14)

This radical position of enabling the natural process of the client is the crux in which the most distortions are considered. The person-centered approach is an 'avant-garde' position, not an 'old guard' position. Several specific distortions that are associated with some who practice person-centered therapy are the following:

• *Distortion 1: The therapist has a systematic intention to help the client change in a certain way.*
This intention is explicit in at least two offshoots of the person-centered approach. One of these offshoots is that of human relations training that evolved from Rogers' conceptual work but, I argue, is a distortion of his hypotheses. Another offshoot is that of experiential therapy which generated from Rogers' work and is intertwined in Gendlin's work on the theory of experiencing (Gendlin, 1974). In human relations training, the distortion, simply put, is that the therapist's intention is to move (or help move) the client through the relationship to understanding and, then, to action. In experiential therapy, the intention of the therapist is ultimately to move clients to experience their 'felt sense'. Thus, the person can experience a certain self- phenomenon (Gendlin, 1990). In both of these offshoots, the natural process of the client is replaced with the intention of the therapist. There is a subtle shift back to the authority and expertise of the therapist, and the self-authority of the client is compromised.

• *Distortion 2: The therapist has objectives to help the client diminish or eradicate problems or particular issues.*
The call for person-centered therapists to attend more to clinical issues was stated in an editorial article which suggests that the failure of person-centered writers to address clinical issues constitutes 'a serious oversight on our part' (Cain, 1993, p. 134). Shlien, responding to an article on psychodiagnosis, succinctly summarizes

the person-centered theoretical position in concrete functional terms: 'But client-centered therapy has only one treatment for all cases' (Shlien, 1989, p. 161). Rogers was also quite explicit about this point. He stated (Rogers, 1942):

> The individual, and not the problem, is the focus. The aim is not to solve one particular problem, but to assist the individual to grow, so that he can cope with the present problem and with later problems in a better-integrated fashion. (pp 28-30)

● *Distortion 3: The therapist is an expert at promoting a particular 'process' in the client.*

There is one group of individuals who investigate client processes in therapy in an effort to identify specific therapist responses that facilitate more effective processing of experience by clients (Rice and Greenberg, 1990). Others have also attended to the process of therapy for the client (Barrett-Lennard, 1990). These works were apparently stimulated by Rogers' process conception emanating from 'moments of movement' for clients in therapy as well as in his 'if – then' delineation of his theory (Rogers, 1951; 1959). The distortion is that Rogers' observations of this process occurring in many clients become instructions for the therapist to make a certain process happen and/or believe that the process must necessarily happen. As Brodley states: 'Rogers adoption of the attitudes' mechanism is incompletely articulated because it implies still undescribed variability of processes of change according to individual differences' (Brodley, 1990, p. 12). The theoretical base of the psychotherapeutic theory as one that enables the client to foster his/her own individual process is ignored. The therapist now knows where the client should go, or knows the natural idiosyncratic process of that particular client, and (depending on the therapist's bent to be an expert) is now in a theoretical position to direct the client through the 'proper and right' process.

● *Distortion 4: The term 'person-centered' is different from 'client-centered' in a fundamental way.*

Although the term person-centered may be representative of evolving manifestations of the principles of client-centered therapy, the term is predicated upon the same basic principles of client-centered therapy. Raskin comments upon the meaning of person-centered therapy by referring to the trust of both the therapist and client's self-directed capacities (Raskin, 1988). He suggests that the trust of the therapist '. . . might bring into play different ways of expressing empathy, the use of intuition, or self-disclosure '. . . while maintaining the same basic respect for the self-directive capacities of the client' (p.1). Raskin suggests that an unsystematic therapist activity '. . . may represent person-centered therapy at its optimal level, with a freely functioning therapist accepting the client as leading the way while not being bound by a set of rules' (p. 1). He differentiates systematic from the unsystematic therapist activities by viewing systematic approaches as having '. . . a preconceived notion of how they wish to change the client and work at it in systematic fashion, in contrast to the person-centered therapist who starts out being open and remains open to an emerging process orchestrated by the client.' (p.2)

Elsewhere I discuss therapist behaviors as dependent in part on the idiosyncrasies of the therapist, client, and situation (Bozarth, 1984). These differences, however, are differences in manifestation and not differences in the foundation block of client-centered theory; i.e., actualization; nor a difference concerning the necessary and sufficient conditions that enable the actualizing tendency of an individual to be fostered. Rogers was clear on his position as a practitioner: '. . . whether I am called upon for help in a relationship deemed to be client-centered or in one that is labeled person-centered. I work in the same way in each.' (Rogers, 1987, p. 13)

• *Distortion 5 : The conditions cited by Rogers are necessary but are not sufficient.* Somehow this distortion has been asserted as one of the predominant findings of research on the necessary and sufficient conditions. The fact is that there is not one shred of direct evidence to support this assertion (Stubbs and Bozarth, 1994; see also chapter 19 in this book).

There are other myths and distortions that have been leveled at the person-centered approach. Most of them are generated by a failure to understand and/or assimilate the radical position of the person-centered approach, which centers on the person of the client as his or her own best expert about his or her life, and that the therapist operates on the premise of trusting the enhanced constructive direction when an appropriate psychological climate is created.

# THE ACTUALIZING TENDENCY: THE FOUNDATION BLOCK

4

The intent of this chapter is to examine Carl Rogers' view of the actualizing tendency as the foundation block of person-centered therapy. Rogers, early in his career, assumed the natural growth tendency as the healing factor in psychotherapy. Later, he discussed the formative tendency of the universe as the larger concept that subsumes the actualizing tendency (Rogers, 1942; 1980).

The fundamental notion of person-centered therapy is that the therapist can trust the growth tendency of the client; hence, the therapist's role is to create an interpersonal climate that promotes the individual's actualizing tendency. In Rogers' view, the emotional disturbance as well as specific problems require that conditions offered by the therapist foster the person's natural recuperative and growth capabilities. The therapeutic attitudes of trust and respect of the therapist can free and promote the client's natural capacities for health and growth. The parameters created by the functional trust in the actualizing tendency reject standard clinical thinking about psychotherapy such as the need for diagnosis and treatment plans with treatment goals and strategies. There is no need for the therapist to engage in interventions, strategies or manipulations based upon speculations concerning the client's disturbance. In addition, it is not the therapist who should determine the frequency of therapy interviews, the length of the therapy, or when the client should stop therapy. Instead, Rogers thought that each client should be approached näively without preconceptions as unique individuals and be allowed to develop their own therapy process. The client, consistent with the theory, controls the therapeutic situation and therapeutic process up to the limits of the therapist's capacity and the demands of the work situation. The therapist's basic task is to embody the attitudinal qualities of congruency, empathic understanding and unconditional positive regard in relation to the client while trusting this natural growth process of the client. Since the experience of these attitudes by the client fosters the actualizing tendency, the person-centered therapist trusts the client to move forward in a constructive direction. In Rogers' schema, the constructive

Adapted with permission from:
Bozarth, J. D. and Brodley, B. T. (1991). Actualization: A functional concept in client-centered therapy. *Journal of Social Behavior and Personality*, 6 (5), 45-59.

forward movement of the client is propelled by the sole and inherent motivation in human beings; that is, the actualizing tendency.

### The attitudes and the actualizing tendency
The specific features of the theory evolve from the organismic theory of the actualizing tendency as it is related to the fundamental philosophy and attitudes of trust in and respect for persons. Rogers wrote about this as early as 1942. He states:

> Therapy is not a matter of doing something to the individual, or of inducing him to do something about himself. It is instead a matter of freeing him for normal growth and development.
>
> (Rogers, 1942, p. 29)

Rogers acknowledged that his ideas about actualization were influenced by the work of Kurt Goldstein, Maslow, Angyal and others but noted that his formulation emerged primarily from his own naturalistic observations. Only after formulating his own theory did he become aware of some of the supporting work of such authors and, additionally, supporting work in biology, (e.g., Bertalanffy, 1960).

Rogers observed that behaviors of organisms (including individuals in therapy) move in the direction of maintaining and enhancing themselves. Emphasizing this observation, he asserted the idea of the actualizing tendency as involving all motivation, expansion and enhancement. The basis for all of his thinking about therapy, human development, personality and interpersonal relationships was the actualization tendency, (Rogers, 1959; 1963; 1986b). He noted:

> In person-centered therapy, the person is free to choose any direction, but actually selects positive and constructive pathways. I can only explain this in terms of a directional tendency inherent in the human organism – a tendency to grow, to develop, to realize its full potential.
>
> (Rogers, 1986b, p. 127)

The rationale for person-centered therapy and the person-centered approach in interpersonal interactions rests on the actualizing construct in the following ways:

1. The actualizing tendency is the basic and sole motivation of persons.
2. The actualizing tendency is constructively directional, aiming toward increasing differentiation and complexity and resulting in growth, development and fulfilment of potentialities.
3. The effects of this sole motivational tendency on the person's experience and behavior can be distorted or stunted by interaction with unfavorable, inadequate or destructive environmental circumstances.
4. These distorted or stunted realizations of the person create the need for psychotherapy.
5. Client-centered therapy is an attempt to create an optimal psychological climate for the person by means of the therapist providing a special kind of relationship that involves certain attitudinal qualities of the therapist.

6. This relationship fosters the person's natural actualizing tendency to function in ways that overcome the effects on his/her organism of unfavorable or destructive circumstances.
7. The result of therapy is that the person's experience and behavior become more purely constructive and more powerfully developmental and enhancing. Using the same logic, the promotion of a person's constructive growth tendency was extended beyond psychotherapy to include any interpersonal relationship where one individual can create a climate that promotes the other individual's actualizing tendency.

## Some characteristics

Rogers' construct of the actualizing tendency is an organismic theory with the fundamental qualities in human nature being viewed as those of growth, process and change. In Rogers' theory, 'Man is an actualizing process' (Van Belle, 1980, p. 70). Actualization is the motivational construct in organismic theory and, thus, is embedded in the organismic growth process and is the motivator for change. The principle characteristics of all organisms, including human beings, have this tendency in common although Rogers' term 'person' is the one used for the distinctly human realization of organismic nature. The major assertions of Rogers' 'actualizing tendency' construct are as follows:

1. The actualizing tendency is individual and universal, (Rogers, 1980). The expression of the tendency is always unique to the individual and also the presence of the tendency is a motivating tendency for all organisms.
2. The actualizing tendency is holistic, (Rogers, 1959). The organism/person is a fluid, changing gestalt with different aspects assuming figure and ground relations depending upon the momentary specific aims of the person and upon the immediate demands of the environment. The actualizing tendency as the motivational force functions throughout all systems of the person. It is expressed in a variable, dynamic and fluctuating manner through the subsystems of the whole person while maintaining wholeness and organization.
3. The actualizing tendency is ubiquitous and constant, (Rogers, 1963; Rogers and Sanford, 1984). It is the motivation for all activity of the person, under all circumstances, favorable and unfavorable to the specific person. It functions as long as the person is alive. The moment by moment living – the moving, responding, maintaining of wholeness, feeling, thinking, striving – are all manifestations of the actualizing tendency.
4. The actualizing tendency is a directional process. Although it involves assimilation and differentiation activities while maintaining wholeness, the wholeness is perpetually changing. It is a tendency towards realization, fulfilment and perfection of inherent capabilities and potentialities of the individual, (Rogers, 1963). It is a selective process in that it is directional and constructive. It tends to enhance and maintain the whole organism/person.
5. The actualizing tendency is tension increasing, (Rogers, 1959). The organism/

person is not a drive reduction system but one that inherently and spontaneously increases tension levels to expand, grow and further realize inherent capabilities. The directionality of the actualizing tendency requires its tension-increasing characteristic.

6. The actualizing tendency is a tendency toward autonomy and away from heteronomy, (Rogers, 1963). The person moves inherently toward self-regulation and away from being controlled.

7. The actualizing tendency is vulnerable to environmental circumstances, (Rogers, 1980; Rogers and Sanford, 1984). Under unfavorable circumstances to the organism the expression of the actualizing tendency may be affected such that the organism becomes distorted although the tendency remains as constructive as possible under the circumstances. Rogers used the metaphor of the potato sprout growing towards the tiny source of light in the dark cellar to clarify his point. He said:

> The conditions were unfavorable, but the potatoes would begin to sprout - pale white sprouts, so unlike the healthy green shoots they sent up when planted in the soil in the spring. But these sad, spindly sprouts would grow 2 or 3 feet in length as they reached toward the distant light of the window. The sprouts were, in their bizarre, futile growth, a sort of desperate expression of the directional tendency I have been describing. They would never become plants, never mature, never fulfil their real potential. But under the most adverse circumstances, they were striving to become. Life would not give up, even if it could not flourish.
>
> ( Rogers, 1980, p. 118)

The above characteristics of the actualizing tendency, according to Rogers, are common to all organisms.

### Concepts related to the actualizing tendency

*Self-Actualization*: The concept identified as 'Self-Actualization' is a construct referring to the actualization tendency manifest in the 'self' – a subsystem that becomes differentiated within the whole person, (Rogers, 1951; 1959). This construct is crucial to Rogers' theory of the development of normal personality and psychological disturbances. He theorizes that under unfavorable conditions the actualization of the self-subsystem (dictated by self-concepts) may become discrepant from and in conflict with organismic experiencing. Such conflict results in loss of the person's wholeness and integration with consequent disturbance. Alternatively, under favorable developmental circumstances, persons are theorized as remaining open to experience and as developing self-concepts which are harmonious with organismic experiencing with the consequence that wholeness and integration of the person is fostered.

*Consciousness*: The concept of consciousness, in the sense of capacity for self-awareness, is viewed as a distinctive human channel of the actualizing tendency, (Rogers, 1980). Consciousness gives the person a greater range of choices for self-regulation and permits potentialities not present in other organisms.

*Social Nature*: Human beings have a social nature, consequently a basic directionality of the actualizing tendency in humans is toward constructive social behavior, (Rogers, 1982). It is true of all directional characteristics of individuals and species, that the better the environmental/social conditions of the organism, the stronger the expression of the directional characteristic. Thus, in humans, the capacities of empathy, affiliation and language result in constructive social behavior under adequate (or better than adequate) conditions. It is important to recognize that in Rogers' thinking all potentialities of individuals and of species are not aspects of the directionality of the actualizing tendency, (Rogers, 1989a, 1989b). Behavioral directionality that is (or seems) dysfunctional occurs because of the thwarting of the actualizing tendency.

*The fully functioning person*: Rogers' concept of the 'fully functioning person' is often misunderstood as being a goal for clients in Rogers' therapy. In fact, Rogers is presenting his views on the meaning of 'the good life' and clarifying the manner in which the actualizing tendency functions in human beings. Rogers formulated his concept of the 'fully functioning person' as well as his whole theory from the context and vantage point of his experience as a client-centered therapist. The characteristics of the 'fully functioning person' are an extrapolation from concrete observation of his individual clients and are based on the common features of his clients who progressed in therapy. The common features that Rogers expressed as the 'fully functioning person' are features of directional development in persons. Rogers said:

> If I attempt to capture in a few words what seems to me to be true of these people (who showed positive movement in client-centered therapy), I believe it will come out something like this: The good life is a process, not a state of being. It is a direction, not a destination. It is not . . . a state of virtue, or contentment, or nirvana or happiness. It is not a condition in which the individual is adjusted, or fulfilled or actualized.
>
> (Rogers, 1961, pp 186-187)

In other words, the 'fully functioning person' does not represent a state of being, a class of persons as in Maslow's 'actualizing personalities' (Maslow, 1970). Neither is it a developmental level in Rogers' theory. Instead Rogers is expressing dimensions of directionality that he believes are inherent and ubiquitous in human beings but which show obvious and accelerated development under favorable psychological conditions, such as the conditions described by Rogers as the necessary and sufficient conditions for constructive personality change and notably associated with person-centered therapy, (Ford, 1994).

There are three major dimensions of the directionality in Rogers' description of the 'fully functioning person'. These are: (1) 'an increasing openness to experience', (2) 'increasingly existential living', and (3) 'an increasing trust in his (or her) organism' (Rogers, 1961, pp.187-189). It is the extent of the development of the three directions in an individual that determines the extent of the psychological freedom of the individual. Psychological freedom is a process of growth, development and realization. Thus, it is through increasing openness to experience, increasingly existential living and increasing trust in one's organism that the inherent actualizing tendency operates more effectively and fully. Rogers has described the psychological dimensions of the expression of the actualizing tendency in human beings in his description of the 'fully functioning person' (Rogers, 1961). These characteristics are considered distinctive to the human organism and are crucial in his theories of personality and psychological disturbance as well as being relevant to therapeutic process.

While viewing the actualizing tendency from the stance of his scientific orientation, Rogers always asserted that it is a hypothesis, 'open to disproof' (Rogers, 1980). Nevertheless, the concept of actualization functions in Rogers' theory as an axiom; that is, it functions as a principle that directs the therapist's behaviors. Specifically, the organism/person is always actualizing because actualization is the motivational concept that accounts for all living activity. In effect, the person is always actualizing him/herself as best as he/she can under the circumstances. Whenever destructive or self-limiting behavior is observed, the actualizing tendency concept directs inquiry toward the circumstances that have distorted or limited constructiveness.

Rogers' and Maslow's theories of actualization are often mistakenly equated. In addition to the differences in their views concerning the 'fully functioning' person, a major difference exists between the theories early in his formulations when he defined the 'actualizing tendency' as the sole motivational construct, (Rogers, 1959). The motivations conceptualized as 'deficiency needs'; i.e., the physiological needs, needs for safety, belonging, love and esteem, hypothesized by Maslow as preceding the self-actualization of persons, are included in Rogers' sole motivational construct.

The person-centered therapist implements the actualizing tendency by creating a specific interpersonal climate during the therapy session. This climate is created by means of the therapist experiencing and communicating certain attitudes toward the client. These attitudes are identified as the qualities of congruency, unconditional positive regard, and empathic understanding. Since the experience of these attitudes by the client fosters that client's actualizing tendency, the person-centered therapist trusts the client to move forward in a constructive direction without intervening and assuming therapeutic expertise about the client. The constructive forward movement of the client is propelled by the sole and inherent motivation in human beings; that is, the actualizing tendency. The fundamental notion of Person-Centered Therapy is that the therapist can trust the tendency of the client and the only role of the therapist is to create an interpersonal climate that promotes the individual's actualizing tendency. Rogers adopted the construct of the actualizing tendency principle as a cognitive underpinning that implies attitudes of trust in and respect for the client in a helping relationship. When a person has emotional disturbances and problems, according to Rogers' organismic theory, what is required to help the person is to facilitate the vitality of the person's innate recuperative and growth capabilities.

The therapeutic attitudes of trust and respect and the desirability of a fostering situation that can free the person's capacities for health and growth created some logical parameters for the therapist's approach. These parameters, in effect, eschew standard clinical thinking about psychotherapy, such as, the need for diagnosis and treatment plans with treatment goals and strategies. Instead, the concept of the actualizing tendency suggests that the therapist should not conceptualize the client's illness, nor conceptualize any concrete goals that might affect the therapist's attitudes or behavior in relation to the client. It was also logically consistent that the therapist need not determine the frequency of therapy interviews, the length of the therapy, nor when the client should stop therapy. Rogers, in fact, thought the client should be approached näively without preconceptions as a unique individual and be allowed to develop his/her own therapy process. The assumption was that the client's innate actualizing tendency could be fostered most effectively by the creation of a distinctive interpersonal environment fundamentally based on the trust and respect that was implied by belief in the actualizing tendency. The client would be given, in effect, control over the therapeutic situation and therapeutic process up to the limits of the therapist's capacity (and the demands of the work situation).

# NOT NECESSARILY NECESSARY BUT ALWAYS SUFFICIENT

5

Over forty years ago, Carl Rogers hypothesized the psychological conditions that he viewed as necessary and sufficient to bring about therapeutic personality change (Rogers, 1957). This hypothesis was meant to clarify and extend knowledge in the field of psychotherapy as well as in other kinds of relationships.

## Varied emphases on Rogers' hypothesis

There were varied emphases on Rogers' hypothesis between 1957 and 1993. These emphases included the following (Rogers, 1957):

1. There was a de-emphasis on techniques and methods identified with client-centered therapy. Rogers delineated this point in his hypothesized statement about the necessary and sufficient conditions for therapeutic personality change:

   The conditions apply to any situation in which constructive personality change occurs, whether we are thinking of classical psychoanalysis or any of its modern offshoots, or Adlerian Therapy, or any other. (p. 101)

2. Rogers' conceptualizations of the necessary and sufficient conditions were operationally defined for use as measurement instruments (Barrett-Lennard, 1962; Rogers, Gendlin, Kiesler, and Truax, 1967; Truax and Carkhuff, 1967) and subsequently developed to train therapists with emphasis on systematic training programs (Carkhuff, 1969, 1971; Egan, 1975; Gordon, 1970, 1976).

3. There were a host of studies that, during the 1960s, resulted in the conclusion that the attitudinal qualities as hypothesized by Rogers and supported by research reports were necessary and sufficient (Truax and Mitchell, 1971).

4. There was an increasingly accepted statement that occurred prior to and into the 1970s, that the conditions were necessary but not sufficient. This

Adapted with permission from:
Bozarth, J. D. (1993b). Not necessarily necessary but always sufficient. In Brazier, D. (ed.), *Beyond Carl Rogers*, pp. 92-105, London: Constable.

view later received credence in reviews of the research (e.g., Parloff, Waskow, and Wolfe, 1978).

5. Psychological literature continued to extend the view that the conditions were necessary but not sufficient as authors used other explanatory schemes in their reviews. There was an extensive overview of the psychological treatment model offered from a psychoanalytic perspective (Gelso and Carter, 1985). They emphasized the importance of the relationship as a forerunner to the therapist interventions implicit in the psychoanalytic approach. One review does not discuss the possibility of the sufficiency of the conditions in their review of process and outcome in psychotherapy (Orlinsky and Howard, 1987). They apparently consider sufficiency to no longer be a viable possibility; hence, they direct their attention to other views of therapeutic involvement.

This chapter examines the substance of the increasingly accepted belief that the conditions posited by Rogers are necessary but not sufficient. This is an important area since current research inquiry, which emphasizes specific treatment for specific dysfunctions is driven, in part, by the assumption of lack of sufficiency of Rogers' hypothesis (Stubbs and Bozarth, 1994). An examination of research results, relevant literature, and the theoretical foundation of the person-centered approach are used as a basis for the examination of the assumption of necessary but not sufficient conditions for therapeutic personality change.

**The necessary and sufficient conditions**
Rogers hypothesized that if six conditions existed over a sufficient period of time then, first, no other conditions are necessary to induce constructive personality change, and, second, these conditions are sufficient to induce therapeutic personality change. These conditions are specifically delineated in Chapter 1 as presented in the integration statement (Rogers 1957).

**Research evidence**
Several temporal categories have been used to delineate the findings of a qualitative analysis of research on psychotherapy efficacy (Stubbs and Bozarth, 1994). The temporal categories were: (1) psychotherapy is no more effective than no therapeutic treatment, 1950s. and 1960s, (2) the 'core conditions' (empathic understanding, unconditional positive regard, and congruency) are necessary and sufficient conditions for constructive personality change, 1960s, and 1970s, (3) psychotherapy is for better or for worse with the findings that some therapists were helpful and others were harmful (early 1960s), (4) the core conditions are assumed as being necessary but not sufficient (late 1970s, and mid 1980s), and (5) there are specific treatments for specific dysfunctions. However, the following temporal categories are viewed in this chapter as they relate to Rogers' hypothesis (Stubbs and Bozarth, 1994). A more direct report on Stubbs' and Bozarth's 'Dodo

Bird. . .' investigation is reported later. The following are the temporal categories as they were initially discussed in relation to Rogers' hypotheses:
   • 1950-1960  Research results principally conducted and reported by investigators from the University of Chicago supported the client-centered position that included the central concept that the conditions were necessary and sufficient for therapeutic personality change (Cartwright, 1957; Chordroff, 1954; Rogers, 1959; Rogers and Dymond, 1954; Seeman and Raskin, 1953). 1960-1970 - The research results over this period are summarized as supporting the necessity and sufficiency of the conditions (Truax and Mitchell, 1971). Their review of the literature found that higher levels of the conditions were related to positive outcomes. Clients of therapists measured at higher levels of the conditions improved significantly more than did clients of therapists measured at lower levels of the conditions.

   • 1970-1980  The research continued to focus upon the relationships of the attitudinal conditions to client outcome. The most general conclusions were that: (1) the relationships among therapists, clients, and techniques are more complex than previous studies suggested (Mitchell et. al., 1977; Parloff, Waskow, and Wolf, 1978); (2) the relationship dimensions are ' . . .rarely sufficient for client change . . .' (Gurman, 1978, p. 503); and (3) the relationship between the conditions and client outcome has not been adequately investigated primarily because ' . . . the absolute levels of high functioning therapist groups are at moderate or low levels of the conditions' (Mitchell, et. al., 1977, p. 488). The reviews suggest that the research evidence did not support the potency and generalizability of the conditions as being as significant as once thought (Mitchell, et al, 1977). However, Mitchell, et al, in addition to their concern about the nebulousness of support by research studies for necessity and sufficiency of the conditions also expressed astonishment at the positive outcome results of clients of 'higher' condition therapists when these therapists were seldom rated higher than minimal levels of therapeutic potency.

   • 1980-1987  The research direction moved away from Rogers' hypotheses to examine facets of therapy in different ways (Gelso and Carter, 1985; Orlinsky and Howard, 1987). Gelso and Carter noted in a theoretical statement that from their perspective (i.e., psychoanalytic) '. . . the conditions originally specified by Rogers are neither necessary nor sufficient although it seems clear that such conditions are facilitative' (p. 220). However, the research summaries were challenged as being unsubstantiated conclusions of research (Patterson, 1984, 1985). Patterson suggests that the inherent biases of the reviews generally distort the accuracy and meaning of the research summaries. His re-evaluation and summary of the research studies suggest strong evidence for the conditions being necessary and sufficient.

Some research in Europe on the attitudinal qualities has supported the notion that the conditions are necessary and sufficient (Tausch, 1978, 1987a). However, Tausch also reported other activities as being helpful to various individuals and pointed to convergencies and rapprochement of the person-centered position with behavior therapy (Tausch, 1982; 1987b). Later, he suggests that it is necessary for clients to have 'client-centered communication' supplemented by other treatment modalities (Tausch, 1990).

Several authors propose that the conditions have not been adequately tested (Bozarth, 1983; Mitchell, et. al, 1977; Watson, 1984). I have pointed out that a common ploy of critics of Rogers is arbitrarily to dismiss the fundamental assumption of the person-centered approach and proceed with criticism from other theoretical frames of reference (Bozarth, 1992a, 1995). (This is elaborated upon in Chapter 1 and other parts of this book) It is also noted that therapist samples so seldom include individuals who hold the basic philosophy of the client-centered/person-centered approach that research results on the conditions are thoroughly confounded (Bozarth, 1983). Most of the studies of client-centered therapy consist of therapists (usually student therapists) who apply reflective or empathic listening or 'client-centered communication' (Tausch, 1990) and designated therapeutic behavior without necessarily incorporating the fundamental beliefs of the approach. Watson (1984) views Rogers' (1957) statements as tenets in a scientific method experiment and suggests that they have never been scientifically investigated because several of the six tenets have been ignored.

The research summaries of the evidence regarding the relationship of the attitudinal qualities to client improvement vary in their conclusions. Some reviewers summarize the research as supportive of Rogers' hypotheses (Bergin and Lambert, 1978; Patterson, 1984, 1985). Others are critical of the positive research results (Parloff, Waskow, and Wolf, 1978). Still others suggest that investigators report that more complex relationships exist among therapist, patients, and techniques (Parloff, Waskow, and Wolf, 1978). Numerous reports have used such information to buttress arguments framed in other theoretical approaches (Fay and Lazarus, 1992; Norcross, 1992; Quinn, 1993). Several articles question the extent to which the hypotheses have been investigated (Bozarth, 1983; Mitchell, et al, 1977; Watson, 1984); Two of these reviews might be better described as optimistic about the potency of the conditions and pessimistic about the research efforts (Bozarth, 1983; Mitchell et al, 1977). The extended qualitative analysis of psychotherapy literature over four decades of efficacy research reaffirm that the attitudes espoused by Rogers are the only consistent thread that emerges in relation to psychotherapy effectiveness (Stubbs and Bozarth, 1994).

There is virtually no direct research that supports the position that the attitudinal qualities are necessary but not sufficient and something else is needed for therapeutic personality change. There are no direct research inquiries concerning additional sufficient applications that even approach the same level of research inquiry directed toward the necessary and sufficient conditions. The conclusion of necessary but not sufficient as it emerges from the research is, at best, a quantum leap of interpretation. It is a conclusion predicated on those research reviews that are critical of the positive research results and which conclude that there is no relationship between the conditions and client outcome. Thus, they conclude that the conditions are not sufficient and that more is needed. There is a leap to the assumption that something else is needed (generally, therapist interventions and techniques) and that these additional therapeutic offerings promote sufficiency.

**Relevant literature**

A review of the general psychological literature might be the logical place to find the origin of the notion that the conditions are necessary but not sufficient; demanding additional 'sufficient' therapist activity.

A common view of the requisite conditions for basic personality change probably is that there is no absolute condition for constructive personality change (Bozarth, 1993). However, the forerunner of the 'necessary but not sufficient' statement appears to be the reference to: 'The Necessary But Insufficient Skill of Empathic Understanding' (Krumboltz's, 1967, p. 224). He referred to the skill of empathic listening as being 'only one, of the many skills which a behaviorally-oriented counselor must learn' (p. 224). He viewed empathic listening as the *sine qua non* of client-centered counseling. He pointed out that his view does not fit the behavioral model since, among other things, the behavioral counselor must learn how to translate client-presented problems into achievable objectives. Krumboltz was quite clear that his discussion had to do with counselors who operated from a behaviorally oriented frame of reference.

The confounding of the behavioral view with the basic assumptions of the necessary and sufficient conditions as hypothesized by Rogers occurred with the proposal of action dimensions (Carkhuff, 1969; Egan, 1975; Gendlin, 1974; Gendlin, 1981; Truax and Carkhuff, 1967). This position reasserted the therapist as an agent who should direct client behaviors towards more effective functioning. It is ironic that models developed from Rogers' conceptualizations incorporated elements that encourage therapist interventions (Truax and Carkhuff, 1967; Carkhuff, 1969). Eventually, the models presented the client-centered component as the initial but incomplete effort because the therapist was expected to encourage clients toward action dimensions. The combination of the influence of the human relations models and the trend of the psychological literature towards cognitive behaviorism seems to have influenced the conclusion that the conditions are necessary but not sufficient. Many authors of the psychotherapeutic literature (as well as authors of research reviews) do not understand or accept the supposition that the clients know best about their lives and improve life when an atmosphere is provided by a therapist who operates on this premise. Authors seem unable to discard the notion that the therapist must intervene in some way, at some point, to set the client going in an appropriate direction. With this presupposition, the logical conclusion has to be that the conditions are not sufficient. The fundamental premise of the person-centered approach is ignored.

The bulk of the psychological literature simply examines Rogers' conceptualizations from frames of reference that are markedly different from

Rogers' contentions. They do not consider the revolutionary stance of the assumption of the extensive trust in the self-authority and resources of the individual of the client (Bozarth, 1993; 1995). As such, no conclusion could possibly be reached that would threaten the intentions for interventions of therapists.

As noted previously, the conclusions in the literature that the conditions are not sufficient are views from other frames of reference (e.g., behavioral, psychoanalytic) that are not predicated on the assumption of the actualizing tendency. Alternative assumptions about therapy have a predominant set that do not accept personal therapeutic growth as a result of only the presence and communication of the attitudinal qualities of the therapist. The therapist from these views is predisposed to act or intervene to influence the client. The operational model is that it is the responsibility of the therapist to know what is going on with clients and what needs to be done about it (Schaff, 1992). Whereas, Rogers' central point is that we are tapping into a tendency that permeates all organized life (Rogers, 1980). Rogers' point is simply not considered in such presentations. Thus, empathic listening cannot be accepted when it is described (somewhat inaccurately) as the *sine qua non* of Rogerian therapy because it does not fit the behavioral paradigm (Krumboltz, 1967). Likewise, proponents of the Human Relations Training Model act on the premise that one must go beyond the client-centered approach since client-centered therapists seldom get to 'action' in their view. In addition, those who argue that the client-centered approach is not enough either do not understand or do not accept the basic foundation of the client-centered/person-centered approach, i.e., the actualizing tendency as a functional stance (Carkhuff, 1969; Gendlin, 1981; Egan, 1975). The concept of the actualizing tendency may be accepted by some as an abstract notion without considering it to be a functional stance in therapeutic encounters (Bozarth and Brodley, 1986). The remainder of this chapter discusses the conceptualization of the necessary and sufficient conditions within the framework of client-centered theory.

**Theoretical foundation**
This section reviews the theoretical foundation of the person-centered approach in relation to the hypothesis of the 'necessary and sufficient conditions for therapeutic personality change'. The following statement is meant to summarize the application of the theoretical foundations of the person-centered approach:

It is when the therapist embodies the attitudinal qualities of congruency, unconditional positive regard, and empathic understanding in a relationship with the client in such a way that the locus of control belongs to the client and the client perceives/experiences these qualities that the actualizing process of the client, unhindered by the therapist can be depended on to flow in the direction of positive growth.

This theoretical statement is viewed from the perceptual stance of the therapist. It was hypothesized that if the therapist could experience unconditional positive regard and empathic understanding of the client's frame of reference and the client perceives the experience of empathic understanding and unconditional positive regard then the process of client change would follow (Rogers, 1959). If these circumstances exist over a period of time, he implicitly presumes that the other theoretical frames-of-reference do not matter if they are not perceived by the client as contradicting the therapist as experiencing unconditional positive regard and empathic understanding. If these conditions exist, no other conditions are necessary. They are sufficient. Stated in linear terms: if the conditions exist over time then nothing else is necessary and the conditions are sufficient. Rogers does not talk about whether or not there might be other factors sufficient to induce therapeutic personality change other than to state his hypothesis that significant positive personality change always occurs in a relationship. It is interesting, however, that he identifies conditions 2 and 6 as: 'the characteristics of the relationship which are regarded as essential by defining the necessary characteristics of each person in the relationship' (p. 96). These conditions state that one person (the client) is in a state of incongruence and the other (the therapist) communicates as a congruent person the experiencing of the other two conditions, unconditional positive regard and empathic understanding, in a way that is, at least, minimally perceived by the client. There is, however, a question: can a person experience the conditions when they are not experienced or communicated by the particular person of the therapist? Is it possible that the vulnerable person's (e.g., client's) actualizing process can be promoted in other ways? The concept of the actualizing tendency seems to me theoretically to suggest that individuals do improve without necessarily being in relationship with therapists; albeit, there might be a perceived relationship with someone.

**Not necessarily necessary**
At this point the question is raised: are the conditions not necessarily necessary? I believe this is a useful secondary inquiry because it brings to the forefront the assumption of the actualizing tendency and the remarkable resiliency of human beings who quite often overcome intolerable circumstances (and perhaps even their therapists) to improve. The concept of the actualizing tendency is the foundation block of the person-centered approach as discussed in the previous chapter. The actualizing tendency is described as the central source of energy and motivation in the human organism. Rogers' conceptualization is that of ' . . . a tendency toward fulfilment, toward actualization, involving not only maintenance but also the enhancement of the organism' (Rogers, 1980, p. 123). Humans are always doing the best they can with a ' . . . flow of movement toward constructive fulfilment of its inherent possibilities' (Rogers, 1980, p. 117). One of the intriguing aspects of the potato metaphor presented in chapter 4 is that the sprouts of the potatoes move toward the distant light. They seek the conditions conducive to growth. Conceivably, individuals also seek and use whatever is available to them for constructive change. There are certainly individuals who report significant change and improved function from experiencing a religious conversion, a sunset, a smile, a traumatic experience, and so on. The wide variety of suggestions and

interventions of therapists that have been reported by clients to be useful to them include such activities as learning to ride a bicycle, learning to dance, learning to meditate, trusting in God, communicating with their loved ones, and not talking about their problems with their loved ones. The non-specific, quite unreliable therapist interventions and suggestions can be used by clients to grow when the core conditions seem to be minimally experienced by them. The remarkable resiliency of humans in terms of the actualizing tendency leads me to conclude that the conditions may not necessarily be necessary.

This chapter challenges conclusions of some research reviews and comments in the psychological literature that the conditions postulated by Rogers as necessary and sufficient for therapeutic personality change are necessary but not sufficient. Examination of several reviews of research, relevant literature, and the theoretical underpinnings of the person-centered approach repudiate the conclusion that the attitudinal qualities as hypothesized by Rogers are necessary but not sufficient. This is further elaborated upon in the chapter on research. The theoretical foundation of the actualizing tendency suggests that it is more accurate to conclude that the conditions are not necessarily necessary but always sufficient.

# A Reconceptualization of The Necessary and Sufficient Conditions for Therapeutic Personality Change

6

In this chapter, I suggest a reconceptualization of Rogers' hypothesis of the necessary and sufficient conditions for therapeutic personality change. A conceptual model entailing the relationship of the three conditions of therapist genuineness, empathic understanding and unconditional positive regard to each other is proposed. It is suggested that these conditions continue to be necessary and sufficient but that their relationship can be reconceptualized in a way that will emphasize their unique conceptual contributions. Genuineness and empathic understanding are viewed as two contextual attitudes for the primary condition of change; i.e., unconditional positive regard. My conclusions come primarily from a re-examination of Rogers' two major theoretical statements (1957; 1959). The first of these statements in 1957 generated a wealth of research in the realm of psychotherapy. However, the theoretical statement of Rogers in 1959 is the most disciplined statement of his theory of psychotherapy, personality and interpersonal relationships. It is the 1959 statement that provides the basis for the view that unconditional positive regard is the primary change agent in client-centered therapy.

### Review of person-centered theory
The foundation block of person-centered therapy is the concept of the actualizing tendency. The implications of this concept is that the therapist can trust the tendency of the client and, hence, the therapist is liberated to concentrate on the role of creating an interpersonal climate that promotes the individual's actualizing tendency (Bozarth and Brodley, 1986) (see chapter 4). The rationale for person-centered theory in interpersonal relationships rests on the actualizing tendency as the foundation block of the theory (Bozarth and Brodley, 1991; Rogers, 1980; see also Chapter 4). The actualizing tendency is promoted by the attitudinal conditions held by the therapist and noted by Rogers as the necessary and sufficient conditions for therapeutic personality change.

Adapted with permission from:
Bozarth, J. D. (1996). A theoretical reconsideration of the necessary and sufficient conditions for therapeutic personality change. *The Person-Centered Journal*. 3 (1) 44-51.

## The 'if – then' delineation

Rogers' most disciplined and rigorous presentation of his theory is an 'if – then' format (Rogers, 1959). That is, he postulates that if certain conditions exist, a certain process in the client will follow, and if that process occurs in therapy, then there is a certain outcome in personality and behavior. It is important, however, to note this is not an instruction but an observation of what happens and a hypothesis of the process. Thus, there is not intent 'to make' such processes occur. Among other things, the process includes certain occurrences in the client. These occurrences include the following:

1. That the client is freer in expressing feelings;
2. That the client's ' . . . expressed feelings increasingly have reference to the self, rather than nonself' (Rogers, 1959: cited in Kirschenbaum and Henderson, 1989, p. 239);
3. That the client's ' . . . experiences are more accurately symbolized' (Rogers, 1959: cited in Kirschenbaum and Henderson, 1989, p. 239);
4. That the client has increasingly more reference to incongruity between certain experiences and concept of self;
5. That the client is more able to experience the threat of incongruence;
6. That the client experiences in awareness feelings which have been denied or distorted in the past;
7. That the client has the concept of self reorganized to include previously distorted or denied experiences;
8. That the client's concept of self becomes congruent with experiences; including those which would have been too threatening in the past;
9. That the client ' . . . becomes increasingly able to experience, without a feeling of threat, the therapist's unconditional positive regard' (Rogers, 1959: cited in Kirschenbaum and Henderson, 1989, p. 239)
10. That the client ' . . . feels an unconditional positive self regard' (Rogers, 1959: cited in Kirschenbaum and Henderson, 1989, p. 239);
11. That the ' . . . client experiences self as the locus of evaluation' (Rogers, 1959: cited in Kirschenbaum and Henderson, 1989, p. 239);
12. That the client ' . . . reacts to experience less in terms of his conditions of worth and more in terms of an organismic valuing process' (Rogers, 1959: cited in Kirschenbaum and Henderson, 1989, p. 239).

The outcomes of therapy include the client becoming:

1. More congruent and open to experience;
2. More realistic and objective in perceptions;
3. More effective in problem solving; this suggests more enhanced psychological adjustment, increased degree of positive self-regard, more acceptance of others, and behavior being perceived as more social and mature by others.

Rogers' statement concerning the person's capacity to experience the threat of incongruence (point 5) is especially appropriate. He quite specifically states: 'The experience of threat is possible only because of the continued unconditional positive regard of the therapist, which is extended to incongruence as much as to congruence, to anxiety as much as to absence of anxiety' (Rogers, 1959: cited in Kirschenbaum and Henderson, 1989, p. 239). Point 12 is also especially relevant to this chapter; i.e., that the individual reacts to experience less in terms of conditions of worth and more in terms of the organismic valuing process. This occurs as the individual experiences unconditional positive regard. In short, the increasing experience of worth (or unconditional positive regard) promotes the organismic valuing process (or the actualizing tendency).

## The theoretical statement of anxiety

Rogers' theoretical statement of anxiety further clarifies unconditional positive regard as being the fundamental component for personality change in the theory. He states that anxiety exists because of ' . . . the threat that if the experience were accurately symbolized in awareness, the self-concept would no longer be a consistent gestalt, the conditions of worth would be violated, and the need for self-regard would be frustrated. A state of anxiety would exist' (Rogers, 1959: cited in Kirschenbaum and Henderson, 1989, p. 247). The crux of Rogers' theory is summarized in his statement on the process of integration of an individual moving in the direction of congruence between self and experience: for threatening experiences to be accurately symbolized in awareness and assimilated into the self-structure, there must be a decrease in conditions of worth and an increase in unconditional *self*-regard. The communication of unconditional positive regard by a significant other is one way to achieve the above conditions. In order for unconditional positive regard to be communicated, it must exist in a context of empathic understanding. When the individual perceives such unconditional positive regard, conditions of worth are weakened and unconditional positive self-regard is strengthened (Rogers, 1959: cited in Kirschenbaum and Henderson, 1989, p. 249). The consequences of threatening experiences being assimilated into the self-structure and unconditional positive regard being perceived:

> . . .are that the individual is less likely to encounter threatening experiences; the process of defense is less frequent and its consequences reduced; self and experience are more congruent; self-regard is increased; positive regard for others is increased; psychological adjustment is increased; the organismic valuing process becomes increasingly the basis of regulating behavior; the individual becomes nearly fully functioning.
> (Rogers, 1959: cited in Kirschenbaum and Henderson, 1989, p. 249)

Rogers is also explicit about the role of unconditional positive regard when discussing his ultimate hypothetical actualized person. In essence, he says that the individual has two tendencies which are (1) an inherent tendency toward actualizing his or her organism and (2) the capacity and tendency to symbolize experiences accurately in awareness; or, in other words, to keep the self-concept congruent with one's experience. The individual needs positive regard and positive self-regard. The first two tendencies are most fully realized when the second two needs are met. Rogers further states that the first two tendencies tend to be most fully realized when:

1. The individual experiences unconditional positive regard from significant others.
2. The pervasiveness of this unconditional positive regard is made evident through relationships marked by a complete and communicated empathic understanding of the individual's frame of reference.

It is significant that although Rogers' writings about empathic understanding included reference to the importance of understanding and clarification of meaning of the person's frame of reference that these writings always included reference to unconditional positive regard or acceptance in one way or another; and that in his formal theoretical statement, unconditional positive regard is the fundamental concept affecting change (Rogers, 1951, 1959, 1980). Although some individuals discuss extrapolations of Rogers' view of therapy, the fundamental base of the theory remains in the 1959 statement (Van Balen, 1990; Van Belle, 1980). Rogers never revised his theory statement to include thoughts that just his presence could be healing (Baldwin, 1987; Rogers, 1959).

**Theoretical relationship of the attitudinal conditions**
Given that unconditional positive regard is the attitudinal condition that is the primary change agent, the attitudes of genuineness and empathic understanding are integrally interrelated. However, the focus on unconditional positive regard as the primary change agent suggests to me that the theoretical relationship of the three necessary and sufficient attitudinal qualities can be viewed in a different way. It is, thus, proposed that the following reconceptualization be considered:

Genuineness is a therapist trait that must exist. It is contextual; that is, this condition is an attitudinal development that enables the therapist to be more able to experience empathic understanding and unconditional positive regard towards the client. It is, for the therapist, a way to prepare him or her self as a maximally receptive therapist. In both the 1957 and 1959 hypothesis statements, congruence (or genuineness) is stated by Rogers as a therapist quality in the relationship but unlike the other two attitudinal qualities it is neither related directly to the client nor viewed as an attitude to be perceived by the client.

Empathy is also contextual. Empathy is the 'vessel' by which the therapist communicates unconditional positive regard in the most pure way. I interpret this to mean that Rogers thought that the therapist's frame of reference tends to contaminate the purity of the therapist's experience of unconditional positive regard. Empathic understanding of the client's internal frame of reference is one of the two attitudinal qualities which needs to be perceived by the client. It is, however, the only attitudinal action on the part of the therapist. The action of understanding the momentary frame of reference of the client is an ultimate confirmation of the person by the therapist; hence, representing the purity of the therapist's experience of unconditional positive regard towards the client.

Unconditional positive regard is the primary theoretical condition of client change in person-centered therapy. Although there may be other ways that unconditional positive regard is communicated and/or perceived by the client, the underlying premise of the theory is unconditional positive regard in which therapist congruence and empathic understanding of the client's frame of reference is embedded. This attitudinal quality is the unconditional acceptance of the person's momentary frame of reference and all that entails (e.g., feelings and perceptions).

In summary, this reconceptualization of the necessary and sufficient conditions for therapeutic personality change entails (1) genuineness (or congruency) being viewed as a therapist state of readiness that enables the therapist to better experience the client with empathic understanding of the client's internal frame of reference and experience unconditional positive regard towards the client; (2) empathic understanding of the client's frame of reference being viewed as the action state of the therapist in which the client's world is accepted as he or she is experiencing it at any given moment. This is the most optimal way for the client to experiencing unconditional positive regard; and (3) unconditional positive regard being viewed as the primary change agent in which the client's needs for positive regard and positive self regard are met, resulting in congruence between his or her experience and self concept and promotion of the actualizing tendency.

## Practical implications

The attitudinal conditions of genuineness, empathic understanding and unconditional positive regard have been considered as skills (Truax and Mitchell, 1971). They have been considered to be preconditions for other actions (Gendlin, 1990; Tausch, 1990), and they have been considered to be attitudinal qualities (Bozarth and Brodley, 1986; 1991; Heppner, Rogers, and Lee, 1984; Rogers, 1951; 1957, 1959, 1980, 1986b). They have rarely (if ever) been viewed in a logical theoretical relationship to each other or to the general theory of personality and behavior change posited by Rogers.

An examination of these conceptualizations in relation to Rogers' theory of psychotherapy, personality theory and interpersonal relationships, suggests that the quality of genuineness is a therapist preparatory attitude and enabler, i.e., for the therapist to be more able to experience empathic understanding of the client's frame of reference and unconditional positive regard toward the client. This view of the concept of genuineness suggests that therapists participate in activities that help them to become more genuine or more able to be more '. . . freely and deeply him (her) self, with his or her actual experience accurately represented by his awareness of himself' (Rogers, 1959: cited in Kirschenbaum and Henderson, 1989, p. 224). Such activities as individual therapy, encounter groups, person-centered community groups might be some ways in which therapists can develop this attitudinal quality.

Empathic understanding of the client's frame of reference is, thus, more aptly experienced by the therapist in a natural way. The view that the attitudinal quality of empathic understanding is the vessel for maximizing the probability of the therapist experiencing unconditional positive regard toward the client, and for the client to perceive unconditional positive regard of the therapist has several pragmatic implications.

First, the idea that understanding by the client of his or her world view is of utmost importance for change is a questionable assumption. The therapist can concentrate on the therapist's intention to understand the client's frame of reference and not be concerned about whether or not the client understands. Second, this could suggest that the intention of the therapist to understand might be as potent as the understanding in and of itself. Third, Rogers' references to his presence as a person in therapy and the use of self as a therapist being, perhaps, more important than providing the attitudinal conditions might be explained within the framework of this reconceptualization (Baldwin, 1987). That is, the presence of total attending to another individual is apt to be perceived by clients as unconditional positive regard. Unconditional positive regard as the fundamental change agent may have greater significance for the focus on 'being' person-centered versus 'doing' person-centered communication. This has implications even more contradictory to the concepts of intervening, directing, controlling and confronting the client's own process than generally associated with person-centered theory. This conceptualization renews the importance of nondirectivity in the framework of person-centered theory. When the client perceives that ' . . . the therapist is experiencing a positive, nonjudgmental, accepting attitude toward whatever the client is at that moment, therapeutic change is more likely' (Rogers, 1986b, p.198). This involves ' . . . the therapist's willingness for the client to be whatever immediate feeling is going on - confusion, resentment, fear, anger, courage, love, or pride' (p.198). Unconditional positive regard of the therapist for the client is the acceptance of the client's totality of experience, feelings, cognitions at any given moment. As stated by Van Belle (1980):

> . . .we are only actualized by others and ourselves at the regard level, if/when the regard that others show us and which consequently we show ourselves, is unconditionally positive, that is, if/when it is such that personality development can be interpersonally assimilated. (p. 90)

The following comments from an interview with a participant in a person-centered community workshop exemplifies the meaning of unconditional positive regard (Stubbs, 1992):

> And in a moment . . . there was a pressure on me to speak more about something . . . the whole group made a pressure on me. Speak, speak, and I was in a tension. And in that moment the facilitator said 'Well you know, if you don't want to speak, it's perfectly okay.' And it was the very first moment that made me good, made me feel

well. And it made me feel safer. That was very, very fine . . .and the change in me was that uh (begins to cry) the great point of that change was that I felt my mother (the facilitator) accepts me with all my mistakes, all my wrong qualities . . . Because I was not accepted by my own mother, long ago in my childhood . . .that moment or when that change had a big influence on my work or in my job, and I don't know why, because I was very happy or very satisfied with that experience, and I uh tried very hard to be a member of this community. I wanted to go on to continue in this process but in my counseling work, in my job, I uh   . . . uh became a little bit more directive (laughs) or maybe freer to be directive after that experience, which is a paradox.  (p.88)

Although this statement is not necessarily one of empathic understanding, the impact of the perceived unconditional positive regard of his facilitator, whom he viewed as similar to his mother, is clear.

My reconceptualization of the necessary and sufficient conditions for therapeutic personality change is, perhaps, reflected in a statement that I heard Rogers make several times more to himself than to others. He stated: 'If I can be all that I am, then that is good enough.' I would add, 'If the individual can be affirmed in being who he or she is at the moment, then that is good enough.'

# EMPATHY FROM THE FRAMEWORK OF CLIENT-CENTERED THEORY AND THE ROGERIAN HYPOTHESIS

7

This chapter examines Rogers' unique conceptualization of empathy as it has evolved in relationship to client-centered theory (Rogers, 1959). The Rogerian hypothesis or 'integrative' statement, of the necessary and sufficient conditions for therapeutic personality change is also examined (Rogers, 1957). Carl Rogers' conception of empathy is central to client/person-centered theory and to the Rogerian hypothesis (Rogers, 1951; 1957; 1959; 1975; 1980; 1986a; 1986b; 1987; 1989b). Although it was Rogers and Kohut who perpetuated empathy as having central importance in psychotherapy, Rogers' view of empathy is different from Kohut's (Kohut, 1959; Rogers, 1980). Rogers considered empathy to be (1) a central therapeutic construct rather than a precondition for other forms of treatment, (2) an attitude towards and therapist's experiencing of the client rather than any particular therapist behavior, (3) an interpersonal process grounded in a non-directive attitude, and (4) a part of a whole attitude wherein the experience of empathic understanding is intertwined with the therapist's congruence and the experiencing of unconditional positive regard towards the client. Rogers also brought attention to a particular way of communicating the empathic attitude which he referred to as, 'Reflection' or 'Reflection of Feelings'. Rogers' unique view of empathy is discussed in the context of his theory and his written comments. This chapter points out that Rogerian empathy is (1) integrally intertwined with congruence and unconditional positive regard as they exist within his hypothesis; (2) found within the context of nondirectivity which is an essential component of Rogerian empathy; (3) a process intending only to understand the client's frame of reference rather than to achieve any particular therapeutic goal and, as such, communicates unconditional positive regard; and (4) an attitude rather than any particular way of responding. This chapter also suggests that Rogerian empathy is primarily the purest way to communicate unconditional positive regard. Rogerian

Adapted with permission from:
Bozarth, J. D. (1997a). Empathy from the framework of client-centered theory and the Rogerian hypothesis. In Bohart, A. and Greenburg, L. (eds.). *Empathy Reconsidered: New Directions in Psychotherapy*, pp. 81-102, Washington D. C.: American Psychological Association Press.

empathy is, in fact, inseparable from unconditional positive regard and, ultimately, I suggest that they are the same condition.

**Theoretical framework**

Rogers' basic assumption is that human thought, feeling and behavior is motivated and directed by one constructive force, the actualizing tendency, which is inherent in the organism (Bozarth and Brodley, 1991). His theory of the process of personality disturbance purports that individuals develop psychological problems resulting from the introjections of conditional acceptance from parents and other significant persons. These introjections of conditional regard create incongruence between organismic experiencing and the self concept. As the self becomes laden with conditions of worth, it results in anxiety and vulnerability for the person. The theory asserts that it is when the person perceives unconditional positive regard in the context of empathic understanding from a congruent individual (the therapist) that the actualizing tendency of the client is promoted (Rogers, 1959). It is from this theoretical base that the 'necessary and sufficient' conditions were posed as the therapeutic attitudes for the therapist to embody. Rogers' statement concerning the conditions within client-centered theory is delineated in chapter 4 on the actualizing tendency. It can readily be seen from Rogers' six point statement that the conditions are integrally related as one hypothesis, especially the therapist's experiencing of and the client's perception of empathic understanding and unconditional positive regard.

**Delineation of Rogerian empathy**

Examination of Rogers' historical and evolutionary delineation of empathy suggests the following assertion:

> • *Assertion 1: Empathy in client-centered theory is a concept that is integrated with the conditions of congruency and unconditional positive regard. It exists within a context of non-directivity and is predicated on the foundation block of the actualizing tendency.*

Rogers brought a distinct view to the concept of empathy by making it central to the therapeutic change process; that is, if only the therapist experiences an empathic understanding and unconditional acceptance of clients, the clients who perceive the conditions will be better able to understand themselves, accept themselves, make behavioral changes that enhance their lives and be more able to relate constructively in their social world.

Rogers' first major theoretical work on 'nondirective therapy' did not mention the term empathy; however, a number of his comments paved the way for the conceptualization. For example, in his discussion of a good therapist he refers to '. . . a capacity for sympathy . . . a generally receptive and interested attitude, a deep understanding which will find it impossible to pose moral judgements' (Rogers, 1942, p. 254). He also refers to . . . a degree of sympathetic identification with (the client) as him (or her), on his (or her) own level of adjustment . . . (p. 255). He also voiced the non-directive element in empathy, describing the therapy relationship as expressing '. . . warmth of acceptance and absence of any coercion or personal pressure. . . (pp. 113-114). He asserted that the therapist '. . . takes no responsibility for directing the outcome of the process' (p. 115).

Early in his career, Rogers asked the question, 'What, if anything, do all these therapeutic approaches have in common?' (Rogers, 1939: Cited in Kirschenbaum, 1979, p. 96) At that time, Rogers identified four qualifications of the therapist for effective therapy with children as: (1) objectivity, (2) respect for the individual, (3) understanding of self and (4) psychological knowledge. Rogers elaborates upon these qualifications (cited in Thorne, 1992):

1. Objectivity, in which he included a 'capacity for sympathy which will not be overdone, a genuinely receptive and interested attitude, a deep understanding which will find it impossible to pass moral judgements or be shocked and horrified.'
2. A respect for the individual: the aim is to leave the major responsibilities in the hands of the child as an individual going towards independence.
3. Understanding of the self, to which he allied the therapist's ability to be self-accepting as well as self-aware.
4. Psychological knowledge, by which he meant 'a thorough basis of knowledge of human behavior and of its physical, social and psychological determinants'.

(Rogers, 1939: cited in Thorne, 1992, p. 10)

Rogers' attempt to identify the core and crucial qualifications of the therapist in work with children appears to be an early forerunner to his general hypothesis of the necessary and sufficient conditions for personality change in all therapies and all therapeutic approaches.

Rogers first focused on his theory as 'nondirective therapy'. He also focused on 'reflection of feelings' which he cautioned not to be practised as a simple technique. Rogers could write in the mid-1940s that (cited in Kirschenbaum, 1979):

. . . to create a psychological climate in which the client feels the kind of warmth, understanding and freedom from attack in which he may drop his defensiveness, and explore and reorganize his life style, is a far more subtle and delicate process than simply 'reflecting feeling.' (p. 160)

It is clear that 'understanding' of the client was couched in, if not subsidiary, to 'warm acceptance' and an atmosphere of freedom toward the client. While Rogers focused on the therapist's activity as one which was meant to clarify the feelings of individuals, he used the terms 'clarification', 'reflection', and 'reflection of feelings'. The role of the therapist's action was that:

Reflection of feelings communicates to the client that whatever his

> feelings and behavior are or have been, no matter how troubling or
> frightening or socially disapproved of, he is still accepted as a worthy
> human being by the therapist.
>
> (Kirschenbaum, 1979, p. 120)

Much of Rogers' work at the University of Chicago, although grounded in the attitudinal principles, focused on therapists' responses. Out of the scientific method and with a behavioral context, Rogers and his colleagues examined the effect of specific client behaviors to specific responses of the therapist. It was not until Rogers became concerned about the misunderstandings of 'reflection' and use of reflection techniques that he talked about the client's 'frame of reference' and, then, began to use the term, 'empathy'. Empathy provided Rogers with a more comprehensive meaning that emphasized attitude rather than a response repertoire.

As Rogers began to employ the term 'empathy', he described it as the therapist's development of an interest in and receptivity to the client and a search for a deep non-judgmental understanding (Rogers, 1951). It involved identification with the client, respect for the client as a whole person and acceptance of the person as he/she is. The search, through interaction with the client and close attention to the client was and is considered a non-directive process. Indeed, the empathic therapist is responsible for his/her attitudes and responsiveness to the client and not for the outcome of the therapy. Later, Rogers' descriptions of the empathic process focused on the therapist's empathic intention (Rogers, 1980):

> . . . to sense the hurt or the pleasure of another as he (or she) senses
> it, and to perceive the causes thereof as he (or she) perceives them .
> . .( p. 210). . . (and it involves) . . . lay(ing) aside all perceptions from
> the external frame of reference. (p. 29)

And:

> It means entering the private perceptual world of the other . . .being
> sensitive, moment by moment, to the changing felt meanings which
> flow in this other person. . . It means sensing meanings of which he
> or she is scarcely aware, but not trying to uncover totally unconscious
> feelings . . . (p. 142)

This is the kind of understanding required in client-centered therapy; namely: ' . . . the therapist's sensitive ability and willingness to understand the client's thoughts, feelings and struggles from the client's point of view. This ability to see completely through the client's eyes, to adopt his frame of reference. . . is the basis for the use of the term "client-centered" . . .' (cited in Kirschenbaum, 1979, p. 164). In these explanations of empathic understanding, Rogers' focus on understanding empathy *per se* is directed towards the therapist's activity and does not include explicit reference to his fundamental therapeutic change agent of unconditional positive regard. Rogers' implicit, and often explicit, assumption in his definition of empathic understanding is that it is integrally related to the unconditional positive regard of the therapist for the client. Indeed, empathic understanding is the unconditional acceptance of the individual's frame of reference.

It should be noted that Rogers was quite insistent that one should perceive the internal frame of reference from the person's view without losing the 'as if' condition. This seemed particular important to Rogers. Perhaps, this was related to a difficulty where he had approached a 'psychotic' breakdown while working with a 'psychotic' client (Kirschenbaum, 1979, p. 191). He did, as previously noted, identify 'objectivity' as one of the qualifications of the therapist in his early speculations about common therapist qualities even though it was couched in the idea of helping the therapist not to pass moral judgements on the client. Whatever the reason, he seemed particularly concerned that the therapist not identify with the client but maintain the 'as if' dimension.

**The integrative statement**

Rogers' formal 1957 statement of the necessary and sufficient conditions for therapeutic personality change accounts for therapeutic personality change as it occurs in all therapy, not only in client-centered therapy (Stubbs and Bozarth, 1996). In this statement as well as in his 1959 formulation of client-centered theory, Rogers asserts the necessity that the client perceive the therapist's experiencing of acceptant empathic understanding for therapeutic change to occur. Neither Rogers' theory of therapeutic change nor the hypothesis of the necessary and sufficient conditions are expressed in terms of behavior. This is a crucial point in understanding Rogerian empathy particularly because most explanations of it and models developed from Rogers' hypothesis have cast the concept into a behavioral framework (e.g., Carkhuff, 1971; Cormier and Cormier, 1991; Corey, 1982; Egan, 1975). The frequent focus on techniques and the therapist's behavioral strategies have been responsible for misunderstanding and trivializing client-centered therapy and its concept of empathy (Bozarth, 1994; Bozarth and Brodley, 1986; Stubbs and Bozarth, 1996). Rogers' theory is expressed in terms of the therapist's attitudes. There is no specific behavior or pattern of behavior which can be considered to be an inevitable expression of empathy nor a necessarily true expression of an empathic attitude. The role of attitudes is conveyed in a statement Rogers (1957):

> (There is) no essential value to the therapy of such techniques as interpretation of personality dynamics, free association, analysis of dreams, analysis of transference, hypnosis, interpretation of life style, suggestion and the like. Each of these techniques may, however, become a channel for communicating the essential conditions. . . But just as these techniques may communicate the elements that are essential for therapy, so any one of them may communicate attitudes and experiences sharply contradictory to the hypothesized conditions of therapy. (p. 101)

There is, in fact, no specific form of communication of the therapeutic attitudes which can describe client-centered therapy or communicate the necessary and sufficient conditions (Bozarth, 1984; Stubbs and Bozarth, 1996; Rogers, 1957; 1959). Although empathic understanding responses earlier referred to as 'reflection of feelings' responses have been identified with client-centered work, such responses are not to be confused with empathy (Brodley, 1993; Rogers, 1986). The limited importance of specific responses is emphasized by Rogers in his comment concerning techniques (Rogers, 1957):

> ... the techniques of the various therapies are relatively unimportant except to the extent that they serve as channels for fulfilling one of the conditions. In client-centered therapy, for example, (even) the technique of 'reflecting feelings'. . . is by no means an essential condition of therapy. To the extent . . . that it provides a channel by which the therapist communicates a sensitive empathy and an unconditional positive regard, then it may serve as a technical channel by which the essential conditions of therapy are fulfilled. . . Feeling may (however) be reflected in a way which communicates the therapist's lack of empathy. (pp. 102-103)

Rogerian empathy is fundamentally the same in his theory and his integrative statement.

### Empathy and the nondirective attitude as the therapist's activity

The therapist has a deliberate and abiding intent to understand empathically and accept the immediate frame of reference and experience of the client while being integrated and congruent in him/herself. The attitudinal action component of the therapist is that of empathy. The therapist's activities involve several categories which are commented upon in this section.

The nondirective attitude is rarely mentioned in recent literature concerning the client-centered/person-centered approach. It is, however, implicit in the theory and suggests the following assertion:

• *Assertion 2: There is, in essence, no room for directivity in Rogers' conceptions of therapy and the therapist's role. Nondirectivity casts a major influence on Rogers' conceptualization of empathy.*

Although the concept of nondirectivity is not explicit in Rogers' generic theoretical statements nor the integrative statement it is implied in nearly all of Rogers' writings (Rogers, 1951; 1957; 1959; Rogers and Sanford, 1989). Rogers was explicit that he had no goals for clients. As he stated, '. . . the goal has to be within myself, with the way I am' (Baldwin, 1987, p. 47). He contends that therapy is most effective '. . . when the therapist's goals are limited to the process of therapy and not the outcome' (Baldwin, 1987, p. 47). He indicated, 'I want to be as present to this person as possible. I want to really listen to what is going on. I want to be real in this relationship' (Baldwin, 1987, p. 47). He continues: 'Am I really with this person in this moment? . . . (these are) suitable goals for the therapist' (Baldwin,

1987, p. 48). Rogers explained the 'nondirective' attitude as he quotes an unpublished article by Raskin who coined the term. Raskin states (cited in Rogers, 1951):

> There is a level of . . .response which . . . represents the non-directive attitude . . . participation becomes an active experiencing with the client of the feelings to which he (or she) gives expression . . . he (or she) tries to get within and to live the attitudes (of the client) expressed instead of observing them, to catch every nuance of their changing nature; in a word, to absorb himself (or herself) completely in the attitudes of the other. And in struggling to do this, there is simply no room for any other type of counselor activity or attitude; if he (or she) is attempting to live the attitudes of the other, he (or she) cannot be diagnosing them . . . cannot be thinking of making the process go faster . . . (p. 29)

In an analysis of the essence of client-centered therapy, I have asserted that the implications '. . .are staggering' (Bozarth, 1990a):

> It (the essence) is a functional premise that precludes other therapist intentions. The therapist goes with the client – goes at the client's pace – goes with the client in his/her own ways of thinking, of experiencing, of processing. The therapist cannot be up to other things, have other intentions without violating the essence of client-centered therapy. To be up to other things – whatever they might be – is a 'yes but' reaction to the essence of the approach. (p. 63)

The essence of Rogerian therapy is embedded in non-directive empathy. The foundation block of the theory is the actualizing tendency. The change agent is unconditional positive regard.

**Therapist techniques and communications**
Rogers' theory is resistant to the systematic use of techniques and is always embedded in the therapeutic attitudes. The next assertion is:

> • *Assertion 3: Rogers' 'techniques' are always embedded in the therapeutic attitudes; that is, grounded in the inner experiences of the therapist in response to the client's frame of reference.*

Rogers' contribution to techniques is a paradoxical one. The formalization of 'reflection', 'reflection of feelings' and the 'restatement rule' provide a powerful tool for the therapist to attain empathic understanding (Rogers, 1980; Teich, 1992). Shlien has suggested that client-centered therapy would never have progressed without the development of the technique of reflection (Rogers, 1986b). Even so, Rogers was clear that the technique was of little value if not embedded in the attitudes of the therapist. Rogers, in fact, referred to the 'appalling consequences' of the schematization of the principle of reflection into a schema of a technique. Brodley and Brody argue that techniques can be used if they are part of the response to client questions or specific requests by the client (Brodley and Brody, 1996). However, they respond: 'Not if they are the result of the therapist's having a diagnostic mind set that determines which goals and techniques are indicated' (p. 369). I believe that the theory militates against the use of techniques but may be consistent with the theory if they emerge from the blending of the therapist and client (Bozarth, 1996b). I have also argued that: 'The primary reason for involving techniques in a client-centered frame of reference is to help the therapist to clear his/her barriers to absorbing the client's perceptual world (Bozarth, 1996b, p. 367).

To Rogers, empathy is a mode of the therapist's experiencing of another person to an extent that is more than a technique, formula, form or cognitive schema. It is integrally intertwined with trusting the client (in the theory: the actualizing tendency), and within a non-directive context. Rogerian empathy and unconditional positive regard are inseparable.

### Unconditional positive regard and empathy

My next assertion is the following:

• *Assertion 4: The empathic and unconditional acceptance of the therapist is, in essence, the same experience.*

Unconditional positive regard is the crucial client perception in the client's change process and it is conveyed by empathy (Bozarth, 1996a). This is clear in Rogers' early speculations and conceptualizations before he used the term, empathy. In Rogers' theory of personality reintegration (Chapter 6), his view is that learned conditions of worth and consequent incongruence between the self and organismic experiencing are reversed by the growth process inherent in the client, i.e., the process of the actualizing tendency. This inherent process is activated when the client perceives the therapist's unconditional positive regard and develops unconditional positive regard towards him/her self. Such regard is communicated through the therapist's acceptant empathic understandings in the context of the therapist's congruence in the relationship. Rogers states that the role of the combined acceptant and empathic attitudes in terms of the processes that take hold in the client as follows (Rogers, 1980):

> (1) The non-evaluative and acceptant quality of the empathic climate enables the client, as we have seen, to take a prizing, caring attitude towards himself. (2) Being listened to by an understanding person makes it possible for him to listen more accurately to himself, with greater empathy towards his own visceral experiencing, his own vague felt meanings. But (3) his greater understanding of, and prizing of himself opens up part of a more accurately based self. His self is now more congruent with his experiencing. Thus, he has become, in his attitudes toward himself, more caring and acceptant, more

empathic and understanding, more real and congruent (pp. 7-9).

Rogerian empathy involves the therapist in a personal commitment to experience acceptance towards the client and to experience the client's inner world. In client-centered work, empathy is both a manifestation of and a communication vessel for unconditional positive regard. The consequences of such empathy for the recipient is twofold according to Rogers (1980). Empathy ' . . .dissolves alienation . . .' and helps the recipient to feel '. . . valued, cared for, accepted as the person that he or she is . . .' and, when this occurs that '. . . true empathy is always free of any evaluative or diagnostic quality' (Rogers, 1980, pp. 151-155). The non-evaluative and acceptant quality Rogers ascribes to empathy is, in fact, the same as his definition of unconditional positive regard wherein the therapist experiences '. . . a warm acceptance of each aspect of the client's experience as being a part of that client' (Rogers, 1957, p. 93).

## Research findings and Rogerian empathy

An overview of relevant research findings related to Rogerian empathy suggests the following assertion:

- *Assertion 5: To a significant extent, current outcome research substantiates Rogers' conceptualization of empathy in relation to effective psychotherapeutic outcome.*

In his classic article on empathy, Rogers cites several general statements about empathy that emerge from research (Rogers, 1975, 1980). These statements, Rogers believed, could be stated with assurance. The statements are:

- The ideal therapist is first of all empathic. They (therapists of many different orientations) are in high agreement in giving empathy the highest ranking out of twelve variables.
- Empathy is correlated with self-exploration and process movement.
- Empathy early in the relationship predicts later success . . .
- The client comes to perceive more empathy in successful cases.
- Understanding is provided by the therapist . . .
- The more experienced the therapist, the more likely he is to be empathic.
- Empathy is a special quality in a relationship, and therapists offer definitely more of it than even helpful friends. . .
- The better integrated within himself, the higher the degree of empathy the therapist exhibits.
- Experienced therapists often fall far short of being empathic.
- Clients are better judges of the degree of therapy than are therapists.
- Brilliance and diagnostic perceptiveness are unrelated to empathy.
- An empathic way of being can be learned from empathic persons.

(Rogers, 1980, pp 146-150)

Rogers continues in this statement to report that there is 'overwhelming' evidence that empathy is clearly related to positive outcome with individuals diagnosed as schizophrenic, with students, counseling center clients, teachers in training, and individuals diagnosed as neurotic in the United States and Germany. The common thread in all of these research conclusions concerning the impact of empathy is that when a person experiences him or herself as being empathically understood with warm acceptance, a set of growth-promoting therapeutic attitudes are developed towards him/herself.

Research provides the soil for renewed consideration of Rogers' hypothesis (e.g., Bohart and Rosenbaum, 1995; Lambert, Shapiro and Bergin, 1986). (See also Chapter 19). Of particular interest is a qualitative study of the reports of psychotherapy outcome literature over four decades of outcome research (Stubbs and Bozarth, 1994). Of five emergent temporal categories of focus, the abiding relationships to outcome that emerged in some form center on those that Rogers identified in his classic integrative statement as necessary and sufficient for therapeutic personality change (i.e., congruence, unconditional positive regard and empathic understanding) (Rogers, 1957).

Duncan and Moynihan (1994) present an intriguing argument for what is, in essence, Rogerian empathy when they propose a model predicated on recent conclusions concerning the research on psychotherapy outcome. They point out that the research suggests the utility of intentionally utilizing the client's frame of reference. Indeed, they resonate the Rogerian view:

> Empathy, then, is not an invariant, specific therapist behavior or attitude (e.g., reflection of feeling is inherently empathic), nor is it a means to gain a relationship so that the therapist may promote a particular orientation or personal value, nor a way of teaching clients what a relationship should be. Rather, empathy is therapist attitudes and behaviors that place the client's perceptions and experiences above theoretical content and personal values (Duncan, Solovey and Rusk, 1992); empathy is manifested by therapist attempts to work within the frame of reference of the client. When the therapist acts in a way that demonstrates consistency with the client's frame of reference, then empathy may be perceived, and common factor effects enhanced. Empathy, therefore, is a function of the client's unique perceptions and experience and requires that therapists respond flexibly to clients' needs, rather than from a particular theoretical frame of reference or behavioral set. (p. 295)

Duncan and Moynihan, like many researchers, dismiss Rogerian empathy because they identify it with specific behaviors rather than from the bedrock of the empathic attitude in the theory. As such, they apparently do not realize that they are actually proposing an operational concept predicated upon psychotherapy outcome research that is essentially the same as Rogers' conception of empathy. The potency of Rogerian empathy as a complete dedication to and acceptance of the client's perceptual world is reasserted by psychotherapy outcome research.

## The empathic stance

One of the prominent questions concerning Rogerian empathy is, 'How do you do it'? It is contended that one of the greatest sources of misunderstanding of the person-centered approach is that of focusing on 'how to do it' (Bozarth, 1992a; Bozarth and Brodley, 1986; Brodley, 1993). This suggests the next assertion:

- *Assertion 6: Rogerian empathy is not necessarily the same as 'communication' of empathy or 'empathic responses'.*

The therapist-provided conditions for therapeutic change are, in fact, all attitudes – inner, subjective, experiences. They are experiences of the therapist. Any behavior that has the appearance of a therapeutic attitude may or may not implement the attitude. Behaviors that do not appear to fit the descriptions of the attitudes may, in fact, be expressions of the therapeutic attitudes. Or, such behaviors may be perceived by a client as expressions of the attitudes.

In a different framework, Mindell (1992) suggests that it is not the response skills that are important but rather that the metaskills which underlie the responses are the truly important dimensions. Metaskills would, in Rogers' theory and hypothesis, refer to the attitudinal qualities of the therapist. One possibility for future investigation of the complex phenomena of ways of being empathic may be Neville's use of Gebser's structures of consciousness model (Neville, 1996). This model suggests several levels of empathy ranging from total union of the individuals to rational verbal kinds of responses.

In discussions of client-centered therapy the technique of reflection is often equated with empathy. The fact that reflection statements might be empathic contributes to this confusion. I have responded to this issue as follows:

1. Reflection is a way for the therapist to become empathic, to check whether or not he or she understands the client, and to communicate this understanding to the client.
2. Reflection is primarily for the therapist and not for the client. Reflection is one way for the therapist to enter the world of the client. It is the walk in the world of the client that assists the client toward growth.
3. Reflection is not empathy. It is a way to help the therapist become more empathic.
4. Empathy is not reflection. Empathy is a process of the therapist entering the world of the client 'as if' the therapist were the client. Reflection is a technique that may aid the process.
5. Other modes of empathy have not been considered. Other modes are usually not as easily observed and analyzed as are the verbal forms of reflective statements. The dedication of Rogers to quantitative, scientific inquiry influenced the nature of what would

> be examined by others, although his major thrust of inquiry has
> been a qualitative, heuristic examination of the nature of things.
>
> (Bozarth, 1984, p. 69)

Particular kinds of responses may or may not be representative of empathic understanding of the individual's frame of reference.

### Empathic responses

As noted earlier, one of Rogers' contributions was the development of a way of communicating empathy. This was once identified by him as 'reflection' or 'reflection of feelings'. In his last statement about reflective responses, Rogers identified such statements as being attempts to test his understandings with the client (Rogers, 1986b). In later writings, he referred to attitudes and still later referred to the relationship rather than to the method or reflection. Rogers consistently referred to empathic responses as those which captured the client's internal frame of reference. These forms of empathic responses, verbal or non-verbal, are responses that attempt to represent the client's internal frame of reference in the immediate interaction. Thus, whatever their means of expression or form, these empathic responses are a kind of as-close-as-possible-following of the client as he/she narrates and expresses him/herself. Also, all empathic responses are inherently tentative, implying the therapist's question to the client: 'Is this accurate?' As such, the actual responses come in a variety of forms. Films of Rogers' demonstrations of client-centered therapy reveal an almost constant flow of expressive movement accompanying verbal empathic communications (e.g., Rogers, 1965; Rogers and Segal, 1955).

### Responses to questions and requests

Another basic therapist-client interaction that often occurs in therapy is when the client is asking the therapist a question or making a request. When the therapist is being addressed and something is being directly asked of the therapist, the values and attitudes of client-centered theory require the therapist to adapt to this situation and express the therapeutic attitudes, often by honestly answering questions. The values of respect for persons and of trust in the inherent constructive self-directive capabilities of persons that are so basic in client-centered theory require that the client's voice be respected and trusted (Grant, 1990). This means that the therapist be inclined to address clients' questions by being genuine and open to honoring their requests, as well as offering empathic responses to verify the therapist's experiences of empathic understanding during the interaction process. It is a manifestation of the therapeutic attitudes, of acceptant empathic attunement to the client, to treat the client's questions and requests respectfully.

### Empathic understanding response process

There is a well developed and demonstrated process that seems to me to be a more elaborate conceptualization of the method of 'reflection' that Rogers focused upon in his years at the University of Chicago. Brodley espouses the concept of the 'empathic understanding response process' (Brodley, 1977, 1988a, 1988b, 1994). This concept allows concrete examples of therapists' responses to be identified in relation to the client's process. This process can be considered as a likely implementation of the client-centered therapist's acceptant empathic attitude. The empathic understanding response process is the process often modelled by Rogers in demonstrations and examples of his therapy (e.g. Rogers, 1965; Rogers and Segal, 1955). It is a process that is inherently nondirective without goals for the client. Examples of Rogers and others demonstrating client-centered therapy often illustrate the empathic understanding response process and are readily available to review in the literature (e.g. Bozarth, 1990b; Bozarth and Brodley, 1991; Brodley, 1993; Brodley and Brody, 1996; Brody, 1991; Ellis and Zimring, 1994; Merry, 1996; Raskin and Rogers, 1989; Rogers, 1986b). For some, it may be the best way to hold an empathic stance and one of the best ways to learn to trust the client. Again, this response process must be understood as expressive of the therapeutic attitudes, not as a technique or strategy.

**Empathic reactions**

Rogers' responses can most often be classified as empathic understanding responses. Nevertheless, he often discussed other aspects of the implementation of the attitudes. Rogers' presence in the relationship seemed to permit him to respond in ways consistent with the client. Although he often responded with the 'reflection method' that fit him best, he also reacted in various ways in which he felt himself to be empathic and present to the client. Kirschenbaum notes that during Rogers twelve years at the University of Chicago, he '. . . moved from the method to the attitudes to the relationship as the key ingredient in the therapeutic process' (p. 202). The earlier review of the development of Rogerian empathy in this chapter suggests that Rogers' first references to empathy are non-specific. He did not use the term until the late 1940s. The therapists' qualifications were more clearly couched in the attitudes of genuineness and unconditional positive regard in his earlier works. Understanding was important but subsidiary to acceptance of the individual's feelings. He then functionally took a behavioral focus in much of his practical work at the University of Chicago. This behavioral focus was related to the method of quantitative inquiry rather than to any behavioral intention. This is not to say that Rogers and his colleagues operated with any behavioral intent. However, there was clear focus on, 'What does the client do when the therapist responds in a certain way'? Hence, How should the therapist respond? It was when Rogers realized the technological (and behavioral?) interpretations given to his work that he used a broader reference than 'the reflection of feelings' and referred to ' . . . adopting the client's frame of reference' (Kirschenbaum, 1979, p. 164). It was only at this time that Rogers started to use the term empathy and developed it in his own unique formulation while popularizing it as a clinical concept in the helping professions.

Later in his life, Rogers was more explicit in his flirtation with holistic experiential blending with clients (Rogers, 1980). He notes, for example, that when he could be in touch with the unknown in himself during a therapy session that whatever he might do '. . . seems to be full of healing' (p. 129). He felt that his sometimes strange and impulsive way in a relationship turned out '. . . to be right, in some odd way: it seems that my inner spirit has reached out and touched the inner spirit of the other' (p. 129). He was to say that when he was '. . . intensely focused on a client, just my presence seems to be healing . . .' (Rogers in Baldwin, 1987, p. 45). He further reflected, 'Perhaps it is something around the edges of those conditions that is really the most important element of therapy - when myself is very clearly, obviously present (in Baldwin, 1987, p. 45). During much of Rogers' life, there was an inner conflict between observing an individual from the outside and understanding a person from the person's frame of reference. The former view was important to him in research and the latter view in his clinical work. The two perspectives, however, pervaded his work until his personal involvement in quantitative research diminished during the last two decades of his life. His experiences in encounter groups and large community groups impacted his view of empathy by his realization that there '. . . is not even hope of understanding what is going on . . .' in any given large group. However, he suggests: '. . . by surrendering yourself to the process, certain things happen' (Baldwin, 1987, p. 50). Rogers has provided the foundation for the importance of empathic reactions as well as more obvious empathic responses. The therapist may experientially and holistically 'absorb' the experience without worrying about providing particular empathic responses. Indeed, in groups, Rogers learned even more to trust individuals to help themselves and, in addition, for them to help others. In fact, Rogers' emphasis on empathic reaction was not new. As early as the Miss Mun sessions, he referred to what goes on in therapy as a willingness of the therapist to go with them in their separate feeling as a person (Rogers and Segal, 1955). In less didactic terms, he concluded that '. . . what the individual experiences in therapy is the experience of being loved' (Rogers and Segal, 1955, post session comments).

Rogers also referred to 'empathic reactions' in the classic 1966 'Gloria' film stating (Rogers, 1965):

> . . . I find myself bringing out my own inner experience statements which seem to have no connection with what is going on but usually prove to have a significant relationship to what the client is experiencing . . . I simply know I was very much present in the relationship, that I lived it in the moment of its occurrence. . .
>
> (Post session transcription, 1966)

There is often discussion about one of Rogers' responses to Gloria. At one point, she says that she would like Rogers for her father. Rogers replied by saying: 'You look to me like a pretty nice daughter . . .' (Rogers, 1965, session transcription). Some discussants think that he had a particular intention. Many say that this might have been helpful but that it was not an empathic response. His response, however, might be viewed as an empathic reaction if we consider Rogers' reference to his inner experience that he claimed to come from some unidentifiable source. It was his presence in the relationship and to the client that stimulated him to respond in this way. Although his comment might not meet the criteria for a valid empathic understanding response, it could well be considered an empathic reaction (that is, coming from Rogers' presence in the relationship while giving total attention to the individual and having no particular intent).

I have provided some examples of 'idiosyncratic empathy' including the following response preceding a longer monologue to a client's question, 'What did you do this weekend'? The therapist responded:

> When I took my Volkswagen engine out, the car rolled down the hill, hit the rabbit pen . . .
>
> (Bozarth, 1984, p. 70)

The client later verified the therapist's monologue as being empathic. Her previous session had been laden with tenseness and difficulty and she needed a reprieve from such struggle to allow her to assimilate her experience of that previous session. The therapist's reaction, according to the client, relieved her whole psychologically exhausted state.

The concept of empathic reactions theoretically suggests that there is an integral link between congruence and empathy. Congruence became the most important of the conditions to Rogers who periodically referred to it as 'transparency'. Rogers increasingly referred to transparency of the therapist in the relationship with the other person and, concomitantly, to the importance of the person-to-person encounter in the relationship. He also periodically, albeit more tentatively, referred to the use of intuition of the therapist. Taking these thoughts into account, I have stated:

> The basic premise is that the role of the person-centered therapist is that of being transparent enough to perceive the world non-judgementally, as if the therapist were the other person, in order to accelerate the formative tendency of the other person toward becoming all that he or she can become.
>
> (Bozarth, 1984, p. 69)

Hence, the therapist must continuously be aware of his/her own feelings as though they were the feelings of the client, perhaps 'as is' rather than 'as if'. The therapist's congruence is viewed as being integrally intertwined with empathy. That is, the more congruent, the more transparent the therapist in the relationship, the higher will be the empathy. I have argued before that if the therapist is authentically and deeply attuned to the client, then most of the therapist's experiences, even bizarre fantasies, will have therapeutic relevance to the client and/or the client-therapist relationship. Empathic reactions of this nature of 'oneness' seems closer to Basch's definition of 'Einfuhlung', '. . . "searching" one's way into the experience of another without specifying or limiting the means whereby this occurs' (Bozarth, 1984, pp.

110-111).

Stubbs and Bozarth (1996) contend that empathic understanding responses as well as empathic reactions may emerge from the search into the experience of the interaction between the client and the therapist. Indeed, the empathic response repertoire may be gleaned from the client's way of understanding (i.e. *Einfuhlung*). The contention is that if the therapist's intent is totally (as much as humanly possible) dedicated to acceptant understanding of the perceptions and experiences of the client then nearly everything the therapist does is meant to achieve this goal and/or to prepare him or herself to be in the relationship in that way. It might, then, entail any form of response or reaction that is idiosyncratic to the client, therapist and dyadic interaction (Bozarth, 1984). It has been suggested that the person-centered model of therapy ' . . . is particularly conducive to the separateness giving way to unity. . .in that the therapist is free to devote his or her entire being to attending to the client' (Spahn, 1992, p. 35). Rogers refers to such moments in several of his later writings and interviews and, as well, to the use of self in therapy (Rogers, 1980; Baldwin, 1987). Analyses reveal that Rogers practised empathy in a way that was simple, economical, idiosyncratic and predominantly focused on the internal frame of reference of the client (Brodley and Brody, 1996; Merry, 1995). Merry also suggests that: 'There is evidence that Rogers' responded to different clients in different ways; the underlying intention appears to be a consistent intent empathically to follow and hence to understand each client afresh' (Merry, 1996. p. 281). Transcripts reveal that he primarily practised with empathic understanding responses. I surmise that this was his primary way of reacting to his absorption of clients' experiences and the most prevalent way that he checked his experience of empathic understanding with them.

Rogerian empathy is fundamentally different from other conceptualizations of empathy in its convergence with other attitudinal qualities and in its role in bringing the self of the therapist to the self of the client without presuppositions and theoretical speculations concerning the client. Rogerian empathy is grounded in self-empowering principles, operationalized on a behavioral schema and is a flirtation with holistic experiential blending with another individual. This chapter has discussed empathy from the frame of reference of client-centered theory and the Rogerian hypothesis. Empathy from this framework is considered in that Rogers considered empathy to be: (1) a central therapeutic construct rather than a precondition for other forms of treatment, (2) an attitude and experience toward the client rather than a particular behavior, (3) an interpersonal process grounded in a non-directive attitude, and (4) a part of a whole attitude wherein the experience of empathic understanding is intertwined with congruence and unconditional positive regard of the therapist for the client.

Several assertions have been presented in relation to Rogerian empathy. These are, firstly, Rogers was involved simultaneously and continuously in developing client-centered/person-centered theory and formulating his hypothesis concerning the necessary and sufficient conditions for therapeutic personality change in general. Rogerian empathy is a central component to both of these efforts. As such, Rogerian empathy is integrally related to the theory and is unique.

Secondly, Rogers' early focus on method provided his theory with a form of response that helped to establish the theory. However, he discovered that the method was misinterpreted as technique and often used as a form that did not capture the principles that he espoused. It was then that Rogers used the term empathy in his reference to the importance of the attitudes. This allowed more variation of form but also opened the way for contamination of his idea of empathy when it was distorted by others to serve directive intention.

Finally, Rogers more recent evolution of the relationship has never been fully developed. It is a 'formless form' more akin to Basch's reference to *'Einfuhlung'* or 'feeling into', i.e., 'finding' or 'searching one's way into the experience of another without specifying or limiting the means whereby this occurs' (Basch, pp. 110-11). It is predicated upon the person-to-person blending of the therapist enmeshed in the world of the client with empathic reactions and 'total' attunement to the other. It is, perhaps as Shlien noted, ' . . .the exquisite awareness of dual experience that restores consciousness of self. A self being, the self-concept can change (Shlien, 1971, p. 164). Rogerian empathy is a unique contribution to psychotherapy, clinical work and to interpersonal relationships in general. Rogers' conceptualization of empathy is on the threshold of new explorations and meanings.

# CONGRUENCE

8

This chapter reviews Rogers' concept of congruence and explores the meaning of this concept. Congruence (or 'congruency', the term frequently used by Rogers) is one of the two necessary and sufficient conditions, along with unconditional positive regard, which have been focused upon less by theorists and researchers than has empathy. This may be due to the more difficult task of operationalizing the terms of 'unconditional positive regard' and 'congruence' for research and teaching purposes. Empathy can be placed in verbal schemas more readily than can either congruence or unconditional positive regard.

Most counselor education programs teach human relations skills training courses which focus upon 'empathic responses'. Herein, they believe they are using the concepts delineated by Rogers. Students can be taught certain verbal repertoires considered to correspond to Rogers' concept of empathy more readily than they can be taught to be congruent or to hold unconditional positive regard toward their clients.

## First considerations
One of Rogers' first considerations of the core conditions for effective therapy included the need for the therapist's 'understanding of self' (Rogers, 1939). He developed his theory, however, without much emphasis upon this characteristic until his integration statement and his formal theoretical statement (Rogers, 1957; 1959). He does not include the term congruence (nor the term genuineness which he often used interchangeably) in the appendix of his book, *Client-Centered Therapy*. In this book, he mostly focuses on the necessity of the therapist attending to the internal frame of reference of the client, and the therapist's 'warm acceptance' of this referent point (Rogers, 1951). The emphasis at that time was that the therapist have a warm and genuine interest in the client. There were, however, precursors to his increasing acknowledgement of the concept of congruence. In Rogers' seminal statement on client-centered therapy, he writes (Rogers, 1940):

> There must be warmth of relationship between counselor and counselee if any progress is to be made. Interviewing 'tricks' will not do. There must be on the part of the counselor a genuine interest in the individual . . . ( p. 162)

Genuineness had to do with the 'realness' of the therapist's 'warm' interest in the individual (1940s). In an applied psychology text book Rogers indicates that a genuine, unaffected interest in the child is the most important feature and no 'tricks' of interviewing compensate for its lack . . (Rogers, 1941, cited in Adomaitis, p 21). The best interview, in general, is the most spontaneous one . . . (Rogers, 1940, pp. 139-140). As Rogers (1946) . . . dropped the last vestiges of subtle directiveness' (p. 420), he sums up the therapeutic relationship of '. . . warmth, understanding, and safety . . .' (p. 419) by saying: '. . . this type of relationship can only exist if the counselor is deeply and genuinely able to adopt these attitudes . . . to be effective (client-centered therapy) must be genuine' (p. 429). Genuineness was the embodiment of the attitudes of warmth and understanding towards the client in order to be effective (1940s).

In his biography of Rogers, Kirschenbaum (1979) reports that Rogers became more interested in therapists' congruency through colleagues and students at the University of Chicago Counseling Center. Those individuals began to acknowledge and share their own emotional reactions with clients in the therapy relationship. Rogers listened, empathized and adapted additional ideas from his colleagues and students. One of these ideas was that of therapist congruency. Kirschenbaum suggests that Rogers was resistant to expressing his own feelings which, in part, explained the observatory nature rather than participatory action of his involvement in this idea. This resistance to his own self expression resulted in his hesitancy to be very expressive in therapy according to Kirschenbaum. This assumption may, in part, be true; however, Rogers was quite consistent in his comments that the sharing of himself was primarily when he had persistent feelings. Expression seemed to be more along the line of the last resort for Rogers. He refers to some exceptions to this by suggesting that spontaneous remarks sometimes 'bubble up' in him. Rogers actually gave credit for the idea of congruency to individuals in the 'Atlanta Group' who worked with Carl Whitaker. This was around 1959, the time that the first edition of the *Roots of Psychotherapy* was written. Rogers wrote with enthusiasm about the second, unrevised, edition (Whitaker and Malone, 1981). Rogers stated on the book jacket the following:

> Carl Whitaker and Thomas Malone are exciting, excellent therapists. Their thinking and their book have influenced therapists in deep and productive ways. I am delighted that *The Roots Of Psychotherapy* is again available since its contribution is as valuable today as it was when this classic work was first issued.

Whitaker and Malone provide an example of genuineness in their dialogue letters preceding the second edition of the book. The following example is reported from the 'Introduction to the Reprint' in the form of a letter to Whitaker from Malone (1981):

> It was 1944, I was seeing a patient just back from the South Pacific. In the middle of the first interview, I suddenly became terrified that he was going to kill me. I excused myself, went across the hall,

interrupted Dr. John Warkentin's interview: 'I need you.' He came to my office. I explained, John, I was sitting here with this guy taking an ordinary history and all of a sudden I'm terrified he's going to kill me'. John looked at the patient. 'I don't blame you. Sometimes I want to kill the bastard myself,' then got up and walked out. This intervention had a magic way of changing the dynamics. I wasn't terrified, the patient wasn't dangerous, and we went on with our interview. (p. xxi)

The importance of congruence is captured in a slightly different way and more explicitly by Malone:

The key concept is congruence. The congruence between the therapist's technique-system and his/her person allows the maximal personal participation in the relationship to the patient. This differs for different therapists. (p. xxviii)

Their ideas apparently had some effect on Rogers' thoughts about congruence; perhaps, providing impetus to the notions being considered by him. Rogers took a different direction from the idea of congruence being a match between the therapist's technique system and personhood. His concept of the term was more the self acknowledgement of the therapist's organismic experiences of any given moment. It was actually more a focus on the therapist not denying organismic experiences that persisted during the client/therapist relationship. The actual term of 'congruence' was coined from the geometric concept of congruent triangles – thus, technically referring to: 'coinciding exactly when superimposed' (American Heritage Dictionary, 1995). One of Rogers' first commentaries on congruence interchanged the words congruence, genuineness, and wholeness (Rogers, 1956). He continued the use of this interchangeable language throughout his career. His discussion of congruence at that time was of the following nature:

. . . it appears essential that the therapist be genuine, or whole, or congruent in the relationship. What this means is that it is important for the therapist to be what he/she is in his/her contact with the client. To the extent that he/she presents an outward facade of one attitude or feeling, while inwardly or at an unconscious level he/she experiences another feeling, the likelihood of successful therapy will be diminished.

(Rogers, 1956, pp. 199-200)

Congruence, used interchangeably with genuineness and wholeness, is still at this time related to successful therapy. Therapist genuineness by this time refers to the therapist not being phoney and being who she is during the therapy sessions (1950s). Rogers continues:

It is only as he/she is, in this relationship, a unified person, with his experienced feeling, his/her awareness of his/her feelings, and his/

her expression of those feelings all congruent or similar, that he/she is most able to facilitate therapy. It is only as the therapist provides the genuine reality which is in him/her, that the other person can successfully seek the reality in him/herself. The therapist is nondefensive about the reality in him/herself, and this helps the client to become nondefensive. ( pp. 199-200)

Thus, Rogers viewed the therapist's feelings, awareness of feelings and expression of feelings as the substance of genuineness. This represents the reality of the therapist that is necessary in order that the client can seek her/his own reality. It continues at this time to be related to effectiveness of the therapy (late 1950s and early 1960s). He presented this in a more personal form earlier. He said (Rogers, 1954):

I have found that the more I can be genuine in the relationship, the more helpful it will be. This means that I need to be aware of my own feelings, insofar as possible, rather than presenting an outward facade of one attitude, while actually holding another attitude at a deeper or unconscious level. Being genuine also involves the willingness to be and to express, in my words and behavior, the various feelings and attitudes which exist in me. It is only in this way that the relationship can have reality, and reality seems deeply important as a first condition. It is only by providing the genuine reality which is in me, that the other person can successfully seek for the reality in him. (p. 33)

The congruent therapist lives in the session in a way that her conscious and unconscious thoughts and feelings, and her actions and behaviors are in harmony. The therapist's congruency fosters the relationship as a reality. It is, then, that therapy is effective. This holds true for Rogers in 1961. By this time, genuineness seems to include more than the therapist's interest in or attitudes toward the client (late 1950s and early 1960s). It emphasizes the fostering of the relationship which is still theoretically the therapist's experience of the client's frame of reference and the therapist's experience of unconditional positive regard towards the client.

**The ambiguity of congruence**
Brodley suggests that the precise meaning of congruence is somewhat ambiguous because (1) Rogers' writings changed somewhat over the years, and the different versions provide some basis for different interpretations. (2) She further points out that there are different functions of congruence in Rogers' theory of therapy and his theory of interpersonal relationships (Brodley, 1995). Brodley believes that Rogers' definition of adjustment and maladjustment were presented in terms that he later used in his definitions of congruence and incongruence (Rogers, 1951). These definitions can be added as forerunners of congruence. Adjustment was defined as follows:

Psychological adjustment exists when the concept of the self is such that all the sensory and visceral experiences of the organism are, or may be, assimilated on a symbolic level into a consistent relationship with the concept of self.

(Rogers, 1951, p. 513)

He defines maladjustment in the following way:
> Psychological maladjustment exists when the organism denies to awareness significant sensory and visceral experiences, which consequently are not symbolized and organized into the gestalt of the self-structure. When this situation exists, there is a basic or potential psychological tension. (p. 510)

Adjustment and congruence '. . . appear to refer to the same phenomena; that is, the capability for, and the activity of, accurate symbolization of experiences in awareness' (Brodley, 1995, p. 2). The only difference between the definition of adjustment and congruence is in relation to congruence being referred to in more temporal and situational states. Rogers' theoretical statement about therapeutic congruence reveals the definition as a distinction between self and experience rather than a distinction about therapist behavior. Rogers states:
> . . . the therapist should be, within the confines of this relationship, a congruent, genuine, integrated person. It means that within the relationship he is freely and deeply himself, with his actual experience accurately represented by his awareness of himself . . . It should be clear that this includes being himself even in ways which are not regarded as ideal for psychotherapy. His experience may be 'I am afraid of this client' or 'My attention is so focused on my own problems that I can scarcely listen to him'. If the therapist is not denying these feelings to awareness, but is able freely to be them (as well as other feelings), then the condition (congruence) we have stated is met.

(Rogers, 1959, p. 97)

Congruence is:
> . . . when self-experiences are accurately symbolized (in awareness), and are included in the self-concept in this accurately symbolized form, then the state is one of congruence of self and experience . . . terms which are synonymous . . .(are) integrated, whole, genuine. (p. 206)

In his theoretical statement of therapy, Rogers is consistent with his statements throughout his professional writings. He takes a slightly different tack in his theory of interpersonal relationships (Rogers, 1959). He states as '. . . the tentative law of interpersonal relationships' that:
> . . . the greater the communicated congruence of experience,

awareness, and behavior on the part of one individual, the more the ensuing relationship will involve a tendency toward reciprocal communication with the same qualities, mutually accurate understanding of the communications, improved psychological adjustment and functioning in both parties, and mutual satisfaction in the relationship. (p. 140)

The communication of the congruent experience is given a lead role in the theory of interpersonal relationships. As stated by Brodley (1995):

This is a striking deviation from the role of congruence in psychotherapy (p. 12).

And:

Congruence is considered by Rogers as the most important of the conditions in psychotherapy, . . . but is meant as a description of the therapist's inner, subjective state or condition while she is providing acceptant empathic understanding.

(Brodley, 1998. p. 12).

It is also clear, however, that also in the theory of interpersonal relationships, the emphasis is upon the experiencing of the congruence as a clear communication. This allows the other party to be more expressive of '. . . a congruence of his own experience and awareness' (Rogers, 1989 p. 252). The reference to communication in the theory of interpersonal relationships is expressed by the following quote:

. . . hence communication in both directions becomes increasingly congruent, is increasingly accurately perceived, and contains more reciprocal positive regard.

(Rogers, 1959, p. 252)

Rogers' theory of interpersonal relationship continues to focus upon the positive regard couched in the communication of congruence.

## A critical dimension

After Rogers adapted the term of congruence, it seemed to become a critical dimension to Rogers. He eventually identified this concept as the most important of the three core conditions (Rogers and Sanford, 1984). He extended this concept to the self of the therapist being fully present in the therapeutic relationship when he stated to Baldwin (1987) that:

I am inclined to think that in my writing perhaps I have stressed too much the three basic conditions (congruence, unconditional positive regard and empathic understanding). Perhaps it is something around the edges of those conditions that is really the most important element of therapy – when myself is very clearly, obviously present (p. 45).

Rogers' congruency became a full expression of his presence with the client. He refers directly to congruence by saying: 'This is the most basic of the attitudinal conditions that foster therapeutic growth'. He comments further that: ' . . . what the therapist is feeling at an experiential or visceral level is clearly present in awareness and is available for direct communication to the client when appropriate (Rogers and Sanford, 1984). Congruence is self acknowledgement and possibly personal revelation to the client (1980s).

Rogers referred to times in therapy when he believed his very presence was healing to the client and that there was a transcendendant aspect to the relationship (Rogers, 1980). The theoretical concept (congruence) of therapist's awareness (1950s) became the clinical practice of 'being' (transparency) (1980s)

**Extensions of congruence**

In later writings, Rogers (1980) explicitly defines congruence in the more expansive manner:

> . . . genuineness, realness, or congruence . . . this means that the therapist is openly being the feelings and attitudes that are flowing within at the moment . . . the term transparent catches the flavour of this condition. (p. 115)

Adomaitis (1991) suggests that post 1954-56 there was a change in emphasis in Rogers' thinking about congruence. This led to the above conclusion. Adomaitis further summarizes this change as follows:

> Rogers held that what the therapist does should be an accurate reflection of his or her thoughts and feelings. The concept of genuineness, as it were, brought the reality of the rest of the therapist into the relationship with the client.
>
> (Adomaitis, 1991, p. 23)

Adomaitis' speculation is predicated upon statements by Rogers that are similar to those above. He also bases this view upon resources other than Rogers' work. Rogers' comments about genuineness in most of these statements are related to the clinical situation without particularly attending to the theoretical ramifications.

When Rogers' major theoretical statements are examined, they contain the interrelationship of congruence to the other core conditions (Rogers, 1957; 1959). I maintain (see chapter 6 on the reconceptualization of the conditions) that congruence is theoretically the '. . . preparation of the therapist . . . to experience the other two core conditions.' Congruence is a state of the therapist in relation to the therapist's experiencing of the other two conditions towards the client. At a macro level, I hypothesize that the three core conditions are so intertwined in Rogers' theory that they are actually one condition. At high levels of integration into one condition, Rogers' theory fits better with his statements concerning the therapeutic effect of the presence of the therapist.

Rogers' reference to the therapist's congruence in his classic integration article of 1957 and his disciplined theory statement of 1959 casts the term in a different context from empathic understanding and unconditional positive regard. The statement for the conditions of the therapeutic process are similar in both the 1957 and 1959 statements. The 1959 statement refers to the conditions as related to the theory and is a bit more precise. The conditions in 1959 refer to the client-centered framework and are directly related to client-centered theory. He uses the term, 'incongruence' to identify the state of the client. The client was considered to be incongruent, vulnerable and anxious in the therapeutic relationship. His reference to the therapist is : 'That the second person, whom we shall term the therapist, is congruent in the relationship.' Congruence, however, is of a different nature from the other two primary conditions of empathic understanding of the client's frame of reference and unconditional positive regard. Congruence unlike empathic understanding and unconditional positive regard, is primarily a state of the therapist. The therapist just 'is' congruent or genuine according to Rogers. The conditions of empathic understanding and unconditional positive regard are explicitly stated as conditions to be experienced by the therapist toward the client. Rogers also explicitly states that these two conditions must be perceived by the client. This slightly different slant lays the theoretical foundation for the more expanded suggestion of congruence when labelled as 'transparency' or 'self-presence' or 'authenticity' or even 'realness' and 'genuineness'. Rogers used transparency and self-presence more in later writings. They are used in defining the state of the therapist in the clinical situation.

### Congruence, authenticity and transparency

Haugh (1998) contends that the understanding of congruency in Rogers' theory has been blurred and misinterpreted. She proposes that person-centered theory suggests that genuineness, authenticity and transparency are *outcomes* of congruence rather than congruence *per se*. She asserts that the literature which is concerned with determining when it is appropriate to communicate genuineness is 'a red herring'. It is necessary to be clear in what is to be communicated before one can determine when it is appropriate to communicate. In this dialogue, she attends to an important point, namely, the focus upon behavioral correlates often replaces (to varying degrees) the attitudinal basics (see chapter 12 for more discussion on this topic). For example, human relations training models have defined genuineness in ways that refer to behavioral ratings from clients or raters to such questions as:

- Did the counselor match the client's predicates and phrases?
- Was the counselor appropriately spontaneous (for example, also tactful)?
- Did the counselor self disclose, or share similar feelings and experiences?

(Cormier and Cormier, 1994, p. 37)

It is clear that the concept has been diminished to behavior referents. Less obvious diminishment occurs in writings by notable scholars of person-centered theory. Lietaer (1993) for example, offers a juxtaposition of genuineness as having 'two sides' in his discussion of authenticity, congruency and transparency. Lietaer comments upon Rogers' definition of genuineness by stating:

> This definition implies clearly that genuineness has two sides: an inner and an outer one. The inner side refers to the degree to which the therapist has conscious access to, or is receptive to, all aspects of his flow of experiencing. This side of the process will be called 'congruence'; the consistency to which it refers is the unity of total experience and awareness. The outer side, on the other hand, refers to the explicit communication by the therapist of his conscious perceptions, attitudes and feelings. This aspect is called 'transparency': becoming transparent to the client through communication of personal impressions and experiences.
>
> (Lietaer, 1993, p. 18)

Rogers' willingness to be totally transparent or 'seen through' by the client undergoes a subtle change to become a communication process of therapist's impressions and experiences. Haugh (1998) points out the danger of this subtle change of meaning. She states that the possible consequence for the practice of person-centered therapy is that the therapist may be encouraged to engage in behaviours with the intention of trying to be experienced by the client as transparent or authentic. Congruence is more accurately met with an intention to match experiencing to awareness according to Haugh. Her solution to the confusion is to view the various terms (e.g., genuineness, authenticity, realness, and transparency) as outcomes of congruence rather than as definitions of congruence. She concludes that the more fully experience is available to therapists' awareness the more likely therapists will be experienced as genuine, authentic, and real. I agree with Haugh's deliberation on this point. She is responding directly to 'coterminous interminglings of doing and being' (see chapter 12) that I view as primarily responsible for much of the misunderstanding of person-centered therapy.

Lietaer who is a notable international scholar, offers a thorough presentation of congruence. As such, he covers several important points and issues. These points and issues are the following:

- that from 1962, Rogers considered congruence (or genuineness) the most fundamental of the three conditions;
- that congruence is the inner side which refers to the degree to which the therapist is receptive to all aspects of the flow of self experiences;
- that transparency is the outer side which refers to the communication of conscious perceptions, attitudes and experiences to the client;
- that congruence requires that the therapist be a psychologically well developed and integrated individual;
- that personal maturity can be considered the therapist's main

instrument in client-centered therapy;
- that a safe atmosphere for students is a must;
- that between 1955 and 1962 the principle of following within the client's frame of reference was expanded;
- that client-centered therapy evolved from nondirective to experiential.

(Lietaer, 1993)

Lietaer's view is reflective of his dedication to empirical research and, subsequently, to his operational definitions of terms. This is often a problem because of the delimiting effects on the conceptual and holistic meanings of concepts. I concur generally with most of his points. I do not agree with his definition of transparency as the actions ascribed to therapists. It severely delimits Rogers' definition of the therapist's willingness to be 'seen through' by the client. I also do not agree with him that client-centered therapy evolved from 'nondirective' to 'experiential'. Lietaer's conclusions seem to be heavily influenced by Gendlin's 'Experiential Therapy' which I consider to be theoretically related to Rogers' theory but ultimately a deviation from the basic premise of client-centered therapy. The intention of the therapist to direct clients to experiencing violates Rogerian theory by not holding to the strongest degree of self-authority and self-determination of clients.

**Influences on the concept of congruence**
Lietaer suggests that three factors influenced the evolution of client-centered therapy to focus more upon genuineness or transparency as critically important in the therapeutic relationship. These factors are: (1) The study with schizophrenics between 1958 and 1964; (2) the influence of such experiential thinkers as Carl Whitaker and Rollo May; and (3) Rogers involvement in the encounter group movement.

**• *The Wisconsin Project***
Lietaer cites Gendlin as the spokesperson for the study of schizophrenics (Gendlin, 1967). Gendlin points out that the therapist can draw on her own momentary experiencing that will foster continued therapeutic interaction with silent or 'unmotivated' or 'externalized' individuals. Lietaer also indicates that therapists such as Rollo May and Carl Whittaker critiqued the therapists in the schizophrenic research project for being too effacing in the therapeutic relationship. Lietaer, I think, is accurate, but the validity of the critique in relation to client-centered therapy is questionable. Gendlin, May and Whitaker make their criticism from outside of the basic assumptions of Rogers' theory and therefore diminish the theoretical emphasis of client-centered theory upon self-determination and self-authority of client-centered theory.

• *The basic encounter group*

The encounter group movement flourished in the 1960s and 1970s and Rogers brought his own brand to the movement. The 'basic encounter group' was coined by Rogers to identify a process based upon person-centered principles (Rogers, 1980); (see Chapter 17). Rogers refers to his role as a facilitator as one of becoming more and more of a participant in the group, expressing himself and being one of the members (Rogers, 1980). Lietaer concludes that the 'willingness to be known' for the individual therapist emerged forcefully in the encounter group movement. He implies that the credo of Group Dynamics of 'feedback in the here and now' was a major influence on the 'evolution' of client-centered therapy from a 'nondirective' to 'experiential' emphasis. This is somewhat questionable to me because of the fundamental attitudes that are the bedrock of the basic encounter group as Rogers described it. I argue (chapter 17) that Rogers' *basic encounter group* is different from other encounter groups because of the different basic assumptions. Like the theory itself, the basic encounter group is a different paradigm.

Lietaer's account of genuineness, congruence and transparency is a thorough examination of the history and evolution of the concept. His account, though, is tainted by a background of subliminal psychoanalytic logic. He refers periodically to such concepts as 'alter ego', the role of 'transference' and ideas of several authors of psychoanalytic thought.

It may be that Lietaer is not using these terms in the usual way. Nevertheless, their use lends a possible contamination to Rogers' theory. There is that subtle departure from the critical message of client-centered therapy; that is, the self-authority and self-determination of clients. His frequent references to therapists' 'interventions' is one example of this contaminant. This is not an unusual referent for those grounded in theoretical frames of reference other than person-centered. It is predicated upon a problem-solution and/or cause-effect rationale. It is therapist-driven and problem-centered, in contrast to being client-driven and person-centered. The therapists 'impose' their own rationale in order to alter the undesirable behaviors and problems.

Lietaer's conclusion that client-centered therapy evolved from being a 'nondirective' approach to become an 'experiential' therapy is a rationale that allows the therapist to insert her own frame of reference. This is theoretically acceptable to Lietaer as long as the therapist keeps returning to the client's experiential track. Lietaer again cites Gendlin as the representative of client-centered therapy and the authority for the conclusion (Gendlin, 1970). This leads Lietaer to say:

> Thus, we deal here with interventions where the therapist starts from his own frame of reference, as is also the case in interpretations, confrontations and proposals for the use of particular techniques, for instance.

> (Lietaer, 1993, p. 32)

This raises several questions: interpretations and confrontations of what? and techniques for what? The door is now open for the therapist to 'intervene' in the client's life with ideas outside of the client's frame of reference. The focus is upon shortcomings and problems of the client rather than upon the freeing of the natural growth process. The interrelationship of the three conditions of congruence, unconditional positive regard and empathic understanding of the person's frame of reference is relegated to a periphery role. The therapist's experience becomes a means for the client '. . . in his exploration of himself and his relationship patterns . . .' (p. 32). Although Lietaer's chapter is thorough and well presented, I consider the subtle references to be somewhat misleading. Congruence or authenticity from the person-centered stance must remain nondirective in dedication to experiencing the client's frame of reference. The experiential interchange does not replace the dedication to the client's self- authority and determinations. There is no room for 'interventions' in the client-centered framework. What does one intervene between? The therapist's task is to be a certain way, and to trust the client's resources to free the growth process of the individual to a greater degree. What is the nature of the intervention? Interventions shift the approach from a trust-oriented and person-oriented stance to a problem- and solution-focused approach. The concept of congruence does not so much give the therapist permission to bring their own frames of reference into the client's world as it helps them to experience more of the world of the other person 'as if' they are that person. Therapists bring themselves into the client's frame of reference and react out of that place.

Congruence may be as simple as that of the therapist who can be a 'real' human being in the client/therapist relationship. Or, it can be as complex as being a preparatory state for the therapist to become more  accepting and understanding of individuals.

**The conditions loop**
I have argued elsewhere (see chapter 7) that empathy and unconditional positive regard are part and parcel of one condition. Likewise, I believe that there is a genuineness-empathy loop wherein the two concepts are ultimately one. The result is that the three conditions are really, ultimately and functionally one condition. As for genuineness, the therapist's 'ability' to be aware of her own experience permits her to be more aware of the client's experience. As the therapist is more aware of the client's experience, the therapist becomes more aware of her own experience in the relationship. Genuineness is a natural awareness of the therapist to her own experience. The reaction may be simply internal awareness or involve a statement to the client. An important common trait for the therapist is that of being genuinely näive, not having preconceptions of what might happen or the way the person might be at some future point. When one is really empathic and attuned to the individual and can let one's self go; whatever happens may have some connection with the client in various significant ways. Rogers referred to this phenomenon a number of times in his writings. He notes in his commentary on the 'Gloria' film that responses 'bubble up' in him. Rogers states that at times

just his presence seems healing (Rogers, 1980). The genuineness of the therapist really feeds into being more empathic with the client's frame of reference so that it becomes the client's world that they are sharing back and forth or, perhaps, the unsystematic reactions of the therapist to the client's world. Rogers references to 'genuineness' as the most important condition is, I believe, because the condition affords the therapist the capacity to experience empathy towards the client. In the theory, it is the therapist's experience of her own unconditional positive regard and her empathic understanding of the client's frame of reference. I am assuming the perception of these two conditions by the client. Lietaer views congruence and the attitude of unconditionality so closely related to each other that they are parts of a more basic attitude of 'openness' (Lietaer, 1984). He agrees with other contentions that openness toward self (congruence) and openness toward the other (unconditionality) reflect this more basic attitude (Truax and Carkhuff, 1967, p. 504). More explicitly, Lietaer comments:

> The more I accept myself and am able to be present in a comfortable
> way with everything that bubbles up in me, without fear or defense,
> the more I can be receptive to everything that lives in my client.
>
> (Lietaer, 1984, p. 44)

This fits my idea of the interrelationship of the three conditions. This idea of differentiation is only an explanatory form when viewing the conditions as somewhat separate. As I have already suggested, the interrelationship is so high that the conditions are ultimately one condition. Later, it will be speculated that the one core condition is the growth hypothesis (the actualizing tendency). Genuineness, unconditional positive regard and empathic understanding become integrally intertwined with this one condition.

Wyatt (1998) suggests that therapists should feel free to be 'the whole of themselves' (p. 1), in order that the actualizing tendency can be fostered in the therapist as well as the client. Congruence is dependent upon, '. . . who the therapist is, who the client is, the quality and stage of the therapeutic relationship and what is happening in the relationship at that time (pp. 6-7).' Her view as a practising therapist is similar to my emphasis on the interaction of the therapist, client and situation at any given time (Bozarth, 1984). She concludes that the principle use of congruence is:

> . . . where the therapist is trusting in the actualising tendency within
> her client and she extends her trust in the actualising tendency to
> come through herself and the therapeutic relationship . . .(p. 18).

She notes that this is an immense demand on the therapist to be fully present to the client without projecting the therapist's incongruencies on the client.

Rogers' concept of congruence is that of the matching of the individual's organismic experience with the symbolization of self. In therapy, the client is in a momentary state of incongruence; that is, the organismic experiences are not congruent with the individual's view of self. The therapist, on the other hand, is viewed as being congruent in the therapy situation. Rogers used the terms of genuineness (especially), authenticity, transparency and realness interchangeably in some of his writings. He viewed the therapist's genuineness as being the realness of the therapist in holding the facilitative conditions of her own experience of empathic understanding of the client's frame of reference and of unconditional positive regard toward the client. Such congruence was related to effectiveness. Later, transparency was referred to as being more the state of the therapist whatever that might be rather than related to embodiment of the conditions or even to effectiveness. There is still, however, the relationship to effectiveness in that transparency fosters the relationship. The relationship constitutes the therapist's experiencing of the client's frame of reference and of unconditional positive regard for the client.

Rogers' comments that the most basic condition, that of congruence, has, in his later works, not been fully understood. My view is that congruence has to be the most basic condition because it enables the therapist to hold unconditionality for the client more completely. Even this idea becomes more questionable at a macro level since the conditions merge with such a force as to become a whole loop of mutual involvement and blurring of boundaries of the concepts. They become ultimately one in the service of the client's natural growth motivation. Rogers designation of congruence as the most important condition may be due to the idea that the therapist is just trying to be a certain way. There may even be the implicit assumption consistent with the theory that when one is congruent that there is an element of unconditionality that exists for the client to perceive. This is commented upon further in the next chapter where Rogers' states that the therapist's unconditional positive self-regard precedes congruence. Theoretically, the therapist is trying to experience her own unconditionality towards a particular person (the client), and to experience to some extent what it is like to be in the world of that other person.

# UNCONDITIONAL POSITIVE REGARD

9

Unconditional positive regard is the curative factor in client-centered theory. This is not to discard the conditions of therapist congruence and empathic understanding of the client's frame of reference. Conditionality is the bedrock of Rogers' theory of pathology. In the chapter on reconceptualization of the conditions, I suggest that the interrelationship of the conditions of congruence, empathy and unconditional positive regard is so high that they are inseparable in the theory. Rogers occasionally discussed the conditions separately, perhaps as a way to provide pragmatic guidelines to therapists and to clarify specific aspects of each dimension. His theoretical statement clearly presents them as interrelated conditions that are necessary and sufficient for therapeutic personality change. For this reason, it is somewhat paradoxical to argue unconditional positive regard as the curative factor in the theory. Nevertheless, one level of discussion necessitates the separate examination of the conditions.

## Psychological dysfunction

Rogers' theoretical foundations for psychological dysfunctions can result in no other conclusion: unconditional positive regard is the curative factor of the theory. Given this statement, it is important to qualify it in relation to the actualizing tendency. The basic curative factor lies in the client's normal motivational drive of actualization. It is this tendency that is the fundamental curative factor lying within the person. The reference to unconditional positive regard as the curative factor assumes the thwarting of the natural tendency; hence, making it necessary that the client become more directly connected with the actualizing tendency through unconditional positive self regard. Lietaer (1984) provides a similar discourse on Rogers' origin of psychological dysfunctions. He states that Rogers considers:

> . . . the conditional love of parents and significant others to be the basic source of alienation. In order to retain the love of the people who are important to him, a person internalizes norms that may be contrary to his desires and experience. A disassociation thus arises between what we strive after consciously and our true self; we become alienated from our deeper core. In therapy, then, the attitude of

> unconditionality of the therapist serves as a 'counterbalancing force',
> as a kind of 'counterconditioning' in the corrective experience which
> the client hopefully has during therapy! (p. 45)

Rogers is clear on this in his formal theoretical statement. The individual's return to unconditional positive self regard is the crux of psychological growth in the theory. It is the factor that reunifies the self with the actualizing tendency. The crux of Rogers' theory is summarized in his statement on the process of integration of an individual moving in the direction of congruence between self and experience: for threatening experiences to be accurately symbolized in awareness and assimilated into the self-structure, there must be a decrease in conditions of worth and an increase in unconditional self-regard. Rogers hypothesizes that one must perceive reception of unconditional positive regard in order to correct the pathological state. The communication of unconditional positive regard by a significant other is one way to achieve the above conditions. In order for unconditional positive regard to be communicated by a therapist, he suggests that it must exist in a context of empathic understanding or, at least, that empathic understanding of the client's frame of reference is the purist way to communicate the unconditonality. When the individual perceives such unconditional positive regard, conditions of worth are weakened and unconditional positive self-regard is strengthened (Rogers, 1959, p.249). People become incongruent and develop problems according to Rogers by the introjection of conditional values from significant others and from society. Individuals lose touch with the unconditional primitive nature of their experiences.

Lietaer's excellent informational chapter on unconditional positive regard also points out a pervasive problem. He states: 'Unconditional positive regard is probably one of the most questioned concepts in client-centered therapy' (Lietaer, 1984, p. 41). This assertion is predicated upon the general idea that therapists have problems maintaining this condition with their clients. More specifically, Lietaer states: These problems include the following:

> (1) There is a potential conflict between genuineness or congruence on
> the one hand, and unconditionality on the other; (2) it is a rare person
> and a rare time in which the constancy of acceptance can be provided
> by any therapist for any client. Thus, while unconditionality is not
> impossible, it is improbable; (3) unconditionality calls upon the therapist
> for a devoted self-effacing that often leads to a compensatory reaction
> in which confrontation becomes a form of self-assertion (p. 41).

This conclusion cries out with a parenthetical theme of : 'The therapist can't do it'. Lietaer reports criticisms of the condition of unconditional positive regard which emanate from other theoretical frameworks. These criticisms buttress the theme that some therapists believe that unconditional positive regard is impossible to attain with consistency. The question, perhaps, is why is this attitude so difficult for these therapists to maintain? Certainly, it is not difficult for many of my personal acquaintances who are seasoned client-centered therapists grounded in person-centered principles. Lietaer believes that some of the difficulties occurred as client-centered therapy became more relationship-centered. He believes that there was a greater focus on genuineness that accompanied relationship-centered therapy. Others support Lietaer's contention of change in Rogers' emphasis (Van Balen, 1990; Van Belle, 1990). They contend that the increased focus upon genuineness by Rogers began to shift the theoretical base from the therapist as an 'alter ego' focusing on empathic acceptance to a 'companion in search' including the therapist's own reactions to the client and eventually to the authenticity of the mutual relationship which might include the therapist's speculations about the client. There is an implicit assertion that therapist's authenticity changed Rogers' theory. Unconditional positive regard is no longer considered the curative factor of the theory due to the focus on the therapist's transparency in the relationship. The therapist is now the colleague in search with the client — which permits more emphasis upon everything and anything. This may or may not interfere with the fundamental notion of unconditional positive regard as the curative factor. Here, I believe Lietaer and his colleagues fall into the trap of defining client-centered and relationship-centered as different. This trap starts with the notion that there was a focus on the therapist as 'alter ego' early in client-centered therapy and this precluded the 'relationship'. Authors increasingly define the differences in terms of therapists' behaviors rather than as basic attitudes of the therapist. Although there is some evidence that Rogers did focus more on the principles than on the techniques at a certain point in his career, the foundations of client-centered therapy really did not change for him. He did not revise either his theory statement of 1959 nor his integration statement of 1957. He actually reconfirmed his allegiance to his basic theory in a posthumous publication (Raskin and Rogers, 1989).

The problem that therapists have with this condition is revealed in part by Lietaer in his behavioral definition of genuineness as involving feedback and confrontation (see chapter 8). The struggles with this basic attitude is from a frame of mind that begins once again to shift the therapist to the role of clinical expert who is trying to influence the client to become a certain way. In Lietaer's view, it is the therapeutic intent to become a more 'fully functioning person' in accord with Rogers' process description of therapy. The purity of this unconditionality begins to shift since the trust in the clients' frame of reference and the actualizing tendency has become contaminated with the therapist's dedication to influence the client in a predetermined direction. The shift to therapists' expertise occurs out of the goal of intentionality of the therapist. There is a subtle but critical difference between the view that there is a natural process within the client that the therapist fosters and the view that the therapist must urge this process. No wonder the therapists begin to have difficulties with their capacity to hold 'unconditionality'. They begin to view clients from the perspective of other theoretical beliefs. Their trust in the client's self-determination and self-authority is diminished.

**Overview of unconditional positive regard**

Although I disagree with several critical arguments of Lietaer, he has provided a major contribution in his summary of unconditional positive regard. As he notes, Rogers did not elaborate upon this basic attitude nor provide detailed explanations of it; subsequently, leaving some ambiguity in the concept. Few others have provided such an overview. As part of his examination, Lietaer points to a number of theoretical positions which assume (1) that the unconditionality is not possible at all (e.g., learning theorists); (2) that humans cannot 'not influence' (Systems Theories); and (3) that work with 'schizophrenics' and with encounter group participants brought more emphases on therapists' genuineness and upon bringing in their own experience (Rogers, et al, 1967; Gendlin, 1970). Lietaer realizes that most of these criticisms, especially the first two, arise from misunderstanding of the concept and are not to the point. However, Lietaer is quick to subscribe to the view that '. . . the client can be helped forward through the feed back with which the therapist confronts him' (Lietaer, p. 46). Lietaer suggests that unconditional positive regard is a multidimensional concept. It comprises positive regard, nondirectivity and unconditionality. Positive regard refers to the therapist's affective attitude towards the client. Nondirectivity refers to respect for the client's uniqueness and independence and to the client's right for her own viewpoint. Unconditionality, for Lietaer, refers to the constancy in accepting the client. Lietaer states: 'So unconditionality implies, among other things, no judgement from the outside and no approval or disapproval stemming from the frame of reference of the therapist' (p. 43). Attention to Lietaer's scholarly analysis of unconditional positive regard provides a wealth of information for understanding Rogers' concept. His analysis also, like his notable chapter on congruence, lends itself to a potential path of distortion of Rogers' meaning and intent. I agree wholeheartedly with Lietaer that client-centered therapy allows high degrees of self-confrontation within clients. Whether or not this is the therapist's aim as stated by Lietaer is another question. I suggest that the 'aim' and the 'goals' and the 'interventions' are part of what begins to lead therapists astray from Rogers' basic concept of client determination and to the instigation of the subtle resurgence of the therapist as the expert of the client's life. This becomes clearer in Lietaer's discourse on unconditionality when he argues that '. . . the contribution of the therapist has been gradually reformulated in more active terms' (Lietaer, 1984, p. 55). Unconditonality seems forgotten by Lietaer in his zealous enthusiasm for therapists to maximize '. . . the experiential process of the client' (Gendlin, 1970, p. 550). He refers to Gendlin's discussions of implicitly felt meanings, and Rice's intent to have the ' . . . therapist try to open up the experience of the client through evoking experiential elements that are not yet integrated into his cognitive construct of self' (p. 55). The claim is that '. . . client-centered therapy is in the process of evolving toward a more broadly conceived experiential psychotherapy (Gendlin, 1974).

It becomes clear in Lietaer's discourse on unconditional positive regard that he moves with Gendlin to the directive self-authority of the therapist who is now 'up to something' with the client, moving the client towards experiential 'felt meanings', and confronting the client with the consequences of the client's behavior as somehow known by the therapist. Such confrontational interventions are not at odds with unconditionality in Lietaer's view because it '. . . does not in any way mean that I reject my client as a person or that I stop trying to understand his experience' (p. 56). True enough, but he has lost the essence of Rogers' theory. That is, the self-authority and the self-determination of the client is undermined by the seeping authority of the therapist who knows what to confront, knows parts of the client better than the client. Congruence of the therapist is deemed the more important attitude that has increasing acceptance for the expertise of the therapist. Congruence as a state of the realness and openness of the therapist is transposed to include expert views. Unconditional positive regard is ignored as the fundamental basis for change of person-centered therapy.

Mearns and Thorne (1988) define unconditional positive regard more holistically in the following way:

> Unconditional positive regard is the label given to the fundamental attitude of the person-centred counsellor towards her client. The counsellor who holds this attitude deeply values the humanity of her client and is not deflected in that valuing by any particular client behaviours. The attitude manifests itself in the counsellor's consistent acceptance of and enduring warmth towards her client.  (p. 59)

Thorne (1991) helps to clarify unconditional positive regard by suggesting that the underlying belief system of the person-centered therapist is critical to the understanding of the theory. He cites a paper presentation by Brodley and myself which identified the essential assumptions related to Rogers' theory. In that paper we asserted that the person-centered therapist believes:

- That every individual has the internal resources for growth.
- That when a counsellor offers the core conditions of congruence, unconditional positive regard and empathy, therapeutic movement will take place.
- That human nature is essentially constructive.
- That human nature is essentially social.
- That self-regard is a basic human need.
- That persons are motivated to seek the truth.
- That perceptions determine experience and behavior.
- That the individual should be the primary reference point in any helping activity.
- That individuals should be related to as whole persons who are in the process of becoming.
- That persons should be treated as doing their best to grow and to preserve themselves given their current internal and external circumstances.
- That it is important to reject the pursuit of authority or control

over others and to seek to share power.
(Thorne, 1991, pp.172-173)

The role of unconditional positive regard as the core curative condition in Rogers' theory is clarified in his statement concerning application to family life. Rogers offers this as a descriptive statement suggestion from his theory of therapy. He states:

> The theoretical implications would include these:
> 1. The greater the degree of *unconditional positive regard* which the parent experiences toward the child:
>     a) The fewer the *conditions of worth* in the child.
>     b) The more the child will be able to live in terms of a *continuing organismic valuing process*.
>     c) The higher the level of *psychological adjustment* of the child.
> 2. The parent experiences such *unconditional positive regard* only to the extent that he experiences unconditional self-regard.
> 3. To the extent that he *experiences unconditional self-regard*, the parent will be congruent in the relationship.
>     a) This implies genuineness or congruence in the expression of his own *feelings* (positive or negative).
> 4. To the extent that conditions 1, 2, and 3 exist, the parent will realistically and *empathically* understand the child's *internal frame of reference and experience an unconditional positive regard for him*.
> 5. To the extent that conditions 1 through 4 exist, the theory of the process and outcomes of therapy and the theory of the process and outcomes of an improving relationship apply.
> (Rogers, 1959, cited in Kirschenbaum and Henderson, 1989, p. 253)

This statement permits us to better understand the importance that Rogers accords to unconditional positive regard in his theory. It is the parent's experience of unconditional positive regard towards the child that creates (1) fewer conditions of worth, (2) greater experiencing of the organismic valuing process, and (3) psychological adjustment in the child. Moreover, the parent must have unconditional self-regard to be congruent in the relationship and, hence, to be able to experience unconditional positive regard and empathic understanding of the child's frame of reference. This statement succinctly describes the condition of unconditional positive regard as the curative attitude not only for the client but also the importance of unconditional positive self regard for the therapist to be congruent.

# Quantum Theory and the Person-Centered Approach

# 10

Quantum theory involves a conception of the universe as an interconnected web of relations that is intrinsically dynamic. This conception is the overall premise of general systems theory, which offers a different view from that of most current models of understanding life. Capra who suggested that physics has been the model for all sciences has argued the importance of a new vision of reality for all sciences (Capra, 1975, 1982).

**The need for a new paradigm**
Capra stated that there is an imminent revolution in the sciences and in our perceptions and values (Capra, 1982). The Cartesian method of analyzing the world into parts and developing cause-effect laws, and the Newtonian, mechanistic view cannot account for the views of the world indicated by atomic physics (e.g., the interchangeability of mass and energy, the inseparability of observation from that being observed, matter that shows 'tendencies to exist'). According to Capra, many difficulties that currently exist in the world are predicated on a crisis of perception similar to the crisis in physics in the 1920s (Capra, 1975). Capra stated that the concepts of space, time, and matter conceptualized in subatomic physics imply a reality that cannot be understood through the view of the Cartesian-Newtonian model of science. He contended:

> What we need, then, is a new 'paradigm'; a new vision of reality; a fundamental change in our thoughts, perceptions, and values. The beginnings of this change, of the shift from the mechanistic to holistic conceptions of reality, are already visible in all fields and are likely to dominate the present decade.
>
> (Capra, 1982, p. 16)

Barclay suggested the need to consider new paradigms for counseling (Barclay, 1984). He suggested that the 19th-Century paradigm can be described '. . . by the philosophy of positivism and the psychology of evaluate and control . . .' (p. 2).

Adapted with permission from:
Bozarth, J. D. (1985). Quantum theory and the person-centered approach. *Journal of Counseling and Development*, 64 (3), 179-82.

This philosophy fragments counseling theories, lacks recognition of the interrelated human function, and is mostly crisis oriented.

Caple (1985) proposes a paradigm, developed from general system theory, which he labels 'self-organization'. Counselors, according to Caple, can benefit from this paradigm shift. The basic reason for considering a new paradigm for society and also for counseling is that the old paradigm cannot account for and often ignores much of the capability and potentiality of humans.

**Principles of the new paradigm**
This new vision of reality, according to Capra is based on a general systems view of life, that is, 'the interrelatedness and interdependence of all phenomena - physical, biological, psychological, social, and cultural' (Capra, 1984, p. 265). A critical aspect of this general systems view is the principle of self-organization. Caple has directed his article toward a comprehensive understanding of the principle of self-organization as a paradigm and the ways counselors are affected and can benefit from this paradigm shift. He has identified several basic conceptualizations that constitute the principle of self-organization.

There are two notable principal dynamic phenomena of the general systems view:

> Self-renewal – The ability of living systems continuously to renew and recycle their components while maintaining the integrity of overall structure.
> Self-transcendence –The ability to reach out creatively beyond physical and mental boundaries in processes of learning, development, and evolution.
>
> (Capra, 1982, p.269)

Capra identified these assumptions as the underpinnings of quantum physics and contended that the concepts of physics provide the foundation for other sciences. Capra summarized these principles of modern physics and offered a parallel to Eastern mystics:

> . . .in modern physics the universe is thus experienced as a dynamic, inseparable whole which always includes the observer in an essential way. In this experience the traditional concepts of space and time, of isolated objects, and of cause and effect lose their meaning. Such an experience, however, is very similar to that of Eastern mystics.
>
> (Capra, 1975, p. 81)

The principles of the new paradigm included emphasis on (1) relationships rather than isolated parts, (2) inherent dynamics of relationships, (3) process thinking, (4) holistic thinking, (5) subjectivity, and (6) autonomy.

**Application to counseling and psychotherapy**
The paradigm cited by Capra offers several premises for the function of counseling

and psychotherapy. Caple suggests that the new paradigm, represented by 'self-organization' principles, provides a better framework for explaining life and behavior and for understanding the processes of change that occur. The implications suggest that with this paradigm, the therapist would be open to surprise in the therapist client relationship and that the specific kind of client change could not be determined in advance. The therapist would also not be limited to any particular method or technique or necessarily need to give up particular methods or techniques.

This new framework would include three principles, the first of which is the principle of self-renewal. The living system tends toward self-renewal and can transcend physical and mental boundaries to achieve a more universal wholeness. Stated in different ways, this tenet has been a major construct in many major therapeutic theories (e.g., the concepts of social interest in Adlerian individual psychology, individuation in Jungian analytical psychology, self-actualization in client-centered therapy, striving toward wholeness in gestalt therapy, and the development of intrinsic potentials in some psychoanalytical approaches). Horney eloquently described the natural process of development:

> We need not to teach an acorn to grow into an oak tree, but when given a chance, its intrinsic potentialities will develop. Similarly the human individual, given a chance, tends to develop his particular human potentialities. . . he will grow substantially undiverted, toward self-realization.

> (Horney, 1956, p 220)

Thus, some theories of therapy do include this principle and, as such, open the possibility for functioning within the new paradigm.

> The second principle is that of the human organism as a dynamic system containing interdependent psychological and physiological patterns embedded in larger systems. In short, the human organism has the capacity of self-organization and transcendence. Functionally, the therapist's role is simply that of a catalyst that will permit the human organism to self-regulate and self-transcend. Jung, for example, indicated that treatment cannot be anything but the product of mutual influence and involves an interaction between the unconscious of the therapist and the patient.

> (cited in Capra, 1982)

The third principle, that the human organism consistently strives toward self-renewal and self-transcendence, is related to the other two principles. Such striving always occurs and is accelerated in certain situations. Specifically, the implication for counseling and psychotherapy is that the primary ingredient is the therapist's reliance on and confirmation of this autonomous, self-organizational phenomenon.

**Premises of the person-centered approach**

A therapeutic approach that operates on premises predicated on these principles currently exists. Person-centered therapy offers a paradigm consistent with the fundamental model of modern physics and with the parallel assumptions of the writings of mystics.

There is nothing new in viewing the person-centered approach as a fundamentally different approach. Rogers described the approach as a revolutionary one (Rogers, 1977). Others, however, often emphasized the more traditional aspects of communication skills and methodological components of the approach (e.g., Gordon, 1955; Martin, 1983; Truax and Carkhuff, 1967). The concepts that are the crux of the person-centered approach and that reflect the essence of a new paradigm have seldom been considered in the literature. Rogers' reference to the politics of the client-centered approach to psychotherapy is, perhaps, the clearest statement of the different view posed by client-centered therapy. Rogers asked a questioner to explain what the questioner meant by the politics of client-centered therapy. The questioner replied:

> I spent three years of graduate school learning to be an expert in clinical psychology. I learned to make accurate diagnostic judgements. I learned the various techniques of altering the subject's attitudes and behavior. I learned subtle modes of manipulation under the labels of interpretation and guidance. Then I began to read your material, which upset everything I had learned. You were saying that the power rests not in my mind but in his [the client's] organism. You completely reversed the relationship of power and control, which had built up in me over three years. And then you say there is no politics in the client-centered approach
>
> (Rogers, 1977, p. 3)

The person-centered view is not just a different approach or a different theory. It is a different view of the world, a different paradigm. Rogers expressed the foundations of the person-centered approach in terms strikingly similar to the new vision of reality (Rogers, 1980). He did not, however, specifically identify the parallel assumptions of the person-centered approach with those of a new paradigm. Most writers have explained the client-centered conceptual model in a manner consistent with the Cartesian-Newtonian model of science to the extent that underlying assumptions are only secondarily considered. The following are the basic premises of the person-centered approach that identify it as a therapeutic paradigm different from other therapy and growth-activating approaches.

The first premise, that the actualizing and formative tendencies of humans are the foundation blocks of the person-centered approach, is the motivational force in the theory of the client-centered-person-centered approach. Rogers (1980) stated:

> Individuals have within themselves vast resources for self-understanding and for altering their self-concepts, basic attitudes, and self-directed behavior; these resources can be tapped if a climate

of facilitative psychological attitudes can be provided (p. 115).

Rogers was explicit that the actualizing tendency, which is a characteristic of organic life, and the formative tendency, which is a characteristic of the universe as a whole, 'are the foundation blocks of the person-centered approach' (p. 114). This formative tendency for the human being (as well as for every organism) moves toward ' . . .constructive fulfilment of its inherent possibilities' (p. 117). 'There is a natural tendency toward a more complex and complete development' (p. 118).

The systems view of life, which is the foundation of the new vision or reality, is no less than this same phenomenon. As Paul Weiss observed, 'Living forms must be regarded as essentially an overt indicator of, or clue to, dynamics of the underlying formative processes' (cited in Capra, 1982, p. 267).

The individual is always in process, always striving toward recognition of his or her inherent potential, never losing the dynamic movement and striving. Van Belle (1980) suggests that change in the person-centered view is the point of unity. He states that human life is 'a continuous ever-changing flow of forward movement' (p. 93). As in concepts of modern physics, in the person-centered approach, the organism is viewed as dynamic, always in flux. As such, the person-centered approach is the only major therapeutic approach that explicitly treats process as integration (i.e. change as the central reality).

Rogers' hypothesis of the formative, directional tendency in the universe is remarkably similar to the systems theory underlying modern physics:

> This is an evolutionary tendency toward greater order, greater complexity, and greater inter-relatedness. In humankind, this tendency exhibits itself as the individual moves from a single cell origin to complex organic functioning, to knowing and serving below the level of consciousness, to a conscious awareness of the organism and the external world, to a transcendent awareness of the harmony and unity of the cosmic system, including humankind.
>
> (Rogers, 1980, p. 139)

The second premise, that individual clients are always their own best experts and authorities on their lives, is still the most revolutionary principle of the approach. The reliance on the client's inherent movement toward growth for direction and action, rather than on therapist expertise, remains a fundamental difference between the person-centered approach and other therapies. The individual knows best the problems and the direction to take, as Rogers (cited in Kirschenbaum, 1979) stated:

> . . . it is the client who knows what hurts, what directions to go, what problems are crucial . . . I would do better to rely upon the client for the direction of movement in the process. (p. 89)

In other prominent therapeutic approaches the therapist is viewed as an expert intervener at some point. Even those approaches based on the common theoretical foundation of the person striving to become a whole do not include the revolutionary assumption that the client is solely his or her own best expert and authority.

# THE BASICS OF PRACTICE

# The Coterminous Intermingling of Doing and Being in Person-Centered Therapy

# 11

This chapter examines the roles of 'being' and 'doing' in person-centered therapy. The examination consists of: (1) reconsideration of the basic principles of the person-centered approach as espoused by the late Carl Rogers, (2) examination of Rogers' responses to his clients, and (3) consideration of some of the reported research findings concerning the function of the person-centered therapist.

The principles of the approach are well known but often not considered from a functional vantage-point. Person-centered therapy is essentially the following:

*The therapist functions as a genuine person who experiences the attitudes of unconditional positive regard and empathic understanding toward the client and the client perceives these therapist attitudes.*

The assumption is that if the therapist can be this way with the other person and that the person of the client, at least, minimally perceives these attitudes then therapeutic personality change will ensue. In therapy, the foundation block of the theory is the actualizing tendency; i.e., the tendency of the organism to grow in a positive and constructive direction; for the person 'to become all of his/her potentialities' (Bozarth and Brodley, 1991). Put another way: when the therapist can be a certain way, then the client's actualizing tendency is promoted. In addition, the self-actualizing tendency is promoted in a way that is harmonious with the experiencing of the actualizing organism; thus the self-concept of the individual is altered.

The essence (the basic nature and the basic core) of person-centered therapy is consistent with these principles (Bozarth, 1990a). After reviewing the results of the Bower (1986) study, examining the evolution of Carl Rogers as a therapist and from my understanding of Rogers' writings, the essence of the approach was defined as follows (Bozarth, 1990a):

The essence of person-centered therapy is the therapist's dedication to going with the client's direction, at the client's pace, and in the

Adapted with permission from:
Bozarth, J. D. (1992a). Coterminous intermingling of doing and being in person-centered therapy. *The Person-Centered Journal.* 1(1), 33-39.

client's unique way of being. (p. 59)

Implications of this theoretical stance are integrally related to the concept of the locus of control. The therapist is promoting a natural individual and general process in the client by the therapist being a certain way; that is, experiencing certain attitudes toward them. Clients are their own best expert on themselves and their lives. The therapist's intent is not to promote feelings or to help the client to become more independent or to get anywhere. The goal is not self-actualization, actualization, independence or to help the client to become a 'fully functioning' person. The goal is only to be a certain way and by being that way promote a natural process.

### Rogers' responses to his clients

Several authors have suggested that Rogers changed his thinking and approach to therapy over the years (Coulson, 1987; Frankel, 1988; Van Balen, 1990; Van Belle, 1990). I consider their points valid in that Rogers' statements over the years were more focused on the principles rather than on the response modes and, perhaps, the meta-principles as a 'way of being' were more important for him to express than the 'way of doing' that was often the focus of his earlier work. He seemed to become more at ease and expressive over the years and, reportedly, expressed and demonstrated increased involvement with intuition (Baldwin, 1987; Brodley, 1991). Rogers, in fact, indicated in an interview that the presence of the therapist in the therapy session had perhaps not been given enough attention (Baldwin, 1987). Rogers stated:

> Over time . . . I have become more aware of the fact that in therapy I do use myself. I recognize that when I am intensely focused on a client, just my presence seems to be healing . . . (and) I am inclined to think that in my writing perhaps I have stressed too much the three basic conditions (congruence, unconditional positive regard, and empathic understanding). Perhaps it is something around the edges of those conditions that is really the most important element of therapy - when my self is clearly, obviously present.
>
> (Rogers cited in Baldwin, 1987, p. 45)

My analyses reveal that Rogers did not change either his basic intent or way of working as a therapist (Bozarth, 1988a; 1990a; 1990b), (also see previous chapters). In addition, Brodley's analysis suggested that he changed little in the way that he worked as a therapist (Brodley, 1988). More recent extensive analysis of Rogers' work further clarifies this issue (Brody, 1991; Brodley, 1991). Brody reports her analysis of Rogers' articulate verbal responses to clients in ten therapy interviews over a 40-year time span, from 1946 to 1986. Brody's major findings are the following:

1. Rogers responds 91% of the time with an Empathic Following Response in which his apparent intention is to check his understanding of the client's

meaning (when eliminating responses to client questions). Almost all of 556 distinct articulate responses were nondirective, empathic following responses. The range of such responses was from 100% with Miss Mun in 1955 to 60% with Mark in 1982.

2. The average percent of responses for categories (including responses to client questions) were: Empathic Following: 86%; Therapist Comment: 11%; Therapist Interpretation: 1%; Therapist Agreement: 1%; Leading Question: 1%.

Brody's general conclusions are also of interest. They are paraphrased below:

1. '. . . empathic understanding, in Rogers' responses, is a complex and rich expression of the client's subjective meaning. Rogers conveys his understanding of the client's meaning in a varied and deeply personal manner. A focus on feeling, or on simply repeating back what a client has said, is an error in empathic understanding as Rogers used it.'
2. Rogers usually answered questions when asked by the client.
3. He occasionally makes unelicited, spontaneous comments from his own frame of reference, but always in what seems to be a non-systematic manner.
4. His verbal behavior in these ten sessions consistently conveys the gestalt of the therapeutic attitudes.

Brody concludes that Rogers did do what he said over the four decade span. As she states: 'The depth of his involvement in the client's internal world is apparent; he is genuine, a real person presenting himself transparently to the client; and he is unconditionally accepting (Brody, 1991, pp.78-80).

**Doing and being**

One of the greatest sources of misunderstanding of the person-centered approach is that of focusing on how to do it. The focus then shifts to technical responding and leads to the emphases on such conceptualizations as reflecting, client-centered listening, client-centered communication and so on. The understanding of the client's meaning in a varied and deeply personal manner as conveyed by Rogers is distorted. In addition, such confusion leads to invalid conclusions such as the statement that client-centered listening may not be sufficient. Tausch's report of research is a classic example of examining the client-centered approach in this manner (Tausch, 1990). Defining the function of the client-centered therapist as 'client-centered communication', he concludes that some clients need to have supplemental treatment because of the lack of therapeutic gain when receiving only client-centered communication (Tausch, 1990). Although Tausch notes that to a certain extent the necessity for supplementation occurs when they are unable to provide the attitudinal conditions to the clients and when they attend mainly to the clients' emotions rather than to person-related cognitions, he states that the necessity of supplementation in these instances is '. . . a client-centered necessity' (p. 447). Moreover, determination of the kind of supplementation decided upon (intended to be in harmony with each client) emerges from the therapist asking such questions as: what is helpful for this client? What does he need to facilitate his emotional health? Which supplementation is accessible to this client? In my opinion, the focus of the Tausch study upon doing 'Client-Centered Communication' violates the principles of 'being' by casting the therapist in the role of determining what should be proposed to the client. Emphasis upon the way to do person-centered therapy leads to confounding of the approach in practice and in research.

## Coterminous interminglings in practice

When therapists are doing something that does not entail 'being' their experiences with clients, then the 'person-centeredness' is contaminated. In this sense, therapists may be as effective with what they do not do, as they are with what they do do. Specifically, for example, contamination occurs when therapists assume that they know what is best for clients, what is wrong with clients or in what direction clients should go. On the other hand, whatever the therapist does as a therapist that is consistent with these principles is 'person-centered'. For example, the question: 'How old is your sister'? would probably be external to the client's frame of reference most of the time and usually important to the therapist from some external theoretical frame of reference that the therapist might hold. However, it might be conceivable that within the context of a client story about being treated a certain way by her sister that the therapist could try to obtain a clearer picture of the client's story by asking such a question. In short, the principles of the approach guide the specific responses of the therapist.

Therapists' responses may be idiosyncratic to the client, therapist, and the unique relationship. Raskin clarified the concept of idiosyncratic empathy with his conceptualization of unsystematic therapist responses (Raskin, 1988). His conceptualization, I believe, may be the crux of the evolution from the label, client-centered therapy to the label of person-centered therapy. The difference between systematic and unsystematic therapist responses and activities is that systematic approaches have '. . . a preconceived notion of how they wish to change the client and work at it in systematic fashion, in contrast to the person-centered therapist who starts out being open and remains open to an emerging process orchestrated by the client' (p. 33). The differences between the labels of client-centered and person-centered include the attention to the form of the empathic understanding response in client-centered therapy and the emerging process of responses that may occur in person-centered therapy. Person-centered therapy may come more out of the therapist's own genuineness while being absorbed in the frame of reference of the client. Uncontaminated dedication to the frame of reference of the client from a genuine person as the therapist seems to me to be the crucial variable in determining particular responses. The more therapists can allow their 'intuitive' responses to arise and their presence to be connected to the client, the greater the range of idiosyncratic responses is apt to be. Intuition and the presence of the therapist take on progressively more importance. However, this is only contingent, I surmise, if the therapist is maximally trusting of the client's actualizing tendency and is truly dedicated to the client's frame of reference.

In short, the range and type of valid person-centered therapist responses are located in the centering of the therapist in the world of the client with trust in the client's self-determination.

# THE INTEGRATIVE STATEMENT OF CARL R. ROGERS

# 12

Carl Rogers formulated a revolutionary hypothesis when he proposed that there are certain necessary and sufficient conditions for therapeutic personality change (Rogers, 1957). This statement was not about client-centered therapy as often assumed. Rather, it is a statement that is meant to integrate therapies and helping relationships through assumptions of common therapeutic variables. The thesis in this chapter is that Rogers' integrative hypothesis has not been thoroughly investigated nor even adequately understood. It is further suggested that the direction of investigation of this hypothesis has resulted in probable limitations to the understanding and manifestations of the hypothesis.

## The statements

Rogers' most significant theoretical statements were published near the same time (Rogers, 1957; 1959). He first postulated an integrative statement related to his theoretical investigations (Rogers, 1957). His second statement was directly related to client-centered theory (Rogers, 1959). Rogers' integrative statement has been widely referred to in the literature and is quoted in earlier chapters of this book (see p. 7). Rogers wrote the 1957 statement while still working on his rigorous theoretical delineation of, 'A theory of therapy, personality, and interpersonal relations as developed in the client-centered framework' which was then published in 1959. There are subtle differences in Rogers' hypothesis as stated in 1957 and his theoretical statement in 1959. The primary differences between his formal statement concerning the necessary and sufficient conditions for therapeutic personality change in 1957 and 1959 is that in the 1959 statement, he no longer states that the therapist must strive to communicate his or her experiencing of empathic understanding and unconditional positive regard to the client. The client, however, must perceive the therapist as experiencing these two conditions, at least,

Adapted with permission from:
Stubbs, J. P. and Bozarth, J. D. (1996). The integrative statement of Carl R. Rogers. In Hutterer, R., Pawlowsky, G., Schmid, P. F. and Stipsits, R. (eds.) *Client-Centered and Experiential Psychotherapy: A Paradigm in Motion*, pp.25-33. New York: Peter Lang.

to a minimal degree. He also no longer designates the pre-condition as being psychological contact in 1959. It is difficult to determine whether or not these subtle differences have any meaning; however, it seems unlikely that Rogers would be cavalier with statements that were incorporated in what he considered the most rigorous expositions of his belief and of his theory. It might mean that if the client-centered therapist's core attitudes are present, Rogers would just expect that they would be perceived by most clients; whereas this might not be the case for therapists operating out of other theoretical frames of reference. There are some minor differences in the statements of the core conditions. The major difference is, however, more momentous.

**The major difference**
The major difference between Rogers' 1957 and 1959 statements has vast implications. This difference is that in 1959 the hypothesis is presented as a core and integral part of client-centered theory but, in 1957, it is considered as essential in all theories of therapy and, indeed, of all helping relationships. In 1959, these conditions which Rogers considered to be so important are embedded within the context of the foundation block of the theory, the actualizing tendency. The 1959 statement also included the importance of the self-concept, nondirectivity and the 'technical' forms (e.g., reflection, restatement rule, empathic understanding responses) for implementation of the theory as part of the package. This is not necessarily so in 1957 where Rogers is quite clear that he is not referring to conditions that are essential for only client-centered therapy. His statement refers to '. . . conditions which apply to any situation in which constructive personality change occurs, whether we are thinking of classical psychoanalysis, or any of its modern offshoots, or Adlerian psychotherapy, or any other (Rogers, 1957, p. 230). He hypothesized the following:

> . . . that effective psychotherapy of any sort produces similar changes
> in personality and behavior, and that a single set of preconditions is
> necessary.

(Rogers, 1957, p. 231)

The 1957 statement is meant as an integrative medium for all psychotherapies and, even for integration of helping relationships into every day life. As Rogers stated: 'It is not stated that psychotherapy is a special kind of relationship, different in kind from all others which occur in everyday life' (p. 231). He explains further:

> Thus the therapeutic relationship is seen as a heightening of the
> constructive qualities which often exist in part in other relationships,
> and an extension through time of qualities which in other relationships
> tend at best to be momentary.

(Rogers, 1957, p.231)

Rogers even refers to the hypothesis being relevant to programs that are aimed at constructive personality change and mentions programs of leadership, educational programs, and 'Community agencies aim(ed) at personality and behavioral change in delinquents and criminals' (p.233). He suggests that if the hypotheses are supported, '. . . then the results, both for the planning of such programs and for our knowledge of human dynamics, would be significant' (p. 233). Thus, Rogers' integrative statement is referring to conditions that exist as qualities for therapists in all therapies and for helpers in all situations that exist for the development of personality change.

## Misunderstanding

Although Rogers is quite clear about his hypothesis being offered for all therapies and other realms of helping, the literature seldom differentiates the integrative concept from his conceptualization of the role of the attitudinal qualities as central concepts in client-centered therapy. The upshot is that the therapist conditions posed as necessary and sufficient for all helping relationships and therapies has been confounded with the conditions as central attitudes in client-centered therapy. Moreover, they have been understood as somewhat separate actions different from other therapist activities rather than viewed as an integral experiencing of the therapist towards a client regardless of the channels of communication.

Nevertheless, the therapist conditions have come to be considered as synonymous with client-centered. We are, then, left with a misunderstanding that may have important implications having to do with such questions as:
- Do the manifestations of the conditions vary according to the situational and theoretical factors that are present at a given time?
- Do the perceptions of the conditions exist at a different level than the behavioral referents that occur?
- Are the conditions more potent change forces when they exist in the context of the theory of client-centered therapy?

Questions such as these may inform the directions of future research.

## Misdirection

Study of the conditions has taken on a decided focus on communication and delineated forms of behavior that are closely associated with particular assumptions in client-centered therapy. This is further complicated by the operational definitions necessary for measuring the conditions. What the therapist is doing or not doing is assessed with varying degrees of specificity rather than examination of the person of the therapist experiencing attitudinal qualities towards the client. An example of a couple of the questions used in rating scales depicts this directional bias. From one checklist for facilitative conditions, the following questions are asked:

*For Empathy*:
Did the counselor reflect implicit, or hidden, client messages?
Did the counselor refer to the client's feelings?
Did the counselor pace (match) the client's non-verbal behavior?

*For Genuineness*:
Did the counselor match the client's predicates and phrases?
Was the counselor appropriately spontaneous (for example, also tactful)?
Did the counselor self-disclose, or share similar feelings and experience?

*For Positive Regard*:
Did the counselor demonstrate behaviors related to commitment and willingness to see the client (for example, starting on time, responding with intensity)?
Did the counselor convey warmth to the client with supporting non-verbal behaviors (soft voice tone, smiling, eye contact, touch) and verbal responses (enhancing statements and/or immediacy)?
(Cormier and Cormier, 1991)

It is clear that the therapist behaviors are perceived as certain communications that convey the therapist's experience of the client. Some sense of the misdirection from an investigative position and from the integrative intent can be realized when Rogers' statements are examined further. When he responds to the theoretical usefulness of his hypothesis, Rogers explicitly cites a variety of techniques that he viewed as having 'essentially' no value to therapy; such as, interpretation of personality dynamics, free association, analysis of dreams, analysis of transference, hypnosis, interpretation of lifestyle, and suggestion. However, Rogers (1957) adds:

Each of these techniques may, however, become a channel for communicating the essential conditions that have been formulated. An interpretation may be given in a way that communicates the unconditional positive regard of the therapist. A stream of free association may be listened to in a way that communicates an empathy that the therapist is experiencing. In the handling of the transference an effective therapist often communicates his own wholeness and congruence in the relationship similarly for the other techniques. But just as these techniques may communicate the elements that are essential for therapy, so any one of them may communicate attitudes and experiences sharply contradictory to the hypothesized conditions of therapy. (p. 234)

An implication of Rogers' integrative statement and of his comments is reflected in his statement that '. . . the techniques of the various therapies are relatively unimportant except to the extent that they serve as channels for fulfilling one of the conditions' (p. 233). Rogers' statement is really quite astounding. He suggests that a person may employ a technique that is conceptually antithetical, for example, to the concept of empathic understanding (e.g. interpretation) while still experiencing and communicating empathic understanding and/or unconditional positive regard.

The misunderstanding of the integrative statement is to think that the experience of empathic understanding and unconditional positive regard for another must be sculptured in a particular form; i.e., technique responses, rather than existing as an *attitudinal* embodiment in the experiencing of one person for another. It is a personal and person-to-person level of a certain type of experiencing. The misdirection emerges from this misunderstanding, in that thinking and research have been designed from the perspective of these conditions as particular forms of communication. Rogers' liberal and inclusive theoretical definitions have given way to pseudoscientific and exclusive definitions. Some forms, such as empathic understanding responses and the restatement rule, may be less interfering and more pure channels to allow for client perceptions of therapist experiencing (Brodley, 1994; Teich, 1992). These response methods are not necessarily called for in the integrative model. (This is also true for the theory but such responses have received more attention in relation to the theory).

## A paradox

A paradox exists if the thesis that the personal embodiment of the conditions transcends behavior and method is correct. That is, a therapist focusing on an external referent may be in some other way communicating the therapist's empathic understanding of the internal frame of reference. In addition, the external referent may somehow even be a channel for the internal referent. How can this be so? One explanation is that the experiencing of unconditional positive regard and empathic understanding with another is a highly personal experience that exists at some other level of communication. The following experiment in a counseling course may give us a basis for exploring this phenomenon.

One person role-played the scenario of a female client who had been seen by a therapist. The woman came to therapy discussing how her four-year-old son was disrupting her family. Four students talked with her for just fifteen minutes each on a rotational basis. The students who were not the active therapist at a given time observed the session until it was their time to be the therapist. The students were asked to operate from a particular model of human relations that I define as fundamentally problem-oriented and therapist-driven (Egan, 1994). As such, all but one of the therapists focused on the problem of the child's disruption of the family. Questions raised included the following examples: Has he been evaluated for a physical problem? Have you tried rewarding him for good behaviors? Does your husband help? What does he (husband) think about it? Have you tried to communicate to your husband? In addition to the questions, the therapists attempted to summarize the client's communications. The client's comments were essentially presented in the following sequence:

My four year old is disrupting the family (This was a continuous communication interlocked with all of her other comments).

My husband works late on construction and isn't there to help.

My husband doesn't really care. He doesn't understand the problem. He thinks

boys will be boys and it's natural.
My husband doesn't give me any support.
I'm just there dealing with it all alone.
The only person I ever talk with is a friend who comes over sometimes. He tries to talk with my boy.

The therapists focused on the boy's behavior, sometimes wondering how her husband could help her more and even suggesting that her husband come with her for counseling in order to increase their communication with each other. One therapist communicated that this might help her husband to understand the situation better. The last therapist primarily summarized his understanding of her in an attempt to embody more of Rogers' integrative model. This model is viewed as more condition-centered and person-driven. With the continuous summarizing of the therapist's understanding of the client's meaning, the client added to her sequence:

I'm just all alone.  No one supports me.
My boy is angry with everyone . . . with me . . .
He's even mad at people he doesn't know very well.
He's even mad at my friend who comes over.
I'm just alone in all of this.

At this point, we stopped to discuss our experiences and observations. These included:

1. The client's intent was to resist telling the therapists that she was having an affair.
2. The therapists experienced something else other than the boy's behavior as going on but continued to focus on the problem as presented. In doing so, they missed hearing several of the client's comments; for example, that she had a male friend visit her. One therapist expressed a sense that she felt everyone was 'flipping her off'. This was not, however, discussed in the session.
3. The role-play session went in a direction remarkably similar to the direction of the actual client. The actual client quit discussing the boy's behavior (never to be mentioned again) during the second session and discussed her affair. She then quit discussing the affair (never to be mentioned again) and talked about her feelings of being alone, discontent etc. This was the direction the role-play was going during the ten-minute integration model.
4. The client felt that she might have eventually discussed the affair with any of the therapists. She felt that their questions kept her active and she felt that she 'knew that they knew' that there was something more than the boy's behavior.

The paradox of the phenomenon is somewhat illustrated in this instance. The student therapists focused on the problem and held a predominantly external assessment.

Yet, they also had a sense of her perceptual view and they seemed to be gaining an understanding of her internal frame of reference. She felt as though she would have talked about her affair and feelings of aloneness if they had continued the session. This may be an example of the resiliency of individuals as clients but the point is that the client 'knew' at some level that the therapists 'knew' at least vaguely that there was something else and that they were acceptant of her.

The salient points of our examination of Rogers' statement as integrative parallels research findings (Bohart, 1994). First, clients most often find what they need to be helped in whatever the therapist offers. That is, client factors account for over forty per cent of psychotherapy efficacy. Second, the relationship factors that account for a major part of therapy efficacy are viewed by us from the perspective that therapists have to find their own best way to communicate experiences of clients. Tom Malone provides a summary of this point in his correspondence with Carl Whitaker when he points out that thousands of therapists of all orientations and training consider themselves to be 'experiential psychotherapists'. Malone states:

> They use a myriad of psychotherapeutic systems and techniques. They use their experience of their persons in psychotherapy and apparently are convinced that technique and system approach is significantly subordinate to their use of their personal experience to catalyze the patient's growth.
>
> (Malone, 1981, xxvii-xxviii)

It is this personal participation in the relationship by which we suggest that the empathic and caring experience is actually conveyed via or even in spite of techniques and therapist activities. If this is so, it is plausible that for therapists to maximize their experiencing of empathic understanding and unconditional positive regard with a client they must achieve first and foremost their own congruence. This congruence must go beyond their own experiencing with their behaviors to include their own 'technique system' maximizing their capacity to experience the core conditions. This may be why Rogers expressed congruency of the therapist as the most important of the conditions.

It is asserted that Carl Rogers' statement concerning the necessary and sufficient conditions of therapeutic personality change is an integrative statement for psychotherapy and helping relationships that is separate from his statements concerning the conditions in client-centered therapy. The failure to consider his statement as integrative has resulted in misunderstandings and misdirection of investigation. The directions of investigation have focused on form of communication rather than upon the experiences of the therapist and the client. It is speculated that therapists must achieve their own congruence including the use of their own 'technique system' in order to maximize their capacity for experiencing empathic understanding and unconditional positive regard for the client.

# FUNCTIONAL DIMENSIONS OF THE PERSON-CENTERED APPROACH IN THERAPY

13

'Client-centered therapy' is a term that is often employed by individuals who mistakenly believe that they are practising the person-centered approach in therapy. This chapter identifies several fundamental premises that are the essence of the client-centered approach and which functionally assist therapists to clarify their therapeutic underpinnings.

Gendlin has suggested that the 'essence of client-centered therapy has not been learned and absorbed' (Gendlin, 1974, p. 211). Gendlin argues that therapists may use many procedures and try out many ideas but that the therapist – in the essence and crux of client-centered therapy – must return to finding out, listening and responding to where the person is in the present moment. He notes that the essence of client-centered therapy can be stated as: 'Stay in touch at all times with the person's directly felt concrete experiential datum – and help the person also to stay in touch with that, and get into it (Gendlin, 1974, p.220).

Our experiences with students and practitioners who believe that they are practising the client-centered approach are that they often have not learned the essence of this therapeutic effort. They are familiar with 'reflection' and with the importance of 'developing relationship'. Too often, however, they equate the client-centered approach to Human Relations Training Models. They view client-centered therapy as only a prerequisite to other kinds of responding and miss the entire essence of the approach.

It is essential that therapists have nearly unfaltering 'faith' that individuals given the opportunity will engage in an optimal mode of experiencing. It is this experience of 'self' and the experience of being accepted and understood by another individual in the present moment which releases energies for self understanding, self acceptance, and the courage to risk change. There are many other things that therapists may choose to do but it is this unfaltering belief that provides the structure and direction for all therapeutic behaviors.

Adapted with permission from:
Bozarth, J. D. and Mitchell, S. (1984). Functional dimensions of the person-centered approach in therapy. *Renaissance*, 1(1), 7-8.

**Can I permit the locus of control to be with the client?**

Although the functional dimension of the person-centered approach associated with this question is closely related to the first dimension, it is a dimension that is often misunderstood by many professing the practice of person-centered therapy. Although Rogers has written about the locus of evaluation and the direction of progress being with the client, the locus of control of the therapy sessions is often a major barrier to the viable application of the person-centered approach. Therapists often have difficulty being with their clients when the clients are 'muddled' or do not clearly communicate expected progress as perceived by the therapist. At the same time, therapists often seem patently unwilling to 'allow' the client to be extremely sad or in pain or psychotic. Their misperception of the person-centered approach in therapy is primarily the view that the relationship can be developed in such a way that the therapist can then guide the client towards appropriate direction and action. Focusing on the therapist's authoritative expertise often becomes more important than creating the atmosphere which allows the client to achieve self-direction and which enables the therapist to share his/her concepts and experiential data in the relationship.

Many therapists assume that their competence and progress is judged relative to how able they are to motivate clients to address and resolve problems in living. Thus the client is viewed in terms of what 'ought to be discussed' or 'what the person should do' (i.e., in terms of the therapist as authoritative expert). Such concerns and preoccupations often substitute for attending fully to what is occurring with the client and the therapist in the present moment.

The person-centered approach requires that the therapist be responsible for initiating the receptive climate of the relationship. It is primarily the client's and sometimes the therapist's experience of the relationship which is the source of relevant data rather than the therapist's perception of 'what ought to be discussed', 'what should be done', or 'what feelings and experiences' should be focused on.

There is a central question for the person who intends to practice the person-centered approach in therapy: 'Can I allow this person to be whatever he/she is in the relationship'? Perhaps a more concrete statement of this issue is to say that a therapist's need to control is the most accurate measure of the therapist's 'lack of faith' in the other person's ability, thus it creates a direct contradiction to the fundamentals of the person-centered approach in therapy.

**Do I have the intent, ability and self-discipline to attend emotionally and intellectually to the client?**

A frequent and misdirected criticism of person-centered therapy is that the approach lacks the potency to effect change. The therapist in such criticisms is described as passive, uninvolved and even detached. The flaw in such assessments is that they overlook the inherent potency in being confronted with one's self. This criticism lacks the experiential and cognitive understanding that client-centered therapy is not passive but, rather, receptive '. . .which implies aliveness, yet openness, going with the other's direction but fully, even creating something together, something

which does not always come from one or the other but is created in the union . .'
(Wood, 1980). The criticism ignores the '. . . tremendous energy to allow the
mysterious 'self-actualizing' forces of the universe to do their work while you are
exercising self-disciplined listening, attuned to the person's experience and to
your own, and being completely alive in the moment' (Wood, 1980).

### Can I be openly attuned to my own experiences in the relationship with the client?

The major component here can be referred to as 'experiencing' (Gendlin, 1974).
The therapist allows the client to say things that are being experienced in the
moment and attends to his/her own experiences in the relationship. The underlying
assumption is that the more completely therapists are able to permit their awareness
of their own experiential flow the more able they will be to tend to the other
individual's experiential flow. For example, if the therapist experiences anger,
boredom, or esoteric fantasy in the relationship and is aware of these experiences
the therapist is more open to all the experiences in the relationship including those
of the client. We believe that such therapist experiences in the relationship often
have applications for the client's struggle. As the therapist is all that he/she is
during the time of the relationship, he/she becomes increasingly aware of his/her
experiences. He or she may make a decision to communicate a particular experience
to the client. This decision to communicate the experience may be based upon the
strength and consistency of the experience and the therapist's sense of
appropriateness at a particular time in the dyadic contact. The therapist's expression
of self is, however, more apt to be based on his/her own spontaneous and intuitive
reaction. The therapist's awareness of experience is reflective of the approaching
unit of counselor/client.

In summary, many practitioners who profess to be using a person-centered
approach to therapy are, in fact, often identifying the approach with Human
Relations Training Models, or operating on mistaken premises that the person-
centered approach is 'reflection', a prerequisite step to client action, or passive
responsibility on the part of the therapist. The essence of this approach in therapy
is always to stay in touch with the person's concrete experiential data and help the
client get into the experience. This is often forgotten by therapists in lieu of emphasis
on therapist guidance, therapist expertise, and 'appropriate' responses.

A concise definition of the client-centered approach for the therapist is that
client-centered therapy '. . . pivots around surrender and trust . . . involve(s)
increasing one's sensitivities to hear and be guided by one's own inner experience,
one's inner teacher, to awaken to one's total living experience organizing this
awareness, this energy, around the center of the person. Not aspiring to, but being,
who I am' (Wood, 1980, p. 24). In therapy, this type of therapist involvement is
the type of involvement that the client will move toward as he/she experiences the
therapist's self-surrender and trust.

The questions which those therapists who expect to practice person-centered
therapy might ask themselves are: (1) Do I believe that individuals will move in

the direction of self-actualization if I provide an atmosphere of acceptance and attend fully to the concrete experiential flow of the client? (2) Can I permit the locus of control to be with the client?' (3) Do I have the intent, ability and self-discipline to attend emotionally and intellectually to the client?' (4) Can I be openly attuned to my own experiences and share these experiences in the relationship with the client?

# CLIENT-CENTERED THERAPY AND TECHNIQUES

# 14

In chapter 12 I offered my view of one of the major difficulties in the understanding and practice of person-centered therapy. This referred to the focus on what the therapist should do rather than upon the therapist assimilating and operating out of the attitudinal qualities. This chapter focuses on the more specific use of techniques in person-centered therapy.

**The question posed is, can one use techniques and still be client-centered?**
Rogers' theoretical position is a view that militates against the use of techniques in counseling and psychotherapy. Techniques are, at best, irrelevant and have no value to the fundamental theory of the client-centered approach. Worse, however, is that techniques may interfere with the client freedom perpetuated by a client-centered stance and can insidiously contaminate the non-directive position of the therapist. Although I believe that techniques may occur in client-centered therapy and be consistent with the theory, such responses are necessarily related to the internal referent of the client and emergent from that internal referent. It is important to keep in mind Rogers' theory since one of the typical discursive traps is ' . . .that of dismissing the fundamental assumption of the approach (that of the actualizing tendency and the self-authority of the client) as untenable or questionable and proceeding with criticism of the theory from other frames of reference' (Bozarth, 1993a, p. 2). I will begin with a statement of my understanding of the position of those who believe techniques are appropriate in client-centered therapy, offer a brief reiteration of the theory, reiterate Rogers' view of techniques in his classic integrative article and discuss the only theoretically consistent integration of techniques in the theory.

**Rationale for the use of techniques**
Art Bohart asks an intriguing question, 'Can one systematically try to facilitate

Adapted with permission from:
Bozarth, J. D. (1996). Client-centered Therapy and Techniques. In Hutterer, R., Pawlowsky, G., Schmid , P. F. and Stipsits, R. (eds.) *Client-Centered and Experiential Therapy: A Paradigm in Motion.* pp. 363-368, New York: Peter Lang.

experiencing, to work through the problematic reaction points, and to resolve unfinished business, and still be consistent with the person-centered philosophical emphasis on people finding their own solutions?' (Bozarth, 1995a, p. 12). A cogent response to this question is offered by Brodley and Brody (1994):

> In our opinion, infusing specific goal-oriented treatments and techniques with client-centered values in ways that influence the actual application of the treatments and techniques might well tend to greatly humanize and improve the efficacy of the treatments and the techniques. But they should not be confused with client-centered therapy. (p. 2)

To go a bit further, why would one want to use techniques if operating from a client-centered stance? Most techniques are developed from other psychological frameworks holding different basic assumptions. For example, the assumption that clients have unfinished business is alien to the theory. There are no pre-conceived (nor post-conceived) systematic problem points. The approach is trust-centered rather than problem-centered. Concepts and their concomitant techniques such as unfinished business are not part of and are probably antithetical to the underlying framework of the theory. The belief that certain techniques are considered powerful influencers of behavior is not a valid argument for including them in a contradictory frame of reference.

Other than the *non sequitur* emanating from other basic assumptions, the only other rationale that I know that argues for the use of techniques is that there is ample research evidence supporting the effectiveness of certain techniques. Brodley and Brody acknowledge that we know of effective specific psychotechnologies such as ' . . . cognitive and behavioral techniques for alleviating depression, getting through panics, for controlling one's focus of attention and for relaxation (p. 9). However, these techniques are deemed to be effective from frameworks of assumptions of expertise of the therapist and predicated upon the questionable 'specificity' assumption. The position assumes the therapist to have certain information and skills available to the client through which goals can be attained or problems alleviated. In the client-centered position, problem resolution is in the trust of the client's capability and unique directions and not in the therapist's arsenal of skill and knowledge.

In addition, the research on the question of efficacy of techniques can be questioned *prima facie*; e.g., generalizability, direct comparison with other treatments, replicability. My skepticism about such data is recorded in a dialogue with Lazarus and Lazarus where I point out the very studies which they use to support their assertion for the tenet of specific techniques for effectiveness in treating particular disorders actually raise questions about their assertion rather than support it (Bozarth, 1991a). Furthermore, we seldom know the extent of influence of the common variables of the relationship and of client motivation when techniques are being studied. In short, do we really know as much about the efficacy of specific techniques as often assumed? We certainly do not have a comparative base that any technique that we offer is better than the clients' emergent directions of self-influence. The recent research reviews on outcome efficacy suggest that application of the research results might better involve an intentional utilization of the client's frame of reference (Bohart, 1994; Lambert, 1992, Lambert, Shapiro and Bergin, 1986; Patterson, 1984; Stubbs and Bozarth, 1994). The most consistent research findings over four decades of research on effectiveness of psychotherapy identify most of the success (70%) accounted for by the therapist-client relationship and the resources of the client. Part of this 70% is accounted for by extratherapeutic variables (which account for 40% of successful outcome) and the client-therapist relationship (which accounts for 30% of successful outcome) (Duncan and Moynihan, 1994). My personal view is that the potency of attending to the client's frame of reference and to the client's unique self-adjusting methods by far exceed other methods when therapists are able to trust clients' constructive forces and their rights to their own expertise about their own life.

**The theory**

Rogers' theory has been summarized in different ways. It may be relevant to repeat here in a slightly different context. Rogers' view of psychological dysfunction is that individuals are thwarted in their natural growth by conditions of worth being introjected from significant others. Psychological growth results from the individual being freed of these introjections. When the individual experiences unconditional positive regard from a significant other, the person begins to develop unconditional positive self-regard. As this occurs, the individual becomes increasingly able to deal with problems and life. If the therapist is congruent in the person-centered relationship, experiences unconditional positive regard and empathic understanding toward the client and if these attitudes are, at least, minimally perceived by the client, then therapeutic personality change will occur (Rogers, 1959). These attitudinal conditions were also, for Rogers, the necessary and sufficient conditions for constructive personality change. In client-centered therapy, the therapeutic atmosphere created by therapists foster the natural process of the actualizing tendency of the client. The greater the extent that therapists honor the authority of clients as the authority of their own lives then the greater the probability of constructive personality change and problem resolution. As constructive personality change occurs, the client will also be better able to solve his or her own problems (Rogers, 1977; Rogers and Wallen, 1946). Hence, the amelioration of particular dysfunctions is a result of personality change that involves the experiencing of unconditional positive regard. Interventive techniques are simply extant of the theory. To reiterate, client-centered psychotherapy is founded on the trust of the person and not on problem-centered assumptions.

**Techniques from Rogers' perspective**

Rogers' perspective of techniques is clearly pronounced in his integrative statement. This statement is not about client-centered therapy but has to do with the commonalties which Rogers' viewed across therapies and helping relationships (Rogers, 1957; Stubbs and Bozarth, 1994). In the integrative statement, Rogers explicitly cites a variety of techniques that he viewed as having 'essentially' no value to therapy; such as, interpretation of personality dynamics, free association, analysis of dreams, analysis of transference, hypnosis, interpretation of lifestyle, and suggestion. However, Rogers' (1957) (see also chapter 11) adds:

> Each of these techniques may, however, become a channel for communicating the essential conditions that have been formulated. An interpretation may be given in a way that communicates the unconditional positive regard of the therapist. A stream of free association may be listened to in a way that communicates the empathy that the therapist is experiencing. In the handling of the transference an effective therapist often communicates his own wholeness and congruence in the relationship similarly for the other techniques. But just as these techniques may communicate the elements that are essential for therapy, so any one of them may communicate attitudes and experiences sharply contradictory to the hypothesized conditions of therapy. (p. 234)

An implication of Rogers' integrative statement and of his 1957 statement is reflected in his comment that '. . . the techniques of the various therapies are relatively unimportant except to the extent that they serve as channels for fulfilling one of the conditions (p. 233). Rogers could not be more clear. He viewed techniques as valuable only in that they were ways for the therapist to channel the core conditions. This view was true for him not only for client-centered therapy but all therapy and helping relationships in general.

### Techniques in client-centered therapy

Techniques must be emergent rather than pre-conceived to be consistent with client-centered theory. Of the techniques that emerge during therapy, there are several contexts that are reasonably prevalent. These contexts are: (1) the client request; (2) the setting; and (3) the clearing of one's self in order to better absorb the client's world.

When the client has a consistent request for the therapist to apply a technique, the therapist needs to be honestly present in the implementation of that desire. In other words, the therapist might indicate reluctance to give advice or enthusiastically endorse a concentrated behavioral effort to effect particular change. I'm reminded of the time that I reluctantly gave advice (without using a specific technique unless it would be called homework) to a couple in marital counseling. During a one time consulting session, the husband was clearly intent on obtaining advice from me. He was a self employed individual who was very goal and activity oriented. Other therapists had given them advice that he liked (namely, that they contract for the wife to have sex with him once a week and he would stop following her around the house when she changed clothes). They had a pattern of talking about their problems from morning through evening. He asked me for advice at the end of the session. My honest presence was that I understood his wish for suggestions and for concrete action to take. I said to him that I didn't usually give advice and, usually, when I did, it didn't work out very well. However, I expressed my understanding of his need and continued by suggesting that they quit talking to each other about 'the problem'. Several weeks later, the wife indicated that things had dramatically improved between them. The husband was delighted with the advice. Several years later they worked out an amiable divorce. Both individuals still, after nearly ten years, express their gratitude to me for the session. I think that the same gratitude would be there had I advised weekly picnics or if we had attempted psychodrama if these would have been present in the clients' frames of reference during the session.

Another prevalent context for using techniques seems to me to be requirements of the setting. Techniques are increasingly considered by agencies and institutions, to meet demands of demonstrating the treatment mode and pursuit of specific problem amelioration demanded by insurance guidelines, HMO's and so forth. The client-centered therapist may need to adjust to the system to survive. The setting may have a decided influence on the actual use of techniques in therapy.

The third and most important rationale for the therapist to use an emergent technique is for the purpose of 'clearing' him or herself in order to be better able to accept and understand the client. A brief example of this point occurred in a community group meeting. I kept losing my attention with one of the members when he talked. Over the couple of days, I found that I reacted nearly every time he spoke. My stomach got tight; I got a headache; I had a complete lack of attention to him. I would get up and leave when he talked. I discussed my reaction with colleagues and attempted to engage him about my reaction several times. Finally, I found myself completely annoyed with him as he droned on in a (to me) narcissistic dialogue. I had lost my capacity to tolerate him. At that point, I got up and stood by the window noticing some mirror tiles that were awaiting construction of the room. Impulsively, I took one of the mirrors to him and asked him to look at himself. I had no thought of possible effect. The only reason for the action was that of clearing myself and making a connection with him. I thought that he might throw it at me. Instead, he looked at himself for a long time. At the end of the workshop, he mentioned this as a meaningful technique for him. Others questioned my reason for using the technique (a Freudian one I believe someone said). It was, however, not a deliberate technique with any intention of result. It was simply a way that emerged for me to clear myself and connect with him. It enabled me to be somewhat more in concert with him.

For those who adopt the integrative model (and not necessarily the client-centered model), the primary justification for systematically using techniques is the provision of a way for the therapist to be maximize his/her congruency to bring his/her personhood to the client. At the risk of being redundant once again, Tom Malone (Whitaker and Malone, 1981) captures this point:

The key concept is congruence. The congruence between the

therapist's technique-system and his/her person allows the maximal
personal participation in the relationship to the patient. This differs
for different therapists (xxviii).

It is ironic that a therapist's techniques that are incongruent with adhering to client
authority but which enable therapists to enhance their personal participation with
clients might even serve as 'conveyors' of the conditions. Perhaps the conditions
may be so strong that they override techniques that are incongruent with the theory.

**Guidelines for the inclusion of techniques**
In general, I agree with Bohart's idea that techniques may emerge in the 'dance of
the client and therapist' (Bohart, 1994). In fact, I believe that one can do many
things as a therapist as long as one is totally dedicated to the theoretical base of
the internal referent of the client and that empathic responding may be multifaceted
and idiosyncratic (Bozarth, 1984). Increasingly, I believe that one of the most
confounding factors in the understanding of the approach is the focus on what the
therapist should do in therapy rather than how the therapist should be (Bozarth,
1992a; also see Chapter 11). The guidelines that I view for using techniques in
client-centered therapy are similar to those I have proposed for using tests and
assessment. The following quote with substitution of technique for tests and
assessment summarizes this position (Bozarth, 1991b; also, see chapter 15):

> Does this theory mean that techniques from the person-centered
> perspective do not exist? Is it plausible to use techniques in person-
> centered therapy and be consistent with the theoretical model? If so,
> what are the conditions for the use of techniques? Responses to
> these questions revolve around the difference between what the
> counselor does in counseling and the philosophical dedication to the
> self-authority of the client. Assuming that the counselor adheres to
> the person-centered philosophy of honoring the client's perception
> of the world, what a counselor does in person-centered counseling
> is quite flexible depending on the idiosyncrasies of the client,
> counselor, and situation (Bozarth, 1984). Raskin's (1988)
> conceptualization of the systematic versus unsystematic
> implementation is significant in this regard. He differentiated
> systematic therapist activities from the unsystematic by viewing
> systematic therapists as having 'a preconceived notion of how they
> wish to change the client and work at it in systematic fashion, in
> contrast to the person-centered therapist who starts out being open
> and remains open to an emerging process orchestrated by the client'
> (p. 2). Techniques and other forms of activity (e.g., dispensation of
> medicine, behavior modification, homework) are consistent with the
> theory in that they may occur as unsystematic actions that are decided
> on by the client from the client's frame of reference in interaction
> with the therapist. Any ethical activity or action that is decided upon

by the client and emerges from the attention to the internal world of the client is a viable and congruent activity in person-centered therapy (p. 45).

Can one use techniques and be client-centered? The answer, for me, is, 'Yes but . . .' The theory militates against the use of techniques. Techniques are generally problem-centered and therapist-driven rather than trust-centered and person-driven. They are generally laden in one way or another with the expertise of the therapist. Unless they are emergent in the blending of therapist and client, techniques distract from the attention of the therapist to the world of the client. The primary reason for involving techniques in a client-centered frame of reference is to help the therapist clear his/her barriers to absorbing the client's perceptual world. Thus, the remarkable potency of trusting the client's own way, direction and pace can be realized. I personally agree with Rogers when he said, 'If I thought that I knew what was best for a client, I would tell him'. Likewise, if I thought that I knew that a particular technique was best for a client, I would use it. I think, though, that the client would usually be better off if I would never have such a thought.

# APPLICATIONS IN PRACTICE

# PERSON-CENTERED ASSESSMENT

# 15

Carl Rogers' doctoral dissertation was entitled, *Measuring Personality Adjustment in Children Nine to Thirteen Years of Age* (Rogers, 1931). He developed an objective and scientific test measuring the attitudes of children. His major reason for studying this topic was to resolve his own inner conflict between the ideas of observing an individual from the outside versus understanding the individual from the person's own perspective. These two perspectives pervaded client-centered therapy and the person-centered approach throughout the remaining fifty-seven years of Rogers' life. He had a perennial need to 'make sense' out of phenomena through both objective and subjective viewing. The objective view, however, remained important to him in research and less and less important to him in his clinical work. The subjective view of the client became pre-eminent in the practical implementation of client-centered therapy (also referred to as client-centered counseling, person-centered counseling or person-centered therapy) (Rogers, 1939, 1942, 1951, 1957, 1959, 1977, 1980).

## The theoretical foundation
The theoretical position of Rogers is a clinical view that militates against the use of systematic testing and assessment in counseling and psychotherapy. If the therapist is congruent in the person-centered relationship, experiences unconditional positive regard and empathic understanding toward the client while endeavouring to communicate the empathic understanding to the client, and if these attitudes are, at least, minimally perceived by the client, then therapeutic personality change will occur (Rogers, 1957). These attitudinal conditions were, for Rogers, the necessary and sufficient conditions for constructive personality change. In the person-centered approach, the therapeutic atmosphere created by the therapist fosters the natural process of the actualizing tendency of the client. The greater the extent that the therapist honors the client as the authority of his/her own life then the greater the probability of constructive personality change

Adapted with permission from:
Bozarth, J. D. (1991b). Person-centered assessment. *Journal of Counseling and Development*, 69 (5), 458-461.

and problem resolution. As constructive personality change occurs, the client will also be better able to solve his or her own problems (see Rogers, 1957, 1959; Rogers and Wallen, 1946).

## Historical review

After developing client-centered theory, earlier comments about testing within a client-centered approach were to offer several cautions that included: (1) be certain that the client knows what the test score means, (2) be certain that the information derived from the test score adheres with something the client has just said, and (3) be sure to allow the client time to react to the information (Rogers and Wallen, 1946). Several authors refer primarily to the use of tests in client-centered vocational counseling (Bixler and Bixler, 1946; Bordin and Bixler, 1946; Bowen, 1947; Combs, 1947; Covner, 1947; Crites, 1974; 1981; Gothard, 1985; Grummon, 1972; Patterson, 1964; Rusalem, 1954; Samler, 1964; Seeman, 1948; Super, 1949; 1950; 1951; 1957). The various authors have emphasized points which include: (1) the counselor should not impose the tests or test results on the client (e.g., Crites, 1974); (2) the client should request the tests (e.g., Patterson, 1964); and should request the type of tests (e.g., Bixler, and Bixler, 1946); (3) the clients should be encouraged to participate in the test selection process (e.g., Crites, 1974); (4) tests should provide information which the client needs and wants (e.g., Patterson, 1964); (5) the clients should be given tests and other information in the form of reports or through reference to another counselor who assumes the directive approach ( e.g., Combs, 1947); (6) the counselor could move from non-directive to directive techniques (e.g., Super, 1949); and (7) the results should be reported in an objective non-judgmental manner (e.g., Crites, 1974). Other articles describe the use of tests as ways to understand the client's world (Fischer, 1989). There has been the call for a 'collaborative method' as a way that tests may be '... entirely compatible with client-centered theory and practice' (Cain, 1989, p. 176).

Patterson summarizes the gist of the use of tests in client-centered counseling by stating: 'The essential basis for the use of tests in career counseling is that they provide information which the client needs and wants, information concerning questions raised by the client in counseling' (Patterson, 1964, p. 449). This is clearly not the predominant viewpoint of the profession of counseling or counseling psychology (e.g., Duckworth, 1990; Walsh, 1990).

The reasons for the diminished involvement of the person-centered approach in vocational and career counseling seem directly related to the traditional reliance on the use of tests and upon the notion of the vocational counselor as expert. Also, Rogers gravitated more towards working with clients and issues that were not vocational or career in nature (see Rogers, 1970, 1977, 1980).

## Assessment via diagnosis

Although Rogers and his colleagues had little interest in tests as diagnostic instruments, Rogers was involved in diagnostic work earlier in his clinical career and was initially convinced of its importance (Kirschenbaum, 1979, p. 67). He actually developed a diagnostic procedure (Kirschenbaum, 1979, p. 64) that was identified as the 'component factor method'. But as noted, Rogers' clinical interest became increasingly focused on the internal referents of clients, and at least by 1946, he did not consider diagnostic knowledge and skill necessary for good therapy.

Recent considerations of psychodiagnosis from the client-centered perspective raise several fundamental issues which include the purpose, tools, and methodology of diagnostic procedures (Boy, 1989). Boy's summary identifies the inconsistency of psychodiagnosis with the client-centered position and urges that the client-centered position be given consideration in the controversy concerning psychodiagnosis. Seeman (1989) concurs but adds his belief in the importance of psychodiagnosis for the assessment of physiological impairment. Shlien (1989) flatly states, since client-centered therapy has only one treatment for all cases and since diagnosis is for the primary purpose of determining treatment, diagnosis in entirely useless. Some authors agree with the criticisms of categorizing clients but still espouse use of psychodiagnostic procedures as a way to know the client better (Cain, 1989; Fischer, 1989).

### Person-centered assessment

Psychological assessment as generally conceived is incongruent with the basic assumptions of client-centered theory. The most basic value of person-centered counseling is that the authority about the person rests in the person rather than with an outside expert (Bozarth and Brodley, 1986). Information about persons for the purpose of making individual predictions or assumptions assumes the role of the expert about another person's life; i.e., ' . . . the entire process involved in collecting information about persons and using it to make important predictions or inferences' (Grayham and Lily, 1984, p. 2). This view is, at best, irrelevant to client-centered theory.

Dedication to the person-centered base leads to the functional deliberation that the counselor seeks to have no presuppositions about what a client might do, or be, or become. The essence of person-centered therapy is that the client has within him/herself the best direction, way, and pace to go and the therapist follows and honors that process (Bozarth, 1990a). Using external frames of reference are, at best, interferences that effect clients' inclinations to find their own directions and ways at their own pace.

Does this mean that assessment from the person-centered perspective does not exist? Is it plausible to use tests and assessment methods in person-centered therapy and be consistent with the theoretical model? If so, what are the conditions for the use of assessment? Responses to these questions revolve around the difference between philosophical dedication to the self-authority of the client and to focusing on the question, 'What does the person-centered counselor do in counseling'? Assuming that the counselor adheres to the person-centered philosophy of honoring the client's perception of the world, what a counselor does in person-centered counseling is quite flexible depending upon the idiosyncrasies of the client, counselor and situation (Bozarth, 1984). Raskin's conceptualization of the systematic vs. unsystematic implementation is significant in this regard (Raskin, 1988). He differentiates systematic from the unsystematic therapist activities by viewing systematic approaches as having ' . . . a preconceived notion of how they wish to change the client and work at it in systematic fashion, in contrast to the person-centered therapist who starts out being open and remains open to an emerging process orchestrated by the client' (p.2). Testing and other forms of activity (e.g., dispensation of medicine, Behavior Modification, homework) are consistent with the theory in that they may occur as unsystematic actions that are decided upon by the client from the client's frame of reference in interaction with the therapist. Any ethical activity or action that emerges from the attention to the internal world of the client is a viable and congruent activity in person-centered therapy.

### Conditions for person-centered assessment
The conditions for the use of tests are that they are used within the framework of the therapist's dedication to the client's world and 'self-authority'. There are fundamentally three conditions that suggest the use of tests in person-centered counseling: (1) the client may request to take tests; (2) the policies of the setting may demand that tests be given to clients; and (3) testing might take place as an 'objective' way for the client and counselor to consider a decision for action that is affected by institutional or societal demands.

*The client request*
Clients may request to take tests. Here is a specific example as it emerged from a client:

>  Client:     Isn't there some way that I could just take a bunch of tests to find out whether or not I can do this stuff?
>  Counselor: An easy answer would be a relief to you (responding more to the previous context). (Pause) There are some tests available at the center that we might look at.

The counselor honors the client by responding to questions and by acting in concert with the client's decision while attending to the client's view.

*Setting*
Tests and assessments are increasingly used for the agency, institution, insurance payment determination, or reasons other than understanding clients. The person-centered counselor working in this kind of setting must usually adjust (even be 'empathic') to the system to survive. An example of the use of tests due to the requirement of the setting follows:

Counselor: The agency requires that a test profile be developed for agency records. At some point, I can go over with you the kind of tests that the agency requires.

Client: What kind of tests? What good will that do me?

Counselor: You wonder what the value of the tests really is? I'm not sure how they will help you. The tests are necessary for the agency records. They include aptitude, achievement, and interest tests. They will provide some information that may help you compare your observations about yourself with the speculations of the tests. We'll try to find some tests that you think might do you some good.

Client: Well, I'm for anything that will do me some good.

Counselor: Um huh. If they help you are all for it. (C: Yeah)

Sometimes a client may seek a counselor for the purpose of taking a battery of tests because of his/her perception of the counselor's role. An excerpt from a vocational counseling session in a university counseling center offers an example:

Client: A friend took a bunch of tests here to help him find a job; I came over to take them, too.

Counselor: Um huh, you're also interested in taking some tests?

(pause)

Client: Well, yeah, it's like mainly, I'm about to finish school and I don't know what I'm going to do or ought to do. (He talks about his courses and number of years in school). I just need to see what those tests can tell me.

Counselor: Need something to give you some ideas?

Client: Yeah, they helped my buddy decide something anyway.

Counselor: Um huh. Maybe that would be something that would help you too, Is that it?

(Pause three minutes)

Client: Yeah, When can I take them?

Counselor: So you would like to get started. (pause) Anytime is okay.

The tests were scheduled for the client after the first session. Although the setting might determine the actual use of tests in counseling, the client's view of this requirement is the primary interest of the person-centered counselor.

## 'Reality testing'

Since tests and assessment have been primarily used by person-centered counselors in vocational and career counseling, several axioms that have been presented for a model of person-centered career counseling seem apropos when using tests in person-centered counseling (Bozarth and Fisher, 1990). These axioms are:

*Axiom 1*: The person-centered career counselor has attitudes and behaviors which focus on promoting the inherent process of client self-actualization (p. 53).

*Axiom 2*: There is an initial emphasis upon a certain area of client concern, that of work (p. 53).

*Axiom 3*: There are opportunities for the client to test his/her emerging concept of personal identity and vocational choice with real or simulated work activities (p. 53).

*Axiom 4*: The person-centered career counselor has certain information and skills available to the client through which a career goal can be implemented (p. 53).

The second axiom refers to the emphasis upon the area of work. The client makes this emphasis. Initial career counseling might very well evolve into individual psychotherapy and so on. However, a continuing focus on vocations or career would more likely result in the use of tests. Tests might be used as a representation of the 'real world' or 'world standardizations' to assist the client to check his or her emerging concept of personal identity and vocational choice (Axiom 3).

The fourth axiom refers to the counselor having certain information and skills available to the client through which a career goal can be implemented. Tests in career counseling are part of the tools and techniques employed by the career counselor and ' . . . are a source of information and reality-testing for the client.' In person-centered career counseling, ' . . . the meaning and implication of that information is left to the client to decide, within his/her unique process of self-actualization' (p.54).

The following example of a career counseling session from a person-centered perspective further illustrates consideration of tests.

(The client discusses his feelings and concerns for about one half of the first session.)

Client:     So how could I find out what I'd be good at? Can you give me some tests like you gave Joe?

Counselor:  [If he insists on testing, I will certainly give it to him and hope that he doesn't think that testing is a magical shortcut. But I'd prefer to help him find his answers internally.] If we get stuck, I can test you, but I'd prefer to use some exercises first, which will help you decide what your options are.

(Bozarth and Fisher, 1990, p. 26)

The counselor is responding to the client's inquiry in an honest and spontaneous way. He also notes his preference for using 'exercises'. In this example, the counselor uses an external referent of 'exercises' that are referred to within the context of the client's request. Person-centered counselors who use tests and assessment as external referents should be especially integrated in their commitment to the philosophy of the clients' self-authority. Otherwise, the fine line between using tests as authority about the person and using them as external referent tools with the client while honoring the self-authority of the client might become quite confounding. The counselors use of exercises is an example of a counselor's belief in the use of certain procedures that could easily be used before the client has had a chance to develop his/her own ideas.

### Test interpretation
Test interpretation by the client-centered counselor can be briefly summarized: the counselor should be honestly present within the testing context. If the counselor believes in the results of particular aspects of a test or doesn't believe in the results, the counselor should 'be there' with the congruency of his/her convictions. Test information should not be instrumental in reaching a decision point of what the client might do, e. g., take a particular job, enter a particular training program. From the person-centered stance, such decisions would come only from the client's frame of reference.

This chapter has discussed the use of tests and assessment in person-centered counseling. Three conditions under which tests seem more apt to be congruent with person-centered theory are: (1) when the client requests testing or testing emerges within the client-counselor dialogue, (2) when the setting requires it, and (3) when the client and counselor use tests or assessment procedures as an 'external' referent to help the client decide how a decision or conclusion compares with external standards. Test interpretation by the person-centered counselor is primarily predicated on the counselor being honestly present within the testing context It is not so much what the counselor specifically does in counseling sessions that is important in person-centered counseling. Tests and other forms of assessment may be as relevant as any other type of activity. The critical factor in person-centered counseling or therapy is that of extensively honoring the self-authority of the client and, thus, facilitating the natural process of the client to be the architect of his or her own life.

# Person-centered Family Therapy With Couples

# 16

This chapter considers the application of the principles of the person-centered approach to work with a family. The rationale for person-centered family therapy is presented in terms of the development of a therapeutic psychological climate. The idea of the formative tendency is used as a conceptual model for looking at the family system as an 'organismic' unit that moves toward its more healthy potential when psychological conditions permit. The application of this rationale is discussed from the standpoint of the way one therapist does therapy using metaphors, personal experiences, and responses that are consistent with this rationale. Some examples of therapy with a family, and with a husband and wife as a couple, are presented to illustrate the therapist's way of working within this person-centered rationale.

## Rationale

Some basic assumptions as person-centered family therapists are: (1) that individuals strive naturally to maintain and enhance themselves within the family unit (actualizing tendency) and (2) that the family system strives naturally toward maintenance and enhancement of its own healthy potential (formative tendency). These assumptions radically influence the role of the therapist in both action and intent compared to other schools of couple and family therapy. The therapist is not an intervener or expert who presumes to know best about the methods, modes, or process of a particular family system. Instead, as in individual person-centered therapy, the therapist's role is essentially that of a catalyst for the inherent growth direction of the individuals. The growth direction of the particular family system is also included in the therapist's conceptualization for family or couple therapy.

The therapist's role, in short, is that of embodying the attitudinal qualities of empathy, genuineness, and unconditional regard in an effort to facilitate the inherent growth direction of the family unit. That is, to allow the members and family unit to find their own ways of coping, their own solutions, and their own ways of conflict resolution. Person-centered family therapy requires complete dedication

Adapted with permission from:
Bozarth, J. D. and Shanks, A. (1989). Person-centered family therapy with couples. *Person-Centered Review*, 4 (3), 280-294.

of the therapist to the family style as well as to the individuals in any particular family unit. The basic premise is as follows: when a facilitative psychological climate is experienced by the client, family, or couple who assume the locus of control for their lives, the actualizing and formative tendencies are promoted.

It is significant to note that, for person-centered family therapy, the formative tendency became one of the two foundation blocks of person-centered theory (Rogers, 1980). The actualizing tendency as a characteristic of organic life was always central in Rogers' theory, but he noted that the formative tendency grew more important in his thinking as the years went by. As he wrote: 'Taken together, they are the foundation for the person-centered approach (Rogers, 1980, p. 114). The actualizing tendency for Rogers was the *sine qua non* for the motivation of people. The formative tendency was for him the broader view of the directional movement of all phenomena in the universe: the evolution of simpler, less complex forms into more organized forms.

The concept of the formative tendency combined with the phenomenological view can be used as a model for viewing family units as systems that will move toward growth when a facilitative psychological climate is provided. The model, in this case, is that of a family structure incorporating both the individual organismic model of actualization and the formative tendency. This model is consistent with the general systems view of life; that is, the principle of self-organizing systems. The model reflects a paradigm of the family as an organismic unit; that is, a living system capable of movement and direction.

General systems theory originally developed as a science of living systems, reflecting an understanding of the unique characteristics of whole systems. Our rationale is reflective of views of general systems theory (Bateson, 1972; Capra, 1982).

Capra's view is predicated on 'the interrelatedness and interdependence of all phenomena – physical, biological, psychological, social, and cultural' (p. 265), (see Chapter 10). Bateson further suggests that the fundamental characteristics of living systems are that they possess the ability to know, to think, and to decide. He states:

> Any attempt to control living systems [is] an epistemological error. We do not live in the sort of universe in which simple linear control is possible. Life is not like that.
>
> (Bateson, 1972, p. 438)

This view, from the phenomenological perspective, is comparable to Levant's thoughts that the family concept is analogous to the self-concept in that it is 'an organized, cognitive-perceptual scheme with associated affects based on experience' (Levant, 1984, p. 255).

**Assumptions**
The primary assumption is that the creation of the appropriate psychological climate by the therapist promotes individual and interpersonal growth. When this climate

is provided, the family unit and individuals will move toward developing understandings of self and of others, will feel more confidence in themselves personally and as a group, and will increase their abilities to choose their behaviors. It is assumed that the family has the capacity for self-directed change and that when a certain psychological environment can be implemented that constructive and growthful changes will take place within individuals and among individuals. In short: 'Persons in an environment infused with these attitudes develop more understanding, more self-confidence, more ability to choose their behaviors. They learn more significantly, they have more freedom to be and become' (Rogers, 1980, p. 133). Thus it is this psychological climate which enables the family (as with individual clients, students, workers, or persons in groups) to tap into the actualizing and formative tendency. The creation of a psychological climate in which individuals, couples, and families have more freedom to be and become is enhanced by the attitudinal conditions offered by the therapist.

The intent in person-centered family therapy is the same as that for individual person-centered therapy. The primary thrust and abiding intent of the therapist is to understand the world of each individual from that individual's perspective, to understand the family world from their perspective, and to create an atmosphere of trust that will promote the natural growth process of the individuals and of the particular family system.

**Working within the rationale: a therapist's view**
This section offers some flavor of the way one therapist (Ann Shanks who was the co-author of the initial article which comprises this chapter) works within the framework of the previously noted rationale. Ann expresses and gives some examples of her ways of working with couples. In her words, she tries:

- To enter into the individual's worlds and into the unique family interaction system. I do this by continuously clarifying my understandings of what it seems like to be a particular person in that family system at the time. I parenthetically ask each family member or each couple: 'Is this what it is like for you'? or 'What is your understanding of this'?
- To allow the unit to go in its own direction, in its own way, at its own pace. I do this by allowing them to make the decisions about who comes to sessions: to choose their own interaction pattern (e.g., sometimes talking one-on-one with the therapist or talking to each other, or choosing the issues that they discuss).
- To be genuine. I sometimes do this by using my own experiences to check my understandings.
- To refrain from arranging artificially the balance of communication with the session. I allow the family to struggle to find its own balance; then that balance can be maintained without outside support. For example, if I am working with a couple and one person begins to dominate the session continuously, I do not attempt to monitor that

person for the benefit of the other. In the clinical example that follows, the wife came to a session ready to speak, and also had her luggage packed outside of the door ready to leave the family. She spoke for 20 or more minutes during which time I responded only to her without any attempt to bring the husband into the conversation.

• Not to attempt to persuade people to 'get in touch' with themselves or each other. I have worked with couples and families who felt much distance from each other. Yet, when they reminisced, rather than staying in the here and now, they got in touch with distant feelings and were able to embrace and experience these feelings, and become close to each other.

• At the same time, I don't attempt to coerce people to deal with the past when they are communicating in the present. I don't attempt to convince people to respond at either a feeling or cognitive level. I do try to match my manner of respond at either a feeling or cognitive level. I do try to match my manner of responding with whatever is presented to me by them. Within families, styles of communication vary. By being flexible, I believe I am giving permission to individual family members to communicate in their own way and at their own pace.

• To share selectively some of the metaphors or images that pop into my mind. I use them to help me understand the family and communicate my understanding, or test that understanding that comes from my experiencing of these particular individuals in the therapeutic relationship.

## Application

The following section is an illustration of the therapist's work with a couple. The therapist (Shanks) is attempting to engage with the husband and wife of a family as a catalyst for their natural growth process.

The family consisted of husband (John, 45), wife (Joan, 42), three boys (10, 13, and 15) and three daughters (5, 6, and 7). Joan first entered therapy depressed and 'feeling trapped.' Her first therapist and clinic supervisor decided that family therapy was desirable. The family was later transferred to Ann when the original therapist left the agency. Over a period of 12 sessions, Ann met with the family in different constellations, for example, husband and wife, husband, wife, and four to six children. These constellations – type and time – were determined by the family.

The couples therapy was also initiated by the family rather than by the therapist. The therapist did not usually know who would come for the session. Only twice did either the couple or the therapist know the composition of the particular session ahead of time. The first was when the couple wanted to meet without the children. One time it was known prior to the session that the parents would not be present at the request of the children. The eighth session is reviewed for illustration. It was a session with the husband and wife only. The themes of the couple during the 12 sessions of family and couple therapy were as follows:

*John's individual theme was*: 'I'm doing my part and always carrying my load or more'.

*Joan's individual themes were*: 'I don't understand things'; 'I don't understand my husband'; 'I don't understand myself'; 'Others don't understand me'; 'My family doesn't understand me'; 'You (therapist) don't understand me'; 'I don't understand myself'; 'I need individual therapy so I can understand myself, and before I can understand or be understood by my family'; 'I want to be able to talk and be heard'.

The themes for the individuals and couple in the eighth session were as follows:

*John's individual themes were*: 'Usually when there is a job to be done, I just buckle down and do it really hard'; 'I have never been restricted (financially) as much as I am now'; and 'Maybe I attack problems too strongly'.

*Joan's individual themes were*: 'I am not happy with myself'; 'I feel trapped'; 'You make me feel like I'm a bad little girl who is being punished'; 'I can't live like that anymore'; 'I am a human being – an adult – your wife – your equal; 'I want to be able to talk and be heard'; 'As it is I have to be walking out of the door to get him to listen to me'.

*John's family themes were*: 'When I think of Joan as a child, it seems that she makes a big thing out of little things'; 'When I consider her as an adult, it seems she doesn't have many privileges'; 'We are a family'.

*Joan's family themes were*: 'We haven't been able to talk about money without it being extremely painful'; 'We do not communicate with one another'; 'We shut each other out'; 'John will not let me be a part of his life'; 'He will not let me in'; 'We are not a family'.

The central themes of the couple and the family unit can be summarized briefly as oppression and repression. Joan felt mentally oppressed and repressed by John. The children felt physically oppressed and repressed by financial difficulties. The natural sequential flow of the couple was that of (1) struggling with Joan's perception of not understanding the family, (2) dealing with Joan's difficulty in understanding herself, (3) reacting to her decision to separate temporarily from the family, and (4) deciding to discontinue couple therapy, and for Joan to resume individual therapy. It is interesting to note that individual therapy was Joan's initial intent when entering therapy. This decision was restructured by her previous therapist. The previous therapist decided that family therapy was more appropriate. Since Joan had entered therapy with the family, she decided to continue with it after Ann became the therapist.

Joan and the other family members focused on her feeling oppressed by her husband and children. She searched for understandings about herself without having to fear that her family would collapse.

Some of the specifics of the eighth session are presented next in order to give a flavor of the interactions, and some sense of the direction of the couple.

Joan:   He can't hear anything I say. Once he puts up that wall, nothing else gets in. I can't get in. There is nothing that I can do to get in. The wall was up and that was it. And I mean all day until I was packing my suitcases to leave . . . nothing. I can't live like that. I cannot put up with that kind of abuse.

Ann:    I get the feeling that you feel that you are being punished, like you feel you are being hurt.

Joan:   Oh yeah, I feel like I'm the bad little girl that is being punished and he thinks that punishing me is a way of making me behave. He is thinking that 'if I make it so miserable for her, then she won't discuss issues I don't want to discuss. She will be good and won't do that.'

Ann:    You have had enough of that in the past, growing up. You're saying that you are not going to be treated like a child?

Joan:   He even told me to go to my room and stay for thirty minutes until I calmed down and then we could talk about it.

Ann:    That must have made you shoot up to the ceiling.

Joan:   And then he wonders why I'm screaming and crying and running away from him. I am not a child; I am a person; I am a human being that is an adult; I am your wife. I am your equal. You are not going to treat me like that.

Toward the end of this session, Joan and John began talking to each other about being adults who have responsibilities and individual rights. John indicated to Joan that he heard her.

During the ninth session, John and Joan were discussing their difficulty communicating with each other. Joan felt that she expressed herself best through writing. John said that he liked to build things. He expressed his love toward Joan and the children by building things and growing food in a large garden.

Joan frequently would try to establish rules for the family as a way to protect them and govern feelings in the family. John attempted to establish rules to govern family finances and certain family behaviors. Both of them wanted to write up contracts for the family to review and sign. Their rules, however, interfered with their communication with each other. They indicated that they had too many rules but felt the need for even more rules in order to give them greater security and a greater sense of order.

They ended the session with the following discourse:

Ann (to John): You feel that she thinks a lot deeper than you.

John:   Yeah, that way she does. Joan can't come up with a quick decision. She can't. She is completely lost. If you said, 'Joan, move that chair', she would look at it for fifteen minutes and couldn't make a decision where she's going to move it; while you can tell me to move a chair and before you walked towards it, I know where I'm going to put it.

Ann:    Things are more cut and dry.

John:   Real clear.

Joan:   And that is good. That's balance that can complement each other very well if we could get together. I feel like I - where he looks straight ahead – I look peripheral. I am looking at all of the little things out there that might have influence or that might change things, and you need both. If we had to live with no peripheral vision, we'd be limited and if we had only to live with only straight ahead vision, we would be real limited.

Ann:    So you can see a lot together.

Joan:   Yeah.

Ann:    You can't see alone but you want him to know that peripheral is just as important as the straight-ahead.
        (Ten minute silence)

Ann:    So once the chairs are in place you want to know that they can be moved without his permission.
        (Laughter by all)

Joan:   I arrange furniture a lot.

Ann:    Scheduling? Rules?

John:   And when can we change rules (laughter). That's the first thing she will say. When we make a decision or the rule or something, she'll say, 'When can we change it?'

Brief illustrations of the tenth, eleventh, and twelfth sessions are offered next in order to show the change the family was making.

During the tenth session, John stated that Joan was opening up more. Joan reported that she didn't quite know what to do with her new-felt freedom and felt confused. She realized that the family wanted to help her. She indicated that she was feeling the need to withdraw but did not want to push her family away. She felt less a part of the family but felt the need to lean on John, even though she still felt 'bullied' by him at times.

Joan often focused discussion on herself while the older children focused on the younger children, and John focused more on Joan. Joan began to focus more on John's needs. She saw more clearly the relationship between herself and her relationships in the family. She summarized her efforts in the session by saying: 'When I have compassion, I have a better perspective of John and the kids. I am more accepting. And when I don't have compassion, I am aware of my own pain and childhood'.

During the eleventh session, Joan indicated that she felt very defeated and that no one was listening to her. She was not sure how to get anyone to listen to her. John, during this session, was very controlling of the children (all family members were present).

During the twelfth and final session, Joan and her three daughters came in without John. She stated that she felt sad because Ann had not understood her.

During some discussion about this, Ann told her how she (Ann) suddenly felt very sad. It was at this point that Joan shared that she had been thinking a great deal about a biblical verse. Later, when Joan read the verse, Ann understood Joan's feelings of oppression and sadness. The verse was the following one:

Next, I observed all the oppression and sadness throughout the earth
– the tears of the oppressed, and no one helping them, while on the
side of their oppressors were powerful allies. So I felt that the dead
were better off than the living. And most fortunate of all are those
who have never been born, and have never seen all the evil and crime
through the earth.

(The Living Bible, Ecclesiastes 4, 1971)

Joan did, however, feel good about the family. She had gotten out of the 'family fog' and was more able to focus on herself. She reported that she now felt capable of doing something for herself. She realized that other family members could work together to allow her to pursue individual therapy.

A retrospective summary of the family contacts with the therapist follows:

Joan entered therapy with the initial therapist in order to deal with
her feelings of depression and of being trapped, and not having control
over her own life. After two sessions, the therapist decided that family
therapy was more desirable, and Joan passively agreed to the
therapist's decision. The therapist left the agency after three sessions
with the family, and one of the authors (Ann Shanks) was assigned
to work with them. She had 12 sessions with them. Six of these
sessions were 'couples therapy'.

During the 12 sessions, Joan expressed her personal concerns
that she did not have control of her own life, and that no one really
cared for or understood her. This included her family members and
the therapist. The family described themselves as chaotic, and the
sessions were often chaotic.

The children were often inattentive and squirming in their seats
until John forced them to sit still. The children indicated that this
was typical of his oppression of them. They felt that they had no
personal freedom because of him. He felt that he could not stand
chaos in his life, and the only way for him to get order was to impose
it on the children and on Joan. He felt pressured by his family
responsibilities and financial problems.

Joan continued to feel trapped and felt that she had no control of
herself or the family. The couple was at the point of separation;
Joan felt 'engulfed' and 'suffocated' by her family. John felt the
others in the family were closing him out.

## Outcome

Joan gained a better understanding of her feelings, and viewed many of the difficulties as being related to her personal development more than to the family situation. She felt that she would be better able to handle her reactions to family members and family pressures if she had individual therapy.

John felt that he understood Joan better and that he could be more receptive to her way of doing things. He became more involved with the family, and Joan became more involved with John. They agreed to get more involved as two parents with the children while the children said things were better some of the time. They indicated that things were better when the parents were getting along better. John and the children expressed their willingness to support Joan's individual needs. Joan decided not to leave the family and found ways to deal with her personal problems as well as with her discontent in the family.

A follow-up session with Joan two years after the 12 family therapy sessions revealed that the family had recently resumed family therapy at the request of a clinician who was seeing one of the teenage boys. Joan believed this was desirable for her because it was the only place that she could be assured of being heard by John. John agreed because there was less turmoil in the family when they were in therapy. She reported that the 12 sessions with Ann two years ago had helped her realize that she could be heard and to understand that her personal background with her parents restricted her ability to be strong enough in the family to stand up to oppression.

Other positive results reported by Joan were that John and Joan were in closer agreement about how to deal with family interactions. John felt during the couple's sessions that they were a family, and Joan felt strongly that they were not a family. They were, from Joan's report, more in agreement that they are sometimes a family. However, they were optimistic about becoming more of a family. One of their ways of dealing with their feelings that they were not a family was to use their current therapy sessions to communicate to each other.

Overall, several factors suggested that the therapy sessions were beneficial. First, the therapist saw evidence that John and Joan better understood each other and their children. John and Joan reported the same view two years later. Likewise, their views of self and family moved from disparate views of the family in early sessions to more mutual perceptions of the family immediately and two years after therapy.

They both verbalized more confidence in themselves personally and in their relationship. They understood each other better, and were more able to assess their individual and joint needs and seek further help in a more determinate and independent way.

## Conclusion

The rationale for person-centered family therapy, as in work in individual therapy or group therapy, is that of creating a psychological climate through the embodiment of certain therapist attitudinal qualities that promote the inherent actualizing processes of individuals seeking help. The couple is viewed as a family unit that is a living system. There is an assumption that the formative tendency of the family unit can be promoted by the development of the same psychological climate as promotes the actualizing tendency of the individual. Functionally, this means that the therapists allow and trust the family to go in its own direction, in its own way, and at its own pace as a family unit. The conceptualization of the family unit as an organism is theoretically consistent with Rogers' theory, and allows a more functional basis for practice as person-centered family therapists.

# THE BASIC
# ENCOUNTER GROUP

# 17

Carl Rogers coined the term, 'The Basic Encounter Group' to identify encounter groups that operated on the principles of the person-centered approach. It is the contention of this chapter that the person-centered basic encounter group is quite unique and, in fact, offers a different paradigm for group therapy. Indeed, the application of the premises of the person-centered approach in group therapy requires a re-examination of many of the usual presuppositions about group function. This includes presuppositions about leader target population, size of group, establishment of goals and ground rules, and facilitator behavior. This contention is contrary to the conclusion that the client-centered basic encounter group '. . . is in the mainstream of approaches for working with groups because of its eclectic nature and its lack of distinguishing features to set it apart from other process models (Boy, 1985, p. 210).

It is important briefly to consider Boy's rationale for two reasons. First, Boy's conclusion, and the conclusions in this chapter, about the person-centered basic encounter group are quite discrepant. Second, Boy's conclusion is founded on the premise that client centered theory '. . . required them [therapists] to focus on and reflect the feelings of groups members' (p. 207). That is, Boy's focus is on what the therapist should do rather than on the development of fundamental attitudinal qualities and beliefs of therapists. This point is considerably important since it represents a focus that has fostered the mistaken identification of client-centered therapy as a way of doing rather than as a way of being, a point elaborated upon in chapter 12.

An examination of the basic encounter group from the perspective of the fundamental premises of the person-centered approach, rather than on response patterns of therapists, offers a rationale that leads to the conclusion that the person-centered basic encounter group is unique. This conclusion is consistent with my experience with groups over the past twenty-five years; and, specifically, with my experience over the past ten years with person-centered basic encounter and community groups where Rogers was facilitator and participant. It is also a

Adapted with permission from:
Bozarth, J. D. (1986). The basic encounter group: an alternative view. *The Journal for Specialists in Group Work*, 11(4), 228-232.

conclusion consistent with recent literature concerned with person-centered groups (Gazda and Bozarth, 1983; Rogers, 1977; Wood, 1982; Wood, 1983).

The remainder of this chapter will review the fundamental premises of the person-centered approach and the applications of these premises in basic encounter groups. It will be concluded that Rogers has been quite consistent in his adherence to the basic premises rather than to the reflective process, and that the application of these premises to the basic encounter group result in a paradigm for group application which is different from other approaches.

**Basic premises**
As indicated periodically throughout this book, there are three basic premises of the person-centered approach that identify it as a therapeutic paradigm different from other therapy and growth-activating approaches. These underlying premises are: (a) that the actualizing tendency is the foundation block of the person-centered approach and is the primary motivational force; (b) that the individual (client) is always his/her own best expert and authority on his/her life; and (c) that the role of the therapist is only that of implementing certain attitudinal qualities (Bozarth, 1985). That is, the intent of the therapist is to be whom he/she is while embodying the attitudinal qualities in order to promote the client's self-actualizing process.

Rogers is quite clear throughout his writings that the therapist's attitudes are important in creating the climate that will promote an individual's actualizing tendency; as he stated recently: 'We became over fascinated with techniques . . . but what you are in the relationship is much more important' (Heppner, Rogers, and Lee, 1984, p. 16). Adherence to the importance of basic attitudes existed even during the early years of the development of the approach, when the therapy was identified by the presence of reflection (Rogers, 1942). Even then, identification of the therapy with reflection was an oversimplification and inadequate reading of Rogers' theory (Raskin, 1948). Although there is disagreement between client-centered therapists about the centrality of particular therapist response patterns, it is clear that the basic attitudes of the therapist/facilitator are the critical foundations of the approach (Temaner and Bozarth, 1984).

The establishment of the reflective process as the core vehicle of the client-centered counselor's response pattern is considered essential by some authors (e.g., Boy, 1985). This, however, does not mean that the response pattern should be equated to the basic premises. My contention is that the technique of reflection when equated to empathy has resulted in (1) conceptual confusion between empathy and reflection; (2) a focus on operational methods for acting empathically; and (3) a limitation of the empathic response modes of therapists (Bozarth, 1984, p. 59). Rogers is explicit about the foundations of the approach. He (Rogers, 1985) succinctly summarizes:

> The person-centered approach, then, is primarily a way of being which finds its expression in attitudes and behavior that create a growth-promoting climate. It is a basic philosophy rather than simply a technique or a method. When this philosophy is lived, it helps the

person to expand the development of his or her own capacities. When it is lived, it also stimulates constructive change in others. It empowers the individual, and when this personal power is sensed, experiences show that it tends to be used for personal and social transformation. (p. 5)

## The transition

The transition of the client-centered approach with individuals to application in group therapy was not philosophically different. The basic assumptions remained the same. As Wood (1983) states:

The goal (and art) of person-centered therapy is to facilitate the creation of a climate in each person and the group of persons. An event in which this takes place is the definition of person-centered group therapy. (p. 239)

The facilitator of the group encounter requires the same fluency as the individual therapist to 'be fluent in the moment-to-moment action of persons in relationship without resorting to speculation and explanations of process' (Wood, 1983, p. 243).

The essence of the person-centered philosophy in leadership behavior includes giving autonomy to persons in groups, freeing them to 'do their thing' (i.e., expressing their own ideas and feelings as one aspect of the group data), facilitating learning, stimulating independence in thought and action, accepting the 'unacceptable' innovative creations that emerge, delegating full responsibility, offering and receiving feedback, encouraging and relying on self-evaluation, and finding reward in the development and achievement of others (Rogers, 1977). This same philosophy underlies the client-centered therapist's role with an individual client. It was, and remains, a revolutionary idea that the client might be his or her own expert, that the client's own ideas and feelings could be more important than the therapist's interpretations and suggestions, that the client could achieve independence in thought and action, that the client might reach 'acceptable', innovative self-creations, and that the client might acquire his or her own full self-responsibility.

It is the fundamental belief system and adherence to the premises of this belief system by the individual therapist or group facilitator that differentiate the person-centered approach from other individual or group therapeutic systems.

## Paradigm foundations in the encounter group

The functional application of the basic premises of the person-centered approach includes 'indwelling the client to move rather than dragging him by the hair toward health' (Coulson, 1984). It includes: being completely present and totally attending to people; promoting equivalency in people; and not presupposing what people will be like, or do, or become during or after the therapeutic encounter. The person-centered approach in groups does not usually presuppose such considerations as the target population, size of the group, establishment of goals and ground rules, or specific facilitator or participant behaviors.

The facilitator engages the world of each group participant and the developing 'group mind' with the same dedication and discipline applied in individual therapy. Behavioral manifestations are different from group to group as they often are with different individuals in one-to-one therapy. Several basic considerations of group work which indicate the uniqueness of the person-centered group are noted below.

## 1) Target population and size of the group

The major selection criterion for group members is that each person be willing to attend and participate in the group experience. Individuals who convene groups may select participants using varied criteria that meet the facilitators' biases and capacities; however, selection criteria, if and when applied, are based on the personal views of the facilitators. Participants nearly always select themselves to be in such groups. They are usually from a variety of geographical locations, jobs, and have multiple reasons for attending groups. Most other group approaches do presuppose the selection of their participants rather than being dedicated to the self-selection process.

The limitation in size of the group is another of the assumptions that has come to be questioned by experiences from person-centered groups. Rogers (1970) once recommended that the best size for encounter groups was eight to ten people. Since that time, further experience with groups has resulted in other considerations. For example, the relativity of group size is commented upon by John K. Wood, who has been one of the facilitators with Rogers in hundreds of groups. Wood (1982) states:

> ... when we worked with 800, many people said, 'I feel uncomfortable in this large group . . . to really be myself. I need to be in a smaller group.' We divided into groups of 100 to 150 and immediately these people expressed relief and there was considerable personal sharing of feelings and meaningful encounter, just like any group of 10 or 12. People can quickly become personal, speaking in one conversation at a time even in a group of 800 participants. (pp. 13-14)

## 2) Goals and ground rules

Group goals are not defined prior to the group experience, since the development of the personal power of individuals is likely to lead in multiple directions. The group may develop goals, but often group plans are more common occurrences than group goals; e.g., plans to schedule meetings at certain times, and decisions to meet for certain lengths of time. Experiences in person-centered groups suggest that idiosyncratic development of personal power dilutes the development of 'group goals' (Bozarth, 1981). The group will often move in a common direction as though the group is one organism (Rogers, 1977). However, such direction is not in the form of goals.

### 3) The facilitator

The role of the facilitator in the person-centered group is that of creating an atmosphere in which members are enabled to discover their power and to own inner sources of healing. The facilitator does not necessarily expect that any particular process will occur, nor will he or she attempt to accelerate any particular process. If there are ground rules for the facilitator, they can be stated as openness to surprise and to their own surrender to unity (Wood, 1982). The facilitator acts on the assumption that participants have the power within themselves to resolve their problems, heal themselves, and move in positive constructive directions. Rogers describes his facilitator role in the following way:

> My hope is gradually to become as much a participant in the group as a facilitator. This is difficult to describe without making it appear that I am consciously playing two different roles. If you watch a group member who is honestly being himself, you will see that at times he expresses feelings, attitudes, and thoughts primarily directed toward facilitating the growth of another member. At other times, with equal genuineness, he will express feelings or concerns that have as their obvious goal the opening of himself to the risk of more growth. This describes me, too, except that I know I am likely to be the second, or risking, kind of person more often in the later than in the early stages of the group. Each facet is a real part of me, not a role.
>
> (Rogers, 1970, pp 48-49)

It is significant that Rogers does not have a goal of encouraging other members to be therapeutic, and does not participate in self-disclosure as a way to encourage others to self-disclose. Rather, he is consistent with the basic premises; that is, treating participants as their own best experts of their lives; and, by being who he is while embodying the attitudinal qualities, promoting the self actualizing tendencies of individuals. Rogers may offer reflective responses, or may explore his own feelings or concerns in a group, or may participate in a structured group experience.

Facilitative involvement predicated on the attitudinal qualities does not preclude a reflective response style nor does it demand a particular style of response. The therapist is free from being the expert for another person and free to allow the individual client or group member to be his/her own best expert (Spahn, 1984). The person-centered approach to group counseling and psychotherapy is a paradigm shift from most other approaches to group counseling. As such, many interpretations of the application of the person-centered approach are not adequately understood and certain facilitator techniques and behaviors are emphasized rather than fundamental assumptions of the approach. Although some client-centered therapists consider the reflective response to be the basic response pattern for client-centered therapists, it is clear that it is the implementation of the attitudinal qualities that are central to the approach (Temaner and Bozarth, 1984).

The fundamental assumption of the person-centered approach in groups is that each individual has the capacity to allow her or his innate potential (inner healer, inner self) to develop in order to become personally empowered to move in a constructive (albeit idiosyncratic) direction for self and society. The facilitator perpetuates this growth process by embodying and communicating his/her attitudinal qualities to the group without presupposing what its members should do, be like, or become.

These fundamental assumptions suggest a different paradigm from other theoretical approaches. Many assumptions about groups are altered and the facilitator does not have the intention of creating any particular group behavior. As such, the person-centered basic encounter group is unique.

# THE LARGE
# COMMUNITY GROUP

# 18

The intent of this chapter is to: (1) describe the history and some features of person-centered community groups; (2) state several theoretical and functional assumptions of these community groups; (3) discuss the role of facilitators (or convenors) in the large groups; and (4) offer some emerging research findings from qualitative research.

## Personal background in relation to groups

First, a note about my background in experiencing person-centered community groups. As I stated earlier, I learned about the person-centered approach working with chronic, long-term hospitalized psychotics and neurotics in state mental hospitals as a Psychiatric Rehabilitation Counselor. My first experience 'leading' a group was with a heterogeneous group of 'patients' who had been placed in group homes outside of the hospital. I was exposed briefly at this time to community group meetings in one state hospital where patients voted on off-grounds passes, medical treatment and other similar decisions for their fellow patients. Other than that I had no experience in therapy or growth groups.

I facilitated many basic encounter groups of rehabilitation agency clients and of graduate students prior to attending the renowned client-centered encounter group known as the La Jolla Program. After the La Jolla Group experience in 1974, I was a participant in person-centered community groups of one kind or another for, at least, once a year to the current date. I also facilitated (or convened) large groups numerous times, more recently (since 1987) co-ordinating and being one of the conveners of the annual Person-Centered Workshop in Warm Springs,

Adapted paper presentations from:

Bozarth, J.D. (1992c). The person-centered community group. *A paper presented at the American Psychological Association symposium, Contributions of client-centered therapy to American psychology's 100 years.* Chaired by Ned Gaylin, Washington D.C.

and

Bozarth, J. D. (1995b). Designated facilitators; unnecessary and insufficient. *A paper presented at the national conference for the Association of the Development of the Person-Centered Approach,* Tampa, Florida.

Georgia.

My first experience as a group 'leader' in the psychiatric hospital was with a group of about fifteen individuals who had entered a group home outside of the hospital after twenty or more years as hospital patients. The group was established in order to permit me to meet with all of the individuals during my community trips each week. In short, nearly every semblance of the group violated the traditional knowledge about groups (since I didn't know much about the group literature at the time). The group usually met in the shade of a tree, the structure consisted of my request for us to meet '. . .to see how things are going'. It was a heterogeneous group that was diagnosed with a variety of labels. For example, members included a sixty year old male with 'chronic alcoholism: undifferentiated type'; a sixteen year old male 'schizophrenic, hebephrenic'; a 'mentally retarded' (IQ: 50s) thirty year old woman; a forty year old male 'manic-depressive'; a thirty-five year old female 'schizophrenic, hebephrenic'; a forty-five year old male 'schizophrenic, paranoid', and a variety of individuals with still other diagnostic labels. They simply had the opportunity to talk (or not talk) about anything. No rules, directions, orientation were ever given. It was years later that I discovered that nearly everything about the group went against guidelines for groups. Nevertheless, standard criteria suggested that every member made clinically significant progress.

It was from this early experience in the psychiatric hospital that I became interested in groups and I was involved as a facilitator and participant many times and in many kinds of groups over the years. These experiences included participation in Gestalt groups, Adlerian groups, Psychodrama, Tiger training, encounter groups, and T-groups. I personally facilitated 'client-centered' groups with graduate students, vocational rehabilitation clients, 'out-patients' from mental hospitals and others. I had some experience observing several therapeutic community groups in mental hospitals but did not experience large community groups until 1974 in the community meetings at the La Jolla program. My dye was probably cast by this time. Every year from that year, I was a participant in groups of some type with Rogers and his various colleagues. I became in effect a participant/observer who, I have been told, Rogers viewed as a puzzle and wondered, 'Why does this guy come to these groups. He never says anything'. As an aside, I have always wondered why he forgot his own admonishment when he thought a Japanese woman who never said anything in any of his classes '. . . couldn't possibly be getting anything from the class'. When she turned out to be the major force promoting the client-centered approach in Japan, Rogers said that he would never again assume that he could predict what a person was learning. I also noticed that over the years in the large groups, he became more silent himself with less need to respond to individuals. It was, at least, somewhat satisfying to me to view Rogers as moving more towards a stance in the community groups that was more akin to my way of thinking about convenor activity in the groups.

In 1986, several client-centered advocates envisioned an annual workshop which developed into what has become known as the Warm Springs experience which held its twelfth meeting in 1998 (eleven of the twelve workshops through 1998 were at Warm Springs, Georgia). This gave me the opportunity to participate in and observe an ongoing experiment with large groups.

**The Historical development**

The person-centered community group evolved from the framework of the client-centered approach as depicted and researched by Rogers and his colleagues. The central theoretical base is that of Rogers'(1959) statement of the client-centered theory of therapy, personality and interpersonal relationships. This statement is summarized in several other chapters in this book.

The community group evolved with Rogers' expanding interests. Rogers more expanded interests and efforts evolved from his interest in individual psychotherapy (1940s and 1950s) to the basic encounter group (the term applied to client-centered encounter groups; see Chapter 17) of eight to ten individuals. The term 'person-centered' crystallized in the 1970s to denote the application of the principles of client-centered therapy to areas other than psychotherapy. Rogers and his colleagues started to experiment with the concept of large community groups of fifty to three hundred or more individuals (Rogers, 1977). This experiment increasingly involved more and more individuals from different cultures and eventually led to an emphasis on cross-cultural groups often represented by twenty or more nationalities. The work of Chuck Devonshire (1991) in developing client-centered training programs in Europe added to the focus on cross-cultural groups. Eventually, the cross-cultural groups provided Rogers with a foundation in which to attempt workshops focusing on client-centered principles for societal change. One of his major intentions was to assist with the diminishing of international tensions among nations. John K. Wood (1984; 1994a; 1994b) has pointed to some of the difficulties in such groups including the difficulty of operating in the way that Rogers proposed. I have been told that in 1987, Rogers was recognized for this societal effort by being one of the individuals nominated for the Nobel Peace Prize. Ironically, when he received this nomination he was in a coma preceding his death.

**Some features**

The person-centered community group usually refers to a group of thirty to three hundred individuals who meet for between three days and two weeks in a psychological atmosphere founded upon the principles of the person-centered approach. The setting is generally one in which participants will have contacts in their daily activities including dormitory rooms with shared baths, cafeteria meals, and facilities which offer opportunities for participants to meet each other. There are generally small groups, topic groups, paper presentations, experiential activities such as expressive therapy; and recreational activities. These may or may not be structured prior to the meeting. They often develop from the large group community meeting. It is the large group meeting of all participants that might be described as the one major activity of person-centered community groups. The large group involves the meeting of all workshop participants who choose to attend a 'nondirective' meeting. There are facilitators who are dedicated to the principles of the approach and who have previously experienced such groups. These facilitators presume various responsibilities depending upon the particular facilitators. However, they are for the most part willing to go with the direction and pace of the group.

In such groups, there are usually periods of silence, anger, attempts to organize, criticism of the facilitators and expression of various emotions as well as, at times, long dialogues by participants. In the case of cross-cultural workshops, the verbal communications are translated into one or two languages. Personal encounters among individuals and power struggles among group factions often occur. These large groups usually meet for three or more hours. They usually meet at least once each day, although they have remained as the only agreed upon meeting of the community in some workshops. The development of the 'formal' activities of the workshop usually emerges from these meetings.

**Person-centered theory**
This basic premise of person-centered theory is that the human being moves naturally towards constructive growth and development of his/her inherent potentialities and that such growth is fostered by an identifiable, attitudinal environment created by the attitudes of the therapist. This critical assumption is repeated in this book as a continuous reminder of the foundation block of the theory (Rogers, 1980). I have also periodically stated that the three conditions of congruency, empathic understanding and unconditional positive regard are integrally interrelated and functionally necessary and sufficient. I have concluded from Rogers' major theoretical statement and his personality theory that the curative condition in the theory is that of unconditional positive regard (Bozarth, 1992b). Genuineness is the state of the therapist/facilitator/convenor that enables him or her to experience empathic understanding and unconditional regard for other individuals. I suggest it is consistent with Rogers' statements to conclude that empathic understanding is the pure vehicle or vessel for communicating unconditional positive regard. I believe that this idea is basic to Rogers' general theoretical statement. I think that this schema of the theory has implications for further consideration of the theory as related to community groups.

**Theory and application in the community group**
The person-centered community group can be summarized as one application of the basic premise of the person-centered approach; i.e., dedication of facilitators to the natural growth process of individuals and of the universe. This is the fundamental theoretical point in the person-centered approach which is true whether or not the approach is implemented in individual therapy, the basic encounter group, person-centered family therapy, organizations, the community group or any other human activity (Bozarth, 1990a, 1991c). Several of the functional manifestations of facilitators operating on this premise in community groups are

that facilitators (or conveners) entrust themselves to: (1) trust 'group wisdom' as well as individual wisdom; (2) become participants in the group as well as facilitators; (3) trust the inherent therapeutic potential of all members, realizing that any particular person may be more therapeutic with any particular group member than any of the facilitators; (4) combine the spontaneous, genuine responsiveness with their desire and efforts to understand, and (5) relinquish control of outcome, direction, or mood (Bozarth, 1988b). The following axioms seem to me appropriate for person-centered community groups:

*Axiom 1*: The basic intent of the person-centered approach is to perpetuate the nature and destiny of humans and, in doing so, to perpetuate the nature and destiny of the universe. By considering the actualizing and formative tendencies, this axiom was developed. The large group exemplifies this axiom in that a major intent of the facilitator is to create the trusting atmosphere that promotes both individual growth and the 'wisdom' of the group.

*Axiom 2*: The primary and abiding intent is to be a genuine person who attempts to understand and who accepts the world of the other person from the perspective of that person. It is interesting that Rogers' comments on understanding in the community group suggests the importance of the intention to understand and the willingness to have no preconceptions of what might occur. He states:

> That's one of the duties of learning to be truly empathic. You may not have known that this would occur - or that would crop up – but your whole mind-set is a readiness to understand, to try to grasp what it is that has meaning for the person at this point and that gets across to the group - that desire to understand.
>
> (Rogers, 1975, p. 63)

*Axiom 3*: Individuals move toward the best growth mode available to them through their own best process. Another comment of Rogers relates to this axiom and is reflective of periodic references. He said, 'The whole aim is to relinquish any attempt to control the outcome, to control the direction, to control the mood' (Rogers,1987, p. 64).

*Axiom 4*: The infusion of one's self into the group as a genuine person and group member helps to facilitate the group. Rogers indicated specifically that one thing about the facilitator 'is the need for genuineness' (Rogers, 1988, p. 68). Genuineness helped him to be 'more one of the group' (p. 68) and to even help a group realize 'that I really was experiencing the whole thing with them' (p. 69). Maintenance of 'spontaneity and openness to the moment-by-moment process of group communication' (p. 68) was one way he referred to the intertwining of genuineness and empathy in the large group.

*Axiom 5*: There is no pre-supposition of what people will be like, or do, or become during or after the group experience. One of the essential points in person-centered theory is that those with designated 'leadership roles', 'accept what is' (Rogers, 1987, p. 65). Rogers' thoughts on this point are relevant here in view of discussions about facilitator roles. In The Association for the Development of the Person-Centered Approach newsletter, *Renaissance*, Rogers states:
> If you're going to expect a certain degree of affect – if you expect that of the process – then that can be artificial. If the degree of affect is what is comfortable, reasonable, or natural for this person, this group, then that's fine.
>
> (Rogers, 1987, p. 65)

And, more specifically stated: 'It's best to be fairly näive or not full of expectations.' (Rogers, 1987, p. 65.)

## The facilitator or convenor

My major conclusions about facilitators in such groups, based on theoretical considerations, Rogers' comments and my own observations and experience, are the following:
1) It is most ideal not to have facilitators;
2) If there are designated facilitators, they shouldn't do very much except be themselves;

and
3) That pre-conceived ideas about groups emanating from other theoretical stances have contaminated person-centered views and practice in groups as well as in individual therapy (Bozarth, 1996).

## Some evolutionary considerations

More recently, my thinking has been influenced by recent research, the Warm Spring workshop experiences, and by mulling over the theoretical underpinnings of Rogers' theory of therapy and interpersonal relationships.

An extensive qualitative study of person-centered community groups offers some fascinating findings (Stubbs, 1992). First, Stubbs found support for the construct of the actualizing tendency as the foundation block of the person-centered approach. Her findings also suggested support for the importance of participants experiencing genuineness and unconditional positive regard during the workshops. In addition, the importance of 'nondirectivity' was supported as a basic theoretical premise. Also of particular interest was the lack of reference and support for experiencing empathic understanding from others. Likewise, there were frequent references of interviewees to perceived facilitators that suggested that the facilitators might have been viewed as important; however, the importance was non-specific. That is, there were no common facilitator characteristics or behaviors that were noted as particularly important.

Mearns (1994) discusses the large unstructured group in relation to training of person-centered counselors punctuated with the comment: 'The release into congruence enhances both the quality and the quantity of the counselor's unconditional positive regard and empathy' (p. 43). This is in accord with my thoughts on the nature of the central concept even though I believe it is more complex due to the intertwining of the conditions (Bozarth, 1993).

Although Rogers often discussed the facilitator as the person who embodies the attitudes, it is the actualizing tendency of the client that is the foundation block of the theory. This is the natural motivational force of each individual of '. . . a tendency toward fulfilment, toward actualization, involving not only maintenance but also the enhancement of the organism' (Rogers, 1980, p. 123). He continues to say that humans are always doing the best they can with a '. . .flow of movement toward constructive fulfilment of its inherent possibilities' (p. 117). The bottom line is explicit in Rogers' theory; that is, it is the client who has the capacities and inner resources. The climate of unconditional positive regard enables individuals to develop their own unconditional positive self-esteem, freeing them from the interjections of conditional regard by society (Bozarth, 1992b).

### Some learnings from the Warm Springs Workshops

The first Person-Centered Workshop at Warm Springs, Georgia took place in 1987. Carl Rogers had died just a week before. The idea of an ongoing workshop was initiated at the first meeting of the Association for the Development of the Person-Centered Approach (ADPCA) in Chicago. The facilitators who were involved were: Barbara Brodley, Chuck Devonshire, Nat Raskin, Dave Spahn, Fred Zimring and myself.

These individuals were identified as staff on the brochure and had somewhat varying ideas of what it meant to facilitate a person-centered group. A core of students acquainted with person-centered principles from the University of Georgia was quite actively involved in creating the psychological environment of the workshop. Warm Springs is the name of the Georgia town in which the Little White House existed during the administration of President Franklin D. Roosevelt. Roosevelt spent much of the year at the center where he was close to treatment resources for polio. This historical site seems appropriate for the person-centered workshops.

Over the twelve meetings through 1998, there was a shift towards not identifying staff or facilitators. This took place to the point that only my name was on the 1996, 1997 and 1998 brochures as the person to whom to send registration forms. Only Dave Spahn, Nat Raskin and myself who had been designated conveners of the 1987 workshop attended the 1997 and 1998 meetings. There were, however, other participants who had attended most of the workshops. The first seven workshops were held for four days while the 1995 and 1996 years were seven days. The 1997 workshop was changed from a seven-day workshop to a three-day workshop due to low enrolment in the first session. Attendance was always mobile and fluid. There were always some individuals who came for only a part of a day and some who came, left and returned. There has always been a structure on the brochure that included the community group, topic groups and small groups. However, the schedule was seldom adhered to in any structured way. The community meeting was the core site of scheduling. Some of my observations about this experience are:

1. The event was in large part emergent. That is, there was virtually no planning and little conventional organization.
2. Although there were no designated facilitators, some individuals assumed that there were and identified other participants as facilitators. A few people assumed that the student co-ordinator and myself were the facilitators. Others assumed prominent individuals were the facilitators. In other words, varying participants chose to perceive varying individuals as the designated facilitators (a point consistent with Stubbs' findings).
3. There were often statements at the end of the workshops that the experience had '. . . changed my life . . .', '. . . been an exceptional experience . . .', '. . .will have a major impact on my life . . .' There were also some who complained that the group should have been different but who continued to come back year after year. About half of the participants never return for reasons which vary dramatically. In addition, there were wide varieties of perception of the event itself from those who attended. After one workshop, I heard a range of explanations to others by participants that included: ' . . . It was a big party', '. . .It was group therapy . . .', '. . . great intellectual experience . . .', '. . . it was a family reunion. . .', '. . . it was so terribly intense . . .'
4. I periodically thought that the 1994, 1995 and 1996 workshops verged on the edge of being laissez-faire. I personally became a bit concerned. Several times, only a couple of individuals of the community came for the scheduled community meetings. Yet, the community group at the end of the workshop was one that reflected cohesion and individual satisfaction.
5. Considerable dissatisfaction was expressed during the 1995 workshop when I did not go to one of the community meetings. It was reported that the group was leaderlessly walking the grounds looking for me. One person was ready to leave and another wanted a refund of her registration fee. The concerned group met for the entire night and the next day had changed their view to that of having had a very positive workshop experience.

I have reached the conclusion from the Warm Springs experience that designated facilitators, workshop format, or the presence or absence of particular individuals are of little relevance. When people feel fundamentally free to be who they are at the moment, they move in constructive directions and that it is often in the struggle that they find freedom and growth. The relevant question to ask might be: 'How is that atmosphere created'? The general answer is ' That the participants are free to be themselves.'

Coulson's comment on encounter groups is, perhaps, relevant in terms of the role of the designated facilitator in the community groups. He suggested that the necessary and sufficient conditions for encounter is that there be an occasion for it. The major characteristic is to have the time for it in an unstructured situation. Coulson (1970) specifically states:

> This occasion, this sole necessary and sufficient condition of the encounter, is one of stopping the action long enough for people really to come to see one another, for them gradually to have with one another the things which are so simple – to weep, to be held, to be loved – that people ordinarily are too embarrassed to mention them (p. 10).

Coulson suggests, though, that people need permission to talk differently from the way they talk in ordinary social discourse. Hence, individuals who have been in previous encounter experiences, or '. . .permission-giving facilitators can help individuals to not . . . while away the time chit-chatting, vying for leadership, or in other ways avoiding honest expression' (p. 10). As to the role of the facilitator:

> But put a facilitator in the room, imply that s/he knows what he's doing and then suggest to him that s/he not do anything, except perhaps to gently express his/her own feeling from time to time, and this assignment of leadership will both prevent people from wasting time with such social manoeuvres as contending over leadership them-selves, and also give them sufficient permission to speak honestly. People need an excuse at first to speak honestly, and the mere presence of an 'expert' can be sufficient excuse – he (she) doesn't have to do anything special.
>
> (Coulson, 1970, p.10)

Although Coulson is referring to the *basic encounter group*, he also echoes the role for conveners in the community groups. Coulson's observations resonate to the importance of the nondirectivity and lack of interference. The important aspect of group facilitation is that an atmosphere exists where individuals are free to be themselves while overall experiencing themselves as being unconditionally accepted by someone. In therapy, Rogers hypothesized that individuals' adoption of unconditional positive regard for themselves is related to experiencing such regard from the therapist as a significant other. In groups, there is no particular reason that the significant other should be the facilitator. In fact, when freedom in the community exists, there are many significant others accepting any given individual.

**Recent research findings**

As mentioned above, an extensive well designed qualitative research study of person-centered community groups offers some considerations for theory and practice of the person-centered approach in community groups (Stubbs, 1992). A more detailed look at Stubbs' study is revealing. She used heuristic methodology to study individual experiencing in person-centered community workshops. She interviewed fifteen individuals from nine countries at four person-centered workshop sites held in Pezinok, Czechoslovakia; Coffeyville, Kansas; Stirling, Scotland; and Modra Harmonia, Czechoslovakia. The range of participants in the groups was from sixty to three hundred and thirty. She summarizes her data analysis in the following words:

> The emergent depictions, portraits, and a synthesized integration of the data produced a dynamic flowing among four categories: (1) the individual factors of personal influencing including the dimensions of identity and societal influencing; (2) the community factors of power and diversity; (3) struggling depicted as organizing, dividing, and communicating; and (4) freeing characterized by accepting, belonging, experiencing, empowering, and trusting. These four categories are interactive with each category flowing into the core category of evolving. The findings of the study indicate a process of individuals evolving and, through that evolving, experiencing struggling and freeing. Within this struggling, the individual synthesizes his or her own personal boundaries with the boundaries of community.
>
> (p. 2 abstract)

As referred to earlier, the results of her study supports the construct of the actualizing tendency as the foundation block of the person-centered approach in community groups. Her findings also suggest support for the importance of participants experiencing genuineness and unconditional positive regard from other group members. In addition, the importance of 'nondirectivity' was supported as an important theoretical premise. Also of particular interest was the lack of reference and support for experiencing the construct of empathic understanding from others. Likewise, the frequent reference of interviewees to facilitators indicated an importance of the facilitators; however, the importance was non-specific. There were no common facilitator characteristics or behaviors that were noted as particularly important. In addition, the importance of personal contact was present as was support for the idea that the group is a microcosm of society.

**Implications of theory, research, axioms and practice**

The implications are, simply put, that individuals who can experience the freedom 'to be who they are' (unconditional positive regard) can find themselves becoming freer to experience growth (actualizing tendency). Facilitators/conveners create this freeing atmosphere by trusting the process (hence, acting in ways that promote that freedom), not interfering with struggles, accepting each individual in his or her right as a human being and by being open to whatever outcome might occur. This is the essence of the atmosphere and the role of the convenor to promote such an atmosphere in person-centered community groups.

# RESEARCH

# Research on Psychotherapy Outcome and the Person-Centered Approach

# 19

Most therapy sessions are, perhaps, founded upon the question of, 'What might be the most effective treatment for a particular client dysfunction?' The recommendations for specific treatments for particular dysfunctions are supposedly based upon research findings, with the research that is considered most viable being the true experimental design which is predicated upon probability theory. Hence, it was my original intention to propose a model for effective psychotherapy which emanates from psychotherapy outcome research. Not surprising to many who know me, this model would be predicated upon Rogers' (1957) integration hypotheses of the necessary and sufficient conditions for therapeutic personality change and be highly sympathetic to his theory of Client-Centered Therapy (Rogers, 1959). I have over my career differed with the party line of psychology and psychotherapy treatment methods which are, in my opinion, paradigmatically different from Rogers' contention. However, my conclusions are more drastic than simply finding research support for my particular frame of reference. The situation is alarming!

Our entire mental health education and treatment system is virtually founded on a sham and the pretense of scientific support for the effectiveness of treatment by techniques and methods and expertise (which I label, the specificity myth). Therapist expertise is foremost in the determination of the 'right' method for the particular dysfunction. Sadder, yet, is that those who perpetuate and those who are educated in the system continue to believe this contention. To add to the alarm, those of us who think we know better do not speak out. The fundamental fictional foundation of the system is that there are specific treatments for specific disorders. It is primarily on this premise that training and credentials are based and upon which a particular type of practitioner experience is perpetuated. It is implied that there is scientific method research to support this incredibly cost-ineffective system that is dedicated to the principle of specific treatments for specific disabilities.

Adapted with permission from:
Bozarth, J.D. (1998) 'Playing the Probabilities in Psychotherapy', *Person-Centred Practice,* Vol.6, No.1, pp 9-21.
Paper originally presented at the Conference of the Association for the Development of the Person-Centered Approach, Las Vegas, NV. (1997, May).

A recent special issue of the *American Psychologist* on Outcome Assessment of Psychotherapy illustrates the rigidity of the perceptual belief in the fundamental assumption of treatment by method for types of dysfunction. In ten quasi-scholarly articles and five 'comments' revolving around Seligman's (1995) assertions concerning the usefulness of The Consumer Reports survey on mental health in a previous issue of the *American Psychologist*, only one author referred to the importance of the relationship in therapeutic 'encounters' (and this only a tangential reference). All articles abound with the terminology of 'interventions' for treatment. The clear focus is upon the therapist *expertise* and *method of treatment* for the *particular disfunction* paradigm (the 'Specificity Myth').

The factors which have most consistently been related to positive outcome over decades of research; i.e., the client-therapist relationship and the self resources of the client, are virtually ignored.

Furthermore, research reviews on the relationship in counseling are likewise embedded in the specificity myth. Sexton & Whiston's (1994) reasonably thorough coverage of research on the relationship in counseling is indicative of the bias even though they seek and encourage a different paradigmatic view predicated upon a 'social constructivist' view. These authors point out that '. . . it is only the counseling relationship that has consistently been found to contribute to the success of the therapeutic process.' (Luborsky et al, 1988; Orlinsky & Howard, 1986, p.7) They summarize:

> The research has confirmed what was widely recognized: the success of any therapeutic endeavor depends on the participants establishing an open, trusting, collaborative relationship or alliance (Frank & Gunderson, 1990). In addition, research has shown that failure to form such an alliance is strongly associated with client noncompliance with treatment plans (Eisenthal, Emery, Lazare, & Udin, 1979); premature termination (Saltzman, Luetgert, Roth, Creaser, & Howard, 1976; Tracey, 1977); as well as poor outcome (Alexander & Luborsky, 1986).
>
> (Sexton & Whiston, 1992, p. 7)

However, this review of the literature on research concerning the relationship in psychotherapy undergoes a subtle shift of focus. This is reflected by the above statement that '. . . failure to form such an alliance is strongly associated with client noncompliance with treatment plans . . .' The relationship is converted to, 'alliance' and defined by 'client noncompliance' when not formed. In part, this shift is due to the authors use of Gelso and Carter's (1985) multidimensional model of the relationship. This model is founded upon psychoanalytic premises resulting in identification of the relationship as real, unreal and as a working alliance. The unreal aspect of the model is based upon the concept of transference. The working alliance is an extrapolation to all therapies, focusing on the agreement of goals and tasks by and the emotional bond of the client and therapist, but still associated with the psychoanalytic approach. As such, the entire model is presented from the stance of 'therapist expertise and method to dysfunction treatment' ideas even when the relationship is the focus of discussion. This basic assumption seems apparent from the authors' periodic references to such terms as 'client compliance', 'interventions', and measuring the alliance as the 'client's collaboration' in therapy. Even when considering the relationship, the fundamental assumption of our treatment system is embedded in the paradigm of the specificity myth.

The following overview of the research on psychotherapy outcome research demonstrates the fallacy of what I consider to be the fundamentally invalid assumption of our mental health system. It is an assumption that permeates and obfuscates conclusions which miss the critical therapeutic variables that might be considered in a way that can develop more viable treatment.

## Method of inquiry

I examined a number of reviews of psychotherapy outcome research studies as well as re-examined my own inquiry into effective psychotherapy over the past three decades. The most prominent conclusions from research reviews are as follows:

1. Effective psychotherapy is primarily predicated upon (a) the relationship between the therapist and the client and (b) the inner and external resources of the client.
2. The type of therapy and technique is largely irrelevant in terms of successful outcome.
3. Training, credentials and experience of therapists are irrelevant to successful therapy.
4. Clients who receive psychotherapy improve more than clients who do not receive psychotherapy.
5. There is little evidence to support the position that there are specific treatments for particular disabilities.
6. The most consistent of the relationship variables related to effectiveness are the conditions of empathy, genuineness and unconditional positive regard.

## The integrative statement of Carl R. Rogers

The person who has, in my view, come closest to identifying the critical elements of psychotherapeutic effectiveness is Carl Rogers (1957). His statement concerning the necessary and sufficient conditions of therapeutic personality change is an integrative statement for psychotherapy and helping relationships that is separate from his statement (Rogers, 1959) concerning the conditions as part of client-centered therapy (Stubbs & Bozarth, 1996). In my view, this is an important point in that Rogers' efforts were mostly directed toward this core of 'necessary and sufficient' attitudes for helping relationships rather than directed towards the development of Client-Centered Therapy as many have assumed. From this perspective, I have speculated that therapists must achieve their own congruence including the use of their own 'technique system' in order to maximize their capacity for experiencing empathic understanding and unconditional positive regard for the client (Bozarth 1966). In short, I assert that techniques and theoretical formulations are for the therapist rather than for particular clients and this, essentially, allows therapists freedom to enter the person-to-person relationship with their clients in the best possible way. Although Client-Centered Therapy most likely maximizes the probability of such a relationship if the therapist holds the principles of the approach, the conclusions of the psychotherapy research suggest, as Rogers proposed, that the conditions can be embedded in other forms of therapy and helping situations. Focus on the relationship and the client's inner and outer resources can occur to some extent in all therapeutic endeavors.

**The data base**
The major reviews that substantiate my conclusions are briefly summarized as follows:

- *Strupp, H. H., Fox, R. E. and Lessler, K. (1969). Patients view their psychotherapy. Baltimore: The John Hopkins Press.*

This study was an early survey of samples from a psychiatric outpatient clinic wherein patients gave their accounts of their treatments. The 'success' patients in this study were those who had high internal motivation, initiative, and viewed discomfort and determination as crucial to their success. The composite 'patient's' view of the 'good' therapist was '. . . that of a keenly attentive, interested, benign, and concerned listener – a friend who is warm and natural, is not averse to giving direct advice, who speaks one's language, makes sense and rarely arouses intense anger' (p.117).

In addition, they found that inexperienced therapists did as well as highly experienced therapists from the clients' view: 'There were no appreciable differences in outcome or quality of the therapeutic relationship, length of therapy or frequency of sessions had no measurable bearing on outcome, and differences in therapeutic competence, as judged by supervisors, were also inconclusive.' (p. 119)

The authors found that their conclusions were 'strikingly similar to the conclusions . . .' which Berenson and Carkhuff (1967) had drawn from their review of counseling and psychotherapy research. Strupp *et. al.* (1969) paraphrase this review:

1. There is substantial evidence that therapists of very different orientations can be equally effective.
2. There is substantial evidence that therapeutic changes occur in a broad front and that they are independent of the therapist's theoretical position and professional affiliation.
3. There is substantial evidence that the efficacy of psychotherapy is primarily a function of a central core of facilitative conditions. These are three: (a) experiential, (b) didactic, and (c) the role model which the therapist provides. This formulation allows for the possibility that within the context of the core facilitative conditions

a variety of techniques may enhance therapeutic effectiveness. These techniques, however, remain to be spelled out.

4. There is substantial evidence that facilitative conditions are not entities in themselves, to be communicated by prescribed techniques, but rather that they are present in all effective human encounters.

5. There is substantial evidence that techniques are rehabilitative when they free the individual to engage more fully in the kinds of life activities in which he would have become involved if the facilitative conditions had been present originally.

6. There is substantial evidence that all interpersonal encounters may have constructive or deteriorative consequences. To the extent that psychotherapy is effective, it maximizes the constructive consequences of the patient-therapist encounter.

7. There is substantial evidence that effective psychotherapy provides the patient with a human experience which is the inverse of the experiences which gave rise to the difficulties in the first place.

8. There is substantial evidence that in effective psychotherapy the patient eventually incorporates into his own life style the facilitative conditions offered him in therapy. He is influenced by the significant sources of learning in therapy to become more open, understanding, and respectful of himself and others. Thus, what he is learning is new techniques of effective living. (pp. 135-136)

Nearly three decades later, the research reviews of psychotherapy outcome research reflect the major notions observed by Berenson and Carkhuff's (1967) review and the Strupp *et. al.* (1969) study of the importance of the relationship - namely, the importance of the clients' involvement in their own treatment and the minuscule influence of 'interventive' techniques.

• *Stubbs, J. P. & Bozarth, J. D. (1994). The dodo bird revisited: A qualitative study of psychotherapy efficacy research. Applied & Preventive Psychology 3: 109-120.*
At the Third International Forum of the Person-Centered Approach in 1987, I first reported that the prominent conclusion of the time concerning Rogers' hypothesis of the necessary and sufficient conditions for therapeutic personality change was that the conditions were necessary but not sufficient (Bozarth, 1993). One was led by the literature to think that this position was well substantiated by research studies. However, my review did not find a single study which supported this position. Dr. Stubbs examined the literature several years later in an unpublished paper and also found the results to be confusing. This led us to the qualitative study of *The dodo bird revisited.*

This qualitative study of psychotherapy research effectiveness reports that Rogers' hypothesis is the most stable major thread running through the effectiveness of psychotherapy throughout, at least, the last four decades. Of five emergent temporal categories of focus, the abiding relationships to outcome that emerged in some form are those that Rogers hypothesized in his classic integrative statement as core ingredients for therapeutic personality change (i.e., congruence, unconditional positive regard and empathic understanding: Rogers, 1957). Stubbs and Bozarth also specifically note that the predominant temporal category that is the forerunner of the specificity question, i.e., the category that the conditions are necessary but not sufficient has virtually no research support. We did not find one direct study which supported this assertion. Conclusions were, at best, extrapolations of flawed logic. That is: the logic that support for Rogers' hypothesis is weak; hence, something more must be needed, and that thing is some form of interventive technique.

The major implications of this study in relation to effective psychotherapy are that (1) the major thread running through the four plus decades of efficacy research is the relationship of the therapist and client and that a strong part of those data refer to Rogers' attitudinal conditions of the therapist; and (2) the research foundation for the 'specificity question' has abysmal research support and the precursor of the 'specificity' assumption is the unsupported theme of Rogers' conditions being necessary but *not* sufficient.

### • *Duncan, B. L., & Moynihan, D. W. (1994). Intentional utilization of the client's frame of reference. Psychotherapy, 31, 294-301.*

Concomitant to the publication of the *Dodo Bird* qualitative study of psychotherapy research, Duncan and Moynihan summarized reviews of quantitative research studies (e.g., Lambert, Shapiro & Bergin, 1986; Lambert, 1992) to propose the application of the outcome research to practice. Duncan and Moynihan's (1994) argument is actually from a very person-centered perspective. They propose a model predicated on recent conclusions concerning the research on psychotherapy outcome. They point out that the reviews of outcome research (Lambert, 1992; Lambert, Shapiro & Bergin, 1986) suggest that 30% of the outcome variance is accounted for by the common factor of the client-counselor relationship across therapies, techniques account for 15% of the variance as does placebo effect and 40% of the variance is accounted for by extratherapeutic change variables (factors unique to the client and his/her environment). Such research findings suggest to them the utility of intentionally utilizing the client's frame of reference. Indeed, their point resonates the Rogerian view of empathy:

> Empathy, then, is not an invariant, specific therapist behavior or attitude (e.g., reflection of feeling is inherently empathic), nor is it a means to gain a relationship so that the therapist may promote a particular orientation or personal value, nor a way of teaching clients what a relationship should be. Rather, empathy is therapist attitudes and behaviors that place the client's perceptions and experiences above theoretical content and personal values (Duncan, Solovey & Rusk, 1992); empathy is manifested by therapist attempts to work

within the frame of reference of the client. When the therapist acts in a way that demonstrates consistency with the client's frame of reference, then empathy may be perceived, and common factor effects enhanced. Empathy, therefore, is a function of the client's unique perceptions and experience and requires that therapists respond flexibly to clients' needs, rather than from a particular theoretical frame of reference or behavioral set.

(Duncan & Moynihan, 1994, p. 295)

Duncan and Moynihan apparently identify Rogerian empathy with specific behaviors and a particular response set rather than from the bedrock of the empathic attitude in the theory. As such, they apparently do not realize that they are actually proposing an operational concept that is representative of Rogers' view of empathy; hence propose their model as one different from all other models.

The Duncan and Moynihan article is important to consider here  because it summarizes the outcome research in a way that focuses on the critical variables in successful outcome. Moreover, it lays out the basis for a therapy model that is predicated upon scientific method, hypothesis-testing research. Although their model is very aligned to the model of Client-Centered Therapy in its purist form, the emphasis upon the influence of the extratherapeutic variables of the client as the greatest contributor to outcome may suggest that more integral consideration of therapist action and reaction within the empathic context may enhance effectiveness.

- *Consumer Reports. (1995, November). Mental health: Does therapy help? pp. 734-739.*

This survey questionnaire to readers of the Consumer Reports concerning the effectiveness of psychotherapy again buttresses the findings from other reports; e.g., refuting the assertion '. . . of the usefulness of specific techniques for specific disorders . . .' As a survey, the study is subject to the usual methodological critiques of the scientific method paradigm such as, lack of random assignment, lack of systematic treatment and other factors threatening internal validity. It is noteworthy, however, that Seligman (1995), who is a major champion of the 'efficacy' study (scientific method, hypothesis paradigm studies), changed his view of the way to study psychotherapy effectiveness. He comments that within this framework, the studies of specific treatment for specific dysfunction (which he terms, 'efficacy' studies) do not consider the realities of therapy. He elaborates that the efficacy designs seldom go beyond the internal validity of the studies. His conclusion is well stated: 'The efficacy study is the wrong method for empirically validating psychotherapy as it is actually done, because it omits too many crucial elements of what is done in the field.' In other words, the nature of the methodological designs and their inherent constraints (e.g., control studies, exclusive and manualized treatments, random assignment, limited treatment times, single diagnoses), ignore many crucial elements of the actual practice of psychotherapy in the field.

The Consumer Reports' survey and Seligman's assessment is important in that the conclusions of this report are consistent with conclusions of reviews of studies with more 'rigorous' research designs (as, for example, summarized by the Duncan & Moynihan report and the Stubbs & Bozarth study) and the viability of such surveys are acknowledged even though outside of the 'efficacy study' paradigm.

• *Bohart, A. C. and Tallman, K. (1996, Summer). The active client: Therapy as self-help. Journal of Humanistic Psychology, 36,3, 7-30.*
This review of psychotherapy outcome studies concludes that it is the active client who is ultimately the therapist. 'What makes psychotherapy work?' In this review, the answer is, 'the active client'. The authors' interpretations of the research buttress the conclusion that the factors clients see as helpful are not usually technique factors but rather more general processes like providing support. It is further concluded that therapists must not only use the client's frame of reference and rely more on the client but '. . . we must truly understand that it is the whole person of the client who generates the processes and solutions that create change.' (p. 26) The therapist provides a safe working place for client dialogue, experiencing and exploration; provides a set of procedures that can be used by clients to create new self experiences as a way to develop new perspectives and solutions; and provide therapist interactive experience and feedback.

• *Silverman, W. (1996). (1996, Summer). Cookbooks, manuals, and paint-by-numbers: Psychotherapy in the 90's. Journal of Humanistic Psychology, 33,2, 207-346.*
This article is a reaction to recommendations of the Division 12 Task Force Report on Promotion and Dissemination of Psychological Procedures (1993, October). The author points out that the Task Force cited eighteen specific treatments interventions from a total of thirty three studies worthy of 'empirically-validated interventions' and actually ignored the conclusions that emerge from several decades of thorough reviews of psychotherapy outcome literature. Silverman's analogy to the Task Force's procedures is worth quoting since their thrust is an acceleration of the fiction of the specificity hypothesis. Silverman states:

> Let us try a group hypnotic induction. Please imagine that you are back in graduate school taking a seminar in Psychotherapy Research. The professor asks you to write a paper about effective psychotherapies. You will share your scholarship with the rest of the students in the class so that they can also become knowledgeable on the subject. After delivering your paper to the professor, you tell her that while you did not do a comprehensive review of the literature, you asked several of your other professors what they believed to be effective therapies and then you documented these impressions. Furthermore, in defining effectiveness you would only consider those studies that manualized the treatment process. Notice the look on

her face as you explain this to her.

Your paper cites approximately thirty papers as evidence of effectiveness out of the thousands of papers that have been published in the last twenty-five years. From these thirty papers, you list eighteen treatments that are valid, fifteen of which are forms of behavioral modification or cognitive behavioral therapy. As you hand in your paper to the professor, examine her hand for signs of tension. You also inform the professor that regardless of the grade you may receive, you will be making specific recommendations to the Director of Training about what sorts of therapy Clinical Supervisors are to accept. You will also ask the Academic Dean to make specific changes in the graduate curriculum to accommodate your findings. What autonomic reactions do you notice displayed by your professor from the generalizations you make? Now I want you to imagine what grade you will receive. Do you find this hypnotic induction too unrealistic? Well, it time to wake up and face reality. (p. 207)

Silverman's analogy is not only a clear statement about the thrust of the particular Task Force but represents the essence of the undermining of effective mental health care by the myth of specific treatment for particular dysfunction hypothesis.

### • *Bozarth, J. D. (1997). Psychotherapy outcome research designs. Preliminary Report.*

In 1996, I decided to do another perusal of the research designs of psychotherapy outcome research. It is clear that the profession of psychology holds the 'gold standard' (the 'efficacy' or true design study) of psychotherapy research as the *sine qua non* for the determination of psychotherapeutic efficacy (Division 12 Task Force Report on Promotion and Dissemination of Psychological Procedures, 1993; Dawes, 1996; Seligman, 1996) even though there seems little evidence that such research even exists. Such inquiry is further complicated in that, when (if) it exists, such '. . . studies are unable to demonstrate either clear-cut efficacy or adequate descriptions of the effective therapist or effective techniques' (Kisch, 1980)

The perusal of the efficacy studies covered a span of two decades from 1970 through 1989. Efficacy in this review, however, is defined as 'the power to produce an effect' (Webster's Ninth New Collegiate Dictionary, 1991), with 'effect' being 'the power to bring about a result.' Seligman (1996) uses the term 'efficacy' to identify scientific method, hypothesis-testing studies (i.e., the true experimental study). It is unclear to me that the terms 'efficacy' and 'effectiveness' have been so differentiated to any significant degree in previous writings. The studies searched, thus, had a more general meaning than that of being only those studies identified as 'true experimental designs'.

My intent was to identify the general types of studies of psychotherapy, first, as to being quantitative, qualitative or other reports. Second, the quantitative studies were identified by type of design; i.e., pre-experimental, true experimental, quasi-experimental, correlational-causal and Ex Post Facto designs (Leedy, 1993). The 'gold standard' is the true experimental design which has adequate random sampling and a control group. By Seligman's definition, all of the studies would be true experimental designs but the more general definition used for this review allowed a few more studies to be examined.

The initial computer searches (Galin, Eric & PsycINFO) came up with nearly 1000 articles. However, this was rapidly reduced to sixty-four articles when those with non-related titles and content (883), non-research papers (21), not having an efficacy issue (23), and exceptionally poor methodology (6), were dropped. There remained 26 quantitative studies, 2 qualitative studies, and 33 general reviews of the research studies. Three additional articles were meta-analysis. It must be noted that this search did not include some of the studies of 'effectiveness' reviewed in previous articles (e.g., Duncan & Moynihan, 1994; Stubbs & Bozarth, 1994) but, as noted above, they were also not limited to studies of 'efficacy' as defined by Seligman.

Of the quantitative studies (it is in this ball park that we would find the 'gold standard' studies), 10 were pre-experimental designs, 5 were quasi-experimental, 4 were correlational-causal and only 6 were true experimental designs. The fact that there were only 6 studies that met the criterion of the 'gold standard' is, of course, revealing in itself. When we examine the studies in slightly greater detail, it is even more revealing. The samples represent varying populations that include stutterers, the elderly, Russians, depressed women and individuals in crisis. The treatments are also variable ranging from unidentified general psychotherapy in two of the studies, 'supportive psychotherapy' in one of the studies, focused intervention, assertiveness training and Rational-Emotive Behaviour Therapy compared to Systematic Desensitization.

In short, these true experimental design studies have little common ground regarding the question of efficacy and there is not a hint of replication. Although some studies not recorded in the particular computer searches were no doubt missed in this search, this inquiry is consistent with other reviews. There are few true experimental designs and as summarized previously by Stubbs and Bozarth (1994), 'The research concerning specificity of treatment, dysfunction, therapist variables and client variables is characterized by fragmentation, few replications and lack of generalizability.' (p.116)

**The data base conclusion**
The conclusion is clear: there is not a research foundation for the underlying assumption of our mental health care system; that is, that there are specific treatments for specific dysfunctions. The specificity myth is replete. I repeat Stubbs and my previous comment that the direction of the research continues to prove '. . . significantly insignificant to help and often obscures what is most significantly helpful.' (Stubbs & Bozarth, 1994, p.117). The most clear research evidence is that effective psychotherapy results from the resources of the client

(extratherapeutic variables) and from the person-to-person relationship of the therapist and client. The specificity and systematizing of these variables remain somewhat murky although they do include Rogers' hypothesized variables of the attitudinal qualities. The research on relationship reviewed by Sexton and Whiston supports the conclusion '. . . that there are significant individual differences among and within clients over time and that these individual differences account for the majority of the variance in counseling outcome.' (Martin, 1990, p. 58) The data increasingly points to 'the active client' and the individuality of the client as the core of successful therapy.

As O'Hara (1995) aptly concludes:

> It isn't the technique, it isn't the therapist, it isn't the level of training, it isn't the new wonder drug, it isn't the diagnosis. It is our clients' own inborn capacities for self-healing, and it is the meeting - the relationship in which two or more sovereign and sacred 'I's' meet as a 'we' to engage with significant questions of existence. (p. 19, 30-31)

It is here that we seek to find a model which can efficiently help clients find their own empowerment. We can, hopefully, find a model to replace the cost-inefficient 'specificity myth', the model of expertise, specific treatment for specific dysfunction that drives our mental health treatment system. An efficient model should be based on the 'true' findings of the last four decades of research on psychotherapy effectiveness. At the core, Rogers' seminal contributions are a foundation for effective treatment.

# IMPLICATIONS

# THE CORE CONDITION IS US: IMPLICATIONS FOR CRITICAL MASS CONSCIOUSNESS

# 20

The critical message in the theory of Carl Rogers is that of the growth hypothesis; i.e., the actualizing tendency. It is the assumption that each of us innately strives in a constructive direction to 'become our potentialities'. This assumption is the foundation of the person-centered approach and also the primary reason for the approach being a different paradigm from other therapeutic approaches. The assumption belies us to trust in the self-authority, self-determination and self-direction of individuals.

Ironically, Rogers contributed to the resistance towards this fundamental assumption through his hard-nosed pragmatism and dedication to logical-positivism inquiry. He presented us with a multilinear theory that could be extrapolated to unknown dimensions of the human mind but cast it in the framework of linear theory meeting the most rigorous demands of behavioristic scientific inquiry. His early dedication to scientific method inquiry led to a focus on forms of response and to operational definitions of terms that were used in ways that distorted the meaning of his concepts. Academic reception of his early scientific method research overshadowed his equally dedicated considerations of other means of inquiry. Other inquiries included those of person-centered qualitative research engaging participants as researchers, speculations of multiple realities, receptivity to transcendental experiences and experimenting with parapsychological phenomena.

This chapter examines the growth hypothesis and extrapolation of Rogers' theory in relation to critical mass consciousness. Critical mass consciousness refers to a turning point of thought by a large number of individuals. Such shifts include different ways of thinking about realities. The term is used as analogous to 'paradigm shift'. A paradigm shift is defined as: '. . . a fundamental change in our thoughts, perceptions, and values . . .' (Capra, 1992). Implications of the theory in the areas of ethical practice, multicultural diversity, and societal impact are briefly considered.

Adapted paper presentation from
*The core condition is us: Implications for critical mass consciousness,* the Conference of The Association for The Development of the Person-Centered Approach. Wheaton College, Massachusetts, (May 1998)

## The person-centered message

Rogers' essential message is that when an individual can be received with unconditionality (unconditional positive regard) the individual moves more to becoming that person's potentialities. This theme has been mentioned throughout this book as the context for discourse about the theory and practice of the approach. Rogers emphasized the therapist's experiencing of empathic understanding of the client's frame of reference and of unconditional positive regard towards the client. The therapist had to be congruent within this experiencing. This conceptualization provided a pragmatic guideline for therapists to embody themselves in a receptive mode towards their clients. Although therapists may vary considerably in multiple ways, the person-centered therapist must be a certain way. It is when the therapist is reasonably open to her own experiences without denying them, and experiences her own unconditionality towards a particular person (the client) and experiences to some extent what it is like for the other person (the client) and this experiencing is perceived by the client  then the client's actualizing tendency is promoted. However, as I have argued earlier, the fundamental curative or promotional factor is the perceived reception of the therapist's experience of unconditional positive regard. It can be no other way in Rogers' theory.  Individuals become disturbed or incongruent because of the introjection of conditional self values from parents and society. It is the client's perception of the therapist's experience of unconditional positive regard that allows the client to experience unconditional positive self regard; thus becoming whole again and to open their organismic experiences without distortion or conditionality.  For Rogers, empathic understanding of the person's frame of reference and unconditionality are integrally intertwined even to the point of being one condition.

The attitudinal conditions that are necessary and sufficient for releasing the natural constructive inner force of individuals have ironically diverted attention away from the critical condition that is core to his theory. This condition is the actualizing tendency itself. The core motivational condition, from a holistic view of the theory, is that the individual has a directional and formative tendency towards the fulfilment of inner potential. Being in touch with one's organism is naturalisitic and universal.

## The foundation of Rogerian theory

The growth hypothesis is the foundation for extrapolation of Rogers' theory towards what some believe is the mystical and transcendental. This core motivational force is consistently identified as the theoretical foundation in Rogers theoretical writings (Rogers, 1957; 1959). In a cogent summary, Rogers (1963) writes:

> We are, in short, dealing with an organism which is always motivated,
> is always 'up to something,' always seeking. So I would reaffirm,
> perhaps even more strongly after the passage of a decade, my belief
> that there is one central source of energy in the human organism;
> that it is a function of the whole organism rather than some portion
> of it; and that it is perhaps best conceptualized as a tendency toward

fulfilment, toward actualization, toward the maintenance and enhancement of the organism. (p. 6)

Our inherent search is to become the ideal 'fully functioning person'. The individual touches her own inner nature, and trusts her organism to function freely. This basic nature of human beings: '. . . is constructive and trustworthy' Rogers (1961). This is accelerated when the human being is functioning freely. Rogers used a metaphor of potato sprouts trying to survive in a cellar devoid of light to illustrate the actualizing tendency (Rogers, 1977). He noted that the tendrils and sprouts of the potatoes were always striving to become their potentialities no matter how poor the conditions. They continued to strive and survive in the best possible way in spite of adverse environmental circumstances. He likened this metaphor to 'patients' who strove for their survival in state mental hospitals. The potato metaphor always interested me beyond the obvious representation of the human who is always striving for constructive growth and directionality. There is a part of the metaphor seldom considered. That is, the tendrils not only seek to survive the oppressive conditions, they strive to find the light. They seek their own growth source. I have pondered whether this is true for Rogers' postulated inner growth source of humans. Like the dynamics of quantum theory: 'The individual is always in process, always striving toward recognition of his or her inherent potential, never losing the dynamic movement and striving' (Bozarth, 1984. p. 181). Our core condition is this inherent potential and continuous dynamic movement and striving towards constructive fulfilment. It is as we shift the strictures of our minds and the structure of our behaviors that our inherent potential takes on unprecedented possibilities. It is here that we can begin to approach the critical mass of consciousness beyond the logical positivist paradigm. Client-centered therapy puts the person back in touch with her organismic valuing process. Rogers states:

> I believe that when the human being is inwardly free to choose whatever he deeply values, he tends to value those objects, and goals which make for his own survival, growth, and development, and for the survival and development of others. I hypothesize that it is characteristic of the human organism to prefer such actualizing and socialized goals when he is exposed to a growth promoting climate.
>
> (Rogers, 1951, p. 139)

Rogers' assumption is that actualization can only be positive and is enhancing of the individual's nature and existence.

**Extrapolation of Rogerian theory**
Van Belle suggests that Rogers moved towards 'Mystical Universalism' in his latter views of therapy. He suggests that Rogers' views on therapy continually changed but that two themes are predominant. These are the themes of (1) profound respect for the individual, and (2) an '. . . almost religious reverence for growth' (p. 47). I disagree with Van Belle's assertion that Rogers continuously changed

his views of therapy, and also with an assertion by Van Belle that Rogers formed his ideas of individuality from his cultural/historical context. Certainly, Rogers cultural/historical experience was in the 'pioneer' milieu of the United States which logically can be speculated upon as having an influence on him. However, Rogers' account for his views of human growth are identified by him as coming from: (1) a revelation from becoming aware of different views of life during his trip to China as a young man, and (2) his naturalistic observations of living organisms; especially, human beings as they progressed through therapy. I do agree with Van Belle's major thesis that Rogers primarily respected individuals for their ability to actualize their potential. Rogers was more dedicated to the growth potential than to respect for individuals. Van Belle offers a succinct summary:

> For Rogers everything that exists, including human beings, is taken up into this total evolutionary process of becoming. This growth process has its own ends in view and its own organizational principle within itself. It is a syntropic force, it has morphological properties. It forms and reforms itself dynamically (Rogers, 1980). Individuals, as microcosms of this total process, each uniquely have the capacity to form themselves or to actualize their potentials but they have this capacity only insofar as they are open to themselves, thus only insofar as they function as the 'organisms' or growth principles that they are ( Van Belle, 1980). Here we have the one and only condition that Rogers posits for growth to occur.
>
> (Van Belle, 1990, p. 49-50)

Contrary to Van Belle's belief that Rogers' views on therapy are characterized by movement from 'structure bound' nondirective therapy to 'process oriented' thinking, I believe that the process oriented growth hypothesis has been the driving force from the beginning. It was always the client who 'knows best' and the 'best way to go' as far as Rogers' theory was concerned, and this is predicated upon the growth hypothesis. I agree with Van Belle that Rogers' process took him from talking about humans 'becoming' to humans 'being' but, in fact, that this way of dialogue is closer to the explicit theory statement (Rogers, 1959). This is discussed in   chapter 8 concerning congruence in which I conclude that the conditions necessitate therapists 'being' a certain way. That is, the therapist is congruent in a particular relationship; the therapist experiences unconditionality towards a particular person; and the therapist experiences herself as if she is the other person. This is the way the person-centered therapist is called upon to 'be'.

Van Belle quotes from Rogers' book, *A Way of Being*, (Rogers, 1980) with such quotes as Rogers' references to: 'the wisdom of the group'; 'participation in a larger whole'; being 'in a slightly altered state of consciousness'; that the 'inner spirit seemed to reach and to touch the inner spirits of others'; and that his 'relationship with others in the group transcended itself and became part of something larger'. Van Belle aptly concludes:

> To live in this world is to experience yourself 'participating in a

larger universal formative tendency' (p. 128), that itself is 'up to something' (p. 313). It shows a 'trend toward even greater complexity' (p. 128). This is now no longer the impulse of life only but of the universe as a whole. All that exists, changes continually and participates in a kind of 'cosmic dance'.

(Van Belle, 1990,  p. 345)

Rogers' theory extrapolates to 'separateness giving way to unity' similar to the tenets of psychic healing (Spahn, 1992), and movement of the person towards her potentialities (the actualizing tendency) with these potentialities open to the whole of cosmic consciousness and interrelationship with the universe (the formative tendency).

## The Sedona experiment
In January 1998, Peggy Natiello and John K. Wood, sent invitations to various individuals to attend a large group experience in Sedona, Arizona. They represented several other individuals who hoped participants from previous person-centered large groups could be part of a group effort to research the large group phenomena. Sedona is an area noted in the United States as an area with high 'psychic' energy. It is identified as a preferred area for individuals to work in transcendental, psychic quests.

Although I had participated in over a hundred person-centered large groups over the past thirty five years, my experiences in this group served as an assimilation of some of my previous observations and experiences. My beliefs were leaning in the direction of greater non-directivity in the large groups prior to attending the Sedona group. I had written the following about non-directivity and trust in the large group:

The more non-directive, the more chaotic; the more chaotic, the more individuals struggle for their own direction and structure.
The more individuals find their own structures and directions, the more they trust themselves and others. It may be in the struggle itself that is the greatest freeing factor.

(Bozarth, 1998a)

My intent in the group was to experience and observe as well as to participate. My major learning from the Sedona group experience was that the group and the individuals often operate on a process level that is not necessarily behaviorally observable. What I partially mean by that in terms of the group is that ostensibly the group members were often not operating with unconditionality or empathic accuracy. The behaviors in the group did not seem to correspond with an underlying process.

## Specifically
Many of the group members often tried to change individuals to be more the way

they wanted them to be. This occurred particularly with one individual in the group who did not seem to be meeting the norms of the group as many thought he should be.

There was little accuracy of most empathic understanding responses. There were frequent responses by several active participants that distracted from certain intense expressions of other participants. The group was verbally dominated by a few individuals.

I cannot speak for the majority of participants with my observations, but the dozen or so individuals with whom I did speak after the workshop agreed with most of my observations. Also, the group was resoundingly successful for the dozen or so individuals with whom I talked after the experience. Their feelings of success were related to 'spiritual', 'magical', 'transcendental', 'transforming' experiences which are behaviorally difficult to communicate. For example, two felt connected to each other while standing under the Sedona sky just observing a medallion that one of them had made out of clay. Another found 'thirty seconds of hugging' with another changed specific attitudes and triggered physiological change. Two individuals reported experiencing a 'cosmic connection' as they labeled it; an experience which included the feeling of an intense internal heat that they had never experienced before. One individual was puzzled by the experience of physiological pain and spasms while another spoke in the group. Later, he discovered that this was the way the speaker felt during the time of her expression in the group. Such reports were more pervasive and extreme and, yet, reminiscent of reports from other large groups. A separate project covering different groups is reported by Kass (1998) who found the participants used the same terms which are noted above to describe their experiences. This is interesting since the group participants came from a broad base of life and beliefs, many of them never before using such terminology. On the larger level of the group, the difference between examination of the 'process' from a behavioral stance and the felt togetherness and success of the group as a whole was striking. All of this is just a reminder that there may be that element of a 'transcendental' nature to which we seldom attend. Rogers' reference to the 'wisdom of the group' and the 'participation in a larger whole' is reflective of such experiences. Rogers' growth hypothesis at the extrapolated level moves '. . . to knowing and sensing below the level of consciousness, to a conscious awareness of the organism and the external world, to a transcendent awareness of the harmony and unity of the cosmic system, including humankind' (Rogers, 1980, p. 133).

## Critical mass consciousness

Rogers' foundation block of person-centered theory, i.e., the actualizing tendency, lends itself as a base to new realms of thinking and broader assumptions for humankind. Evolution of his theoretical assumption of growth suggests the possibility of an emergent newera in psychotherapeutic treatment similar to the new era in medical treatment (Dossey, 1994). The three eras of medicine identified by Dossey are:

> Era I: the mechanical or physical medicine era which refers to any form of therapy focusing on aspects of the body;
> Era II: Mind-body medicine, which refers to the effects of consciousness within a particular body; and
> Era III: transpersonal medicine, which refers to any therapy in which effects of consciousness bridge between different persons (pp. 40-41).

Era II treatments are now accepted by most practitioners. These treatments include those of biofeedback, hypnosis, relaxation therapy, and psychoneuroimmunology. Era III approaches in medicine or therapy are seldom accepted. These treatments include distant healing, diagnosis at a distance, telesomatic events and non-contact therapeutic touch.

What are the limitations if we are open to our organismic experiences? What are the limitations of the growth hypothesis? I submit that we can approach answers to these questions only by having a healthy mix of skepticism and openness. The mix of openness to our own experiences, to anecdotal reports, survey studies, qualitative research, and quantitative design studies of true, quasi and correlational design.

### Some far out considerations

What are some of the suggestions from various sources for extending our belief systems? Here are a few which intrigue me about certain phenomena:

*Out-of-body experiences – remote viewing*
Thousands of anecdotal reports are now recorded in addition to the studies of Robert Monroe (1995) (the hard-headed businessman cited by Rogers) and his colleagues on out of body experiences and remote viewing. In addition, the CIA and Army Intelligence has documented files on experiments on remote vision from units such as Stargate, a government espionage unit involved with psychic espionage. David Moorhouse tells his personal account as a 'Psychic Warrior' which is corroborated by the existence of such governmental units (Moorhouse, 1996).

*Psychic healing*
Results of a true design, double-blind study with heart patients that concludes that there is significant improvement in the group which was offered prayer is reported by Dossey (1994). Likewise, there is at least one tightly designed study demonstrating significant effects of the effect of distant healing as an adjunct to standard antidepressant medication (Greyson, 1996).

*Talking with angels*
James Van Praagh (1998), a medium, has demonstrated highly specific 'hits' with information he views as coming from angels. Within minutes of discussion with

audience members via telephone, he has specific hits that are obviously beyond chance.

There are domains of experience not readily considered in our usual lexicon of therapy.

## The purpose of such inquiry

The purpose of mentioning such phenomena as remote viewing, psychic healing and even 'talking with angels' is to point out that there are domains which demand our openness. The extrapolation of the growth hypothesis lends itself to such possibilities. Rogers' conceptualization of the formative tendency should remind us of his continuous open inquiry:

> The crucial point is that when a person is functioning fully, there are no barriers, no inhibitions, which prevent the full experiencing of whatever is organismically present. This person is moving in the direction of wholeness, integration, a unified life. Consciousness is participating in this larger, creative, Formative Tendency.
>
> (Rogers, 1980, p. 128)

Greater openness to study of such areas may eventually lend itself to affirming some of Rogers' experimenting with the transcendental and, moreover, extend Rogers' theory of the growth hypothesis. The growth hypothesis is a likely foundation for new realms of thinking reflective of openness to inner resources of individuals. Rogers refers to times when his therapy relationship '. . . transcends itself and becomes a part of something larger . . .' ( Rogers, 1980, p. 129). Thorne (1991) is convinced that Rogers' words must be taken seriously in order '. . . to ensure the vitality and the development of the client-centered tradition . . .'(p.183). As Rogers stated in a personal paper first written in 1974:

> . . . we are wiser than our intellects . . . that our organisms as a whole have a wisdom and purposiveness which goes well beyond our conscious thought . . . I think men and women, individually and collectively are inwardly and organismically rejecting the view of one single culture-approved reality. I believe they are moving inevitably toward the acceptance of millions of separate, challenging exciting informative individual perceptions of reality. I regard it as possible that this view - like the sudden and separate discovery of the principles of quantum mechanics by scientists in different countries - may begin to come into effective existence in many parts of the world at once. If so, we would be living in a totally new universe, different from any in history. Is it conceivable that such a change can come about?
>
> (Rogers, 1980, pp. 106-107)

The implications of the growth hypothesis affect several areas of concern which I will briefly comment upon.

## Ethics

The fundamental assumption of the person-centered approach is also the basic ethical premise for person-centered practitioners. The manifestation of the assumption is that the practitioner is dedicated to the self-authority and self-determination of the client. As such, the principle suggests new interpretations and even different statements concerning ethical standards. Such revision does not suggest fewer ethical restraints, rather it suggests stronger ethical principles and more attention to the nature and substance of professional relationships.

Psychotherapy is the search for and integration of one's own biologically intrinsic and authentic values. Psychotherapy, for Rogers, like Maslow (1962), was a process of recovery of 'specieshood' or of 'healthy animality', of self-discovery, and of integration leading toward greater authenticity of being and spontaneous expressiveness. This assumption is significantly different from underlying assumptions of most ethical standard statements. Most ethical assumptions in therapy are embedded in psychoanalytic theory. The assumptions are: (1) that therapists must be controlled in their behavior with clients; that is, they can not be trusted; (2) that the client is helpless in the relationship with the therapist (and that feelings are transference towards the therapist); (3) that the therapist is more powerful than the client and can easily coerce the client.

It is not my purpose here to argue ethical virtues of a different assumptive base. Rather, the implications of the growth assumption for ethical behavior is examined.

The job of the person-centered therapist is to be a certain way and that way involves maximal experiencing of self in relation to the client. The intent is to dedicate particular kinds of one's experience towards the client during the time of the therapeutic contact. It is assumed that this promotes the positive growth of the individual. The difference between the client and therapist is not therapist expertise but the therapist's congruence (versus client incongruence) in the relationship and the therapist's dedication and intent of experiencing the client in certain ways; i.e., unconditionally and 'as if' the therapist were the client. The abiding person-centered ethic is to operate from these attitudinal qualities. This is the way the person-centered therapist strives to 'be'. Person-centered ethics are predicated on attitudinal qualities of the therapist. When the therapist is this way, the therapist can be trusted to act in accord with the positive growth directions of the client.

## Multicultural diversity

There have been numerous critiques of Rogers' theory in relation to cultural values, frames of reference of various races and even gender perceptual stances (Holdstock, 1990; O'Hara, 1997). The position is often taken that Rogers' values were middle class America values and out of the U.S. culture of valuing independence, individual resourcefulness and materialistic accomplishments. As I noted in a previous chapter, I consider this a flawed argument that fails to consider the essence of the theory as an organismic, natural and universal theory. The qualities of the biological core are intrinsic to the human nature of each individual. Denial and unawareness of the core lead to psychological illness. Evil is a product of social conditioning and reaction to introjected values of conditional love according to Rogers. The more one becomes what one truly is, the less evil one finds within and the more one permits evil feelings to surface the less potent and burdensome they become. Moreover, the more one actualizes, the more one is able to interface with the environment and others even when at odds with strictures of the norm group. The latter point concerning adjustment, although not necessarily agreement, with particular societal norms for individuals at higher levels in the actualizing process is important to understanding part of Rogers' position. The theoretical assumption applies to all human species and indeed, to all living organisms (and even beyond: see Rogers, 1980). When the theory is cast in a way that is considered inappropriate in particular instances, it is always cast in the format of the way individuals have learned to 'do' client-centered/person-centered therapy. I have argued that focusing on how to do person-centered therapy is one of the more inhibiting factors to the creation of the freeing environment for the individual. As such, the arguments that person-centered therapy cannot apply to certain other cultures are predicated upon this way of 'doing' therapy. The foundational premise of a universal and natural force is ignored as the basic premise.

## Societal impact

In the area of management and organizations, Plas (1996) recommends person-centered principles for enhancing management skills. Her key ideas of related individualism, authenticity, and acceptance of strength and weakness provide the guidelines for change. She develops these guidelines with only passing reference to Rogers' works. The ideas emerge from successful managers and from successful organizations. Rogers wrote a book concerning the meaning of his theory for society (Rogers, 1977); he believed that the most notable influence on society was related to power and control in relationships. In his words, 'Most notably it has altered the thinking about power and control in relationships between persons . . .' (p. xii). Rogers' summarizes the impact of his approach in his book on personal power. One of his quotes is appropriate to convey his thoughts. He states:

> A person-centered approach, when utilized to encourage the growth and development of the psychotic, the troubled, or the normal individual, revolutionizes the customary behaviors of members of the helping professions. It illustrates many things: (1) A sensitive person, tying to be of help, becomes more person-centered, no matter what orientation she starts from, because she finds that approach more effective. (2) When you are focused on the person, diagnostic labels become largely irrelevant. (3) The traditional medical model in psychotherapy is discovered to be largely in opposition to person-centeredness. (4) It is found that those who can create an effective person-centered relationship do not necessarily come from the professionally trained group. (5) The more this person-centered approach is implemented and put into practice, the more it is found

to challenge hierarchical models of 'treatment' and hierarchical methods of organization. (6) The very effectiveness of this unified person-centered approach constitutes a threat to professionals, administrators, and others, and steps are taken' consciously and unconsciously – to destroy it. It is too revolutionary.

(Rogers, 1977, p. 28)

He notes: 'From the perspective of politics, power, and control, person-centered therapy is based on a premise which at first seemed risky and uncertain: a view of man as at core a trustworthy organism' (p. 7). Rogers' revolutionary proposition founded upon the growth hypothesis faces us with different ways of thinking, and practising, and being.

# References

Adomaitis, R. (1991) *On being genuine: a phenomenologically grounded study of the experience of genuineness and its place in client-centered theory.* Unpublished Doctoral dissertation, Northwestern University, USA.

Alexander, L. B. and Luborsky, L. (1986) The Penn helping alliance scales. In L. S. Greenberg and W. M. Pinsoff (eds.) *The Psychotherapeutic Process.* New York: Guilford. pp. 325-366

American Heritage Dictionary. (1995) Microsoft Word Version.

American Psychological Association. (1993, October) *Task force on promotion and dissemination of psychological procedures: a report by the Division 12 Board.* Washington DC: APA.

American Psychological Association. (1996, October) *Special issue: Outcome assessment of psychotherapy.* Washington DC: APA.

Baldwin, M. (1987) Interview with Carl Rogers on the use of the self in therapy. In M. Baldwin and V. Satir (eds.) *The Use of Self in Therapy.* New York: The Haworth Press. pp. 45-52.

Barclay, J. R. (1984) Searching for a new paradigm in counseling. *Personnel and Guidance Journal*, 62, 2.

Barrett-Lennard, G. T. (1962) Dimensions of therapist response as causal factors in therapeutic change. *Psychological Monographs,* 76 (43. Whole No. 562).

Barrett-Lennard, G. T. (1990) The therapy pathway reformulated. In G. Lietaer, J. Rombauts and R.Van Balen (eds) *Client-Centered and Experiential Therapies in the Nineties.* Leuven: Leuven University Press. pp. 123-153.

Basch, M. F. (1985) Empathic understanding: a review of the concept and some theoretical considerations. *Journal of the American Psychoanalytic Association,* 31, 101-126.

Bateson, G. (1972) Conscious purpose versus nature. In G. Bateson, *Steps to an ecology of mind.* New York: Chandler. pp. 438-459.

Berenson, B. G. and Carkhuff, R. R. (1967) *Sources of gain in counseling and psychotherapy.* New York: Holt, Rinehart and Winston.

Bergin, A.E., and Lambert, M. J. (1978) The evaluation of therapeutic outcomes. In S. L.Garfield and A. E. Bergin (eds) *Handbook of Psychotherapy and Behavioral Change: an Empirical Analysis (2nd edition).* New York: John Wiley and Sons. pp. 139–189.

Bertalanffy, L. (1960) *Problems in life.* New York: Harper Torchbooks.

Bixler, R. H. and Bixler, V. H. (1946) Test interpretation in vocational counseling. *Educational and Psychological Measurement*, 6, 145-156.

Bohart, A. C. (1994) The person-centered therapies. In A. S. Gurman and S. B. Messer (eds) *Modern Psychotherapies.* New York: Guilford. pp. 59-75.

Bohart, A. C. and Rosenbaum, R. (1995) The dance of empathy: empathy, diversity, and technical eclecticism. *The Person-Centered Journal,* 2, (4), 6-16.

Bohart, A. C. and Tallman, K. (Summer 1996) The active client: therapy as self-help. *Journal of Humanistic Psychology*, 36 (3), 7-30.

Bordin, E. S. and Bixler, R. H. (1946) Test selection: a process of counseling. *Educational and Psychological Measurement,* 6, 361-373.

Bowen, M. V. (1991) Intuition and the person-centered approach. *Paper presented at the Second International Conference on Client-Centered and Experiential Therapy, University of Stirling, Stirling, Scotland.*

Bowen, O. H. (1947) The client-centered approach to educational and vocational guidance. *The Personal Counselor.* 2, 1-5.

Bower, D. (1985) Assumptions of the Rogerian person-centered approach to counseling: implications for pastoral counseling. *(Research Project), Atlanta: Columbia Theological Seminary.*

Bower, D. (1986) Attributes of person-centered therapists: a pilot study. *Unpublished paper.* The University of Georgia.

Bower, D. and Bozarth, J. D. (1988) Features of client-centered/person-centered therapists. *Paper presented at the International Conference on Client-centered and Experiential Psychotherapy.* Book of abstracts (pp. 23-25). Belgium: Leuven.

Boy, A. V. (1985) Main streaming the basic encounter group. *The Journal for Specialists in Group Work*, 10 (4), 205-210.

Boy, A. V. (1989) Psychodiagnosis: a person-centered perspective. *Person-Centered Review*, 4, (2), pp. 132-151.

Bozarth, J. D. (1983) Current research on client-centered therapy in the USA. In M. Wolf-Rudiger and H. Wolfgang (eds) *Research on Psychotherapeutic Approaches: Proceedings of the 1st European Conference on Psychotherapy Research*, Trier, Frankfurt: Peter Lang. pp. 105-115.

Bozarth, J. D. (1984) Beyond reflection: emergent modes of empathy. In R. Levant and Shlien, J. (eds) *Client-centered therapy and the person-centered approach: new directions in theory, research, and practice.* New York: Praeger. pp. 59-75.

Bozarth, J. D. (1985) Quantum theory and the person-centered approach. *Journal of Counseling and Development.* 64 (3), 179-182.

Bozarth, J. D. (1986) The basic encounter group: an alternative view. *The Journal for Specialists in Group Work*, 11, (4), pp 228-232.

Bozarth, J. D. (1988a) Examination of Rogers' sessions with Miss Mun, Gloria and Kathy. In F. Zimring (Chair), Re-examination of client-centered therapy using Rogers' tapes and films. *Symposium conducted at the meeting of the American Psychological Association, Atlanta.*

Bozarth, J. D. (1988b) The person-centered large community group – premise, axioms, and speculations. *Paper presented at the Person-Centered Approach Workshop, Warm Springs, GA.*

Bozarth, J. D. (1990a) The essence of Client-Centered Therapy. In G. Lietaer, J. Rombauts, and R. Van Balen (eds) *Client-Centered and Experiential Psychotherapy in the Nineties.* Leuven: Leuven University Press. pp. 59-64.

Bozarth, J. D. (1990b) The evolution of Carl Rogers as a therapist. *Person-Centered Review*, 2 (1), 11-13.

Bozarth, J. D. (1991a) Rejoinder: perplexing perceptual ploys. *Journal of Counseling and Development*, 69 (5), 466-468.

Bozarth, J. D. (1991b) Person-centered assessment. *Journal of Counseling and Development*, 69, 458-461.

Bozarth, J. D. (1991c) Serving the older worker with a disability: The role of Rehabilitation. In L. Perlman and C. Hanson (eds) *Ageing, Disability and the Nation's Productivity.* Washington D.C.: National Rehabilitation Association, pp. 18-24.

Bozarth, J. D. (1992a) Coterminous intermingling of doing and being in Person-Centered Therapy. *The Person-Centered Journal*, 1(1), 33-39.

Bozarth, J. D. (1992b) A theoretical reconceptualization of the necessary and sufficient conditions. *The Person-Centered Journal,* 3 (1) 44-51.

Bozarth, J. D. (1992c) The person-centered community group. *Paper presented at the American Psychological Association symposium. Contributions of client-centered therapy to American psychology's 100 years.* Chaired by Ned Gaylin, Washington D. C.

Bozarth, J. D. (1993a) Misunderstandings of the person-centered approach. *Paper presented at the annual conference of the Association for the Development of the Person-Centered Approach, Maryville, TN.*

Bozarth, J. D. (1993b) Not necessarily necessary but always sufficient. In D. Brazier (ed) *Beyond Carl Rogers.* London: Constable. pp 92-105

Bozarth, J. D. (1995a) Person-centered therapy: a misunderstood paradigmatic difference? *The Person-Centered Journal,* 2 (2), 12-17

Bozarth, J. D. (1995b) Designated facilitators: unnecessary and insufficient. *A paper presented at the annual conference for the Association of the Development of the Person-Centered Approach, Tampa, FL.*

Bozarth, J. D. (1996a) A theoretical reconsideration of the necessary and sufficient conditions for therapeutic personality change. *The Person-Centered Journal,* 3 (1), 44-51.

Bozarth, J. D. (1996b). Client-centered Therapy and Techniques. In R. Hutterer, G. Pawlowsky, P. F. Schmid & R. Stipsits (Eds.) Client-Centered and Experiential Psychotherapy: A Paradigm in Motion (pp. 363-368). Peter Lang: New York.

Bozarth, J. D. (1997a) Empathy from the framework of Client-Centered Theory and the Rogerian hypothesis. In A. Bohart and L. Greenburg (eds) *Empathy Reconsidered: new directions in psychotherapy.* Washington DC.: American Psychological Association. pp. 81-102.

Bozarth, J. D. (1997b) Review study of psychotherapy outcome. *Preliminary study, Discussion Paper. The University of Georgia.*

Bozarth, J. D. (1997c) The person-centered approach. In C. Feltham (ed) *Which psychotherapy?* London: Sage. pp. 12-32.

Bozarth, J. D. (1998a) Some observations on large community groups. *Unpublished manuscript,* Sedona, Arizona.

Bozarth, J. D. (1998b) The core-condition is us: implications for critical mass consciousness. *Paper presentation at the Association for the Development of the Person-Centered Approach,* Wheaton College, Massachusetts, USA.

Bozarth, J. D. and Brodley, B. T. (1986) Client-centered psychotherapy: A statement. *Person-Centered Review,* 1 (3), 262-271.

Bozarth, J. D. and Brodley, B. T. (1991) Actualization: A functional concept in client-centered psychotherapy: a statement. *Journal of Social Behavior and Personality,* 6, (5), 45-59.

Bozarth, J. D. and Fisher, R. (1990) Person-centered career counseling. In W. B. Walsh and S. Osipow (eds) *Career Counseling.* Hillsdale, NJ: Erlbaum. pp. 45-78.

Bozarth, J. D. and Shanks, A. (1989) Person-centered family therapy with couples. *Person-Centered Review,* 4 (3), 280-294.

Brodley, B. T. (1977) The empathic understanding response. *Unpublished manuscript. University of Illinois, Chicago.*

Brodley, B. T. (1986) Client-centered therapy: What it is? What it is not? *Paper presented at the First Annual Meeting of the Person-Centered Approach, Chicago.*

Brodley, B. T. (1988a) A client-centered psychotherapy practice. *Paper presented at the Third Annual Meeting of the Association for the Development of the Person-Centered Approach, New York.*

Brodley, B. T. (1988b) Carl Rogers' therapy. In F. Zimring (Chair), *Re-examination of client-centered therapy using Rogers' tapes and films. Symposium conducted at the meeting of the American Psychological Association, Atlanta.*

Brodley, B. T. (1990) Client-centered and experiential: two different therapies. In G. Lietaer, J. Rombauts and R. Van Balen (eds) *Client-Centered and Experiential Therapies in the Nineties.* Leuven: Leuven University Press. pp. 87-107.

Brodley, B. T. (1991) Some observations of Carl Rogers' verbal behavior in therapy interviews. *Paper presented at the Second International Conference on Client-Centered and Experiential Therapy, University of Stirling, Stirling, Scotland.*

Brodley, B. T. (1993) Some observations of Carl Rogers' behavior in therapy interviews. *Person-Centered Journal,* 1(1), 37-47.

Brodley, B. T. (1994) Meanings and implications of the non-directive attitude in client-centered therapy. *Revision of paper presented at the ninth annual meeting of the Association for the Development of the Person-Centered Approach.* Kendall College, Evanston, Illinois.

Brodley, B. T. (1995) Congruence and its relation to communication in Client-Centered Therapy and the Person-Centered Approach. *Unpublished paper, Illinois School of Professional Psychology – Chicago/Chicago Counseling and Psychotherapy Center.*

Brodley, B. T., and Bozarth, J. D. (1986) Core Values in Client-Centered Therapy. *Paper presented at the First Annual Meeting of the Person-Centered Approach, Chicago.*

Brodley, B. T. and Brody, A. F. (1996) Can one use techniques and still be Client-centered? In R. Hutterer, G. Pawlowsky, P. Schmid, and R. Stipsits, R. (eds) *Client-Centered and Experiential Psychotherapy: a paradigm in motion.* New York: Peter Lang. pp. 369-374.

Brodley, B. and Zimring, F. (1992) Person-centered practice: A therapy transcript. *The Person-Centered Journal,* 1 (1), 77-90.

Brody, A. F. (1991) Understanding client-centered therapy through interviews conducted by Carl Rogers. *Clinical Research Paper in partial fulfilment of requirements for the Doctor of Psychology Degree in Clinical Psychology, Illinois School of Professional Psychology.*

Cain, D. J. (1989) The client's role in diagnosis: Three approaches. *Person-Centered Review,* 4 (2), 171-182.

Cain, D. J. (1993) The uncertain future of client-centered counseling. *Journal of Humanistic Education and Development,* 331, 133-139.

Caple, R. B. (1985) Counseling and the self-organization paradigm. *Journal of Counseling and Development,* 64, 173-178.

Capra, F. (1975) *The Tao of Physics.* Boulder: Shambala.

Capra, F. (1982) *The Turning Point.* New York: Simon and Schuster.

Carkhuff, R. R. (1969) *Helping and Human Relations, Vol 1.* New York: Holt, Rinehart and Winston.

Carkhuff, R. R. (1971) *The Development of Human Resources.* New York: Holt, Rinehart and Winston.

Cartwright, D. S. (1957) Annotated bibliography of research and theory construction in client-centered therapy. *Journal of Counseling Psychology,* 4, 82-100.

Chordroff, B. (1954) Self perception, perceptual defense and adjustment, *Journal of Abnormal Psychology,* 49, 508.

Combs, A. (1947) Non-directive techniques and vocational counseling. *Occupations,* 25, 261-267.

Consumer Reports (1995, November) *Mental health: does therapy help?* pp. 734-739.

Corey, G. (1982) *Theory and Practice of Counseling and Psychotherapy (2nd ed.)* Monterey: Brooks/Cole.

Cormier, W. H. and Cormier, A. (1991) *Interviewing Strategies for Helpers*. Belmont, CA.: Brooks/Cole Publishing Co.

Coulson, W. R. (1970) Rejoinder. *The Counseling Psychologist*, 2 (2), 56-60.

Coulson, W. R. (1987) *The Californication of Carl Rogers*. Fidelity. pp. 20-31.

Covner, B. J. (1947) Non-directive interviewing techniques in vocational counseling. *Journal of Consulting Psychology*, 11, 70-73.

Crites, J. O. (1974) Career counseling: a review of major approaches. *The Counseling Psychologist*, 4 (3), 3-23.

Crites, J. O. (1981) Career Counseling Models, Methods and Materials. New York; McGraw Hill.

Dawes, R. M. (1994) *House of Cards: Psychology and psychotherapy built upon myth*. New York: The Free Press.

Devonshire, C. (1991) The person-centered approach and cross-cultural communication. In E. McIlduff and D. Coghlan (eds) *The person-centered approach and cross-cultural communication: an international review*. Dublin, Ireland: Center for Cross-Cultural Communication. pp. 15-44.

Dossey, L. (1994) *Healing Words*. San Francisco: Harper and Row.

Duncan, B. L., Hubble, and Miller (1997) *Psychotherapy with 'Impossible' Cases: the effective treatment of therapy veterans*. New York: W. W. Norton and Company.

Duncan, B. L., and Moynihan, D. W. (1994) Applying outcome research: intentional utilization of the clients frame of reference. *Psychotherapy*, 31, 294-301.

Duncan, B., Solovey, A., and Rusk, G. (1992) *Changing the Rules: a client-directed approach to therapy*. New York: Guilford.

Duckworth, J. (1990) The counseling approach to the use of testing. *The Counseling Psychologist*, 18 (2), 198-204.

Egan, G., (1975) *The Skilled Helper: a model for systematic helping and interpersonal relating*. Belmont, CA: Wadsworth.

Eisenthal, S., Emery, R., Lazare, A. and Udin, H. (1979) 'Adherence' and the negotiated approach to patienthood. *Archives of General Psychiatry*, 36, 393-398.

Ellis, J. and Zimring, F. (1994) Two therapists and a client. *The Person-Centered Journal*, 1 (2), 79-92

Evans, R. I. (1975) *Carl Rogers: the man and his ideas*. New York: Dover Publications.

Fay, A. and Lazarus, A. A. (1992, August) On Necessity and Sufficiency in Psychotherapy. *Paper presented at the 100th annual convention of the American Psychological Association, Washington, D.C.*

Fischer, C. T. (1989) The life-centered approach to psychodiagnostics: attending to lifeworld, ambiguity, and possibility. *Person-Centered Review*, 4 (2), 163-170.

Ford, G. (1994) Extending Rogers' thoughts on human destructiveness. *The Person-Centered Journal*, 1 (3), 52-63.

Frank, A. F., and Gunderson, J. G. (1990) The role of the therapeutic alliance in the treatment of schizophrenia. *Archives of General Psychiatry*, 47, 228-236.

Frankel, M. (1988, May) The category error and the confounding of the therapeutic relationship. *Paper presented at the Second Annual Meeting of the Association for the development of the person-centered approach, New York City*.

Gazda, G.M. and Bozarth, J. D.(1984) Personality change: personality change groups. In R. K. Conyne (ed) *The group workers handbook: varieties of group experience*. Boston: Marger.

Gelso, C. J., and Carter, J. A. (1985) The relationship in counseling and psychotherapy: components, consequences, and theoretical antecedents. *The Counseling Psychologist*, 13, 155-433.

Gendlin, E. T. (1970) A short summary and some long predictions. In J. I. Hart and T. M.

Tomlinson (eds), *New Directions in Client-Centered Therapy*. Boston: Houghton Mifflin. pp 554-562.

Gendlin, E. T. (1974) Client centered and experiential psychotherapy. In D. Wexler, and L. Rice (eds) *Innovations in Client-Centered Therapy*. New York: John Wiley and Sons.

Gendlin, E. T. (1981) *Taped Interview, La Jolla Program*.

Gendlin, E. T. (1990) The small steps of the therapy process. How they come and how to help them come. In G. Lietaer, J. Rombauts and R. Van Balen (eds) *Client-Centered and experiential psychotherapy in the nineties*. Leuven: Leuven University Press. pp. 205-224.

Goodyear, R. K. (1987) In memory of Carl Ransom Rogers (January 8, 1902 – February 4, 1987). *Journal of Counseling and Development*, 63, 561-564.

Gordon, T. (1970) *T.E.T.: Teacher effectiveness training*. New York: New American Library.

Gordon, T. (1976) *T.E.T in Action*. New York: Wyden.

Gordon, T. (1985) *Group-Centered Leadership*. Boston: Houghton Mifflin.

Gothard, W. P. (1985) *Vocational guidance: theory and practice*. London: Croom Helm.

Grayham, J. R. and Lily, R. S. (1985) *Psychological Testing*. Englewood Cliffs, NJ: Prentice Hall.

Grant, B. (1990) Principled and instrumental nondirectiveness in person-centered and client-centered therapy. *Person-Centered Review*, 5 (3) 77-88.

Greyson, B. (1996) Distance healing of patients with major depression. *Journal of Scientific Exploration*, 10 (4), pp. 10-18.

Grummon, D. L. (1972) Client-Centered Theory. In B. Steffler and W. H. Grant (eds) *Theories of Counseling* (12th Edition) New York: McGraw Hill. pp. 73-135.

Gurman, A. S. (1978) The patient's perception of the therapeutic relationship. In A. S. Gurman and A. M. Razin (eds) *Effective Psychotherapy: a handbook of research*. New York: Pergamon pp. 503-543.

Haugh, S. (1998) Congruence: a Confusion of Language. *Person-Centred Practice* 6, (1), 44-50.

Heppner, P. P., Rogers, M. E., and Lee, L. A. (1984) Carl Rogers: Reflections on his life. *Journal of Counseling and Development*, 63, 14-63.

Holdstock, T.L. (1990) Can Client-Centered Therapy transcend its monocultural roots? In G.Lietaer, J. Rombauts and R. Van Balen (eds) *Client-Centered and Experiential Therapies in the Nineties*. Leuven: Leuven University Press. pp. 109-121.

Horney, K. (1956) The search for glory. In C. E. Moustakas (ed) *The Self*. New York: Harper and Row. pp. 39-51.

Kass, J. (1998, May) Research results from converging studies. *Paper presentation at the Twelfth Meeting of the Association for the Development of the Person-Centered Approach, Wheaton, Massachusetts*.

Kirschenbaum, H. (1979) *On Becoming Carl Rogers*. New York: Dell.

Kirschenbaum, H. and Henderson, V. (eds) (1989a) *The Carl Rogers Reader*. Boston: Houghton Mifflin Company.

Kirschenbaum, H. and Henderson, V. (eds) (1989b) *The Carl Rogers Dialogues*. Boston: Houghton Mifflin Company.

Kisch, J. (1980) Meaningfulness versus effectiveness: paradoxical implications in the evaluation of psychotherapy. *Psychotherapy: Theory, Research and Practice*, 17, 401-413.

Kohut, H. (1959) Introspection, empathy, and psychoanalysis. *Journal of the American Psychoanalytic Association*, 7, 459-483.

Krippner, S. (1984) *Advances in Parapsychological Research*. London: McFarland and Company.

Krumboltz, J. E. (1967) Changing the behavior of behavior changers. *Counselor Education and Supervision*, Spring, Special Publication, 222-227.

Lambert, M. (1992) Psychotherapy outcome research. In Norcross, J. C. and Goldfried, M. R.(eds.) *Handbook of Psychotherapy Integration*. New York: Basic Books. pp. 94-129.

Lambert, M. J., Shapiro, D. A., and Bergin, A. E. (1986) The effectiveness of psychotherapy. In S. L. Garfield and A. E. Bergin (eds) *Handbook of Psychotherapy and Behavior Change*. New York: John Wiley and Sons. pp. 157-212.

Lazarus, A. A. (1993) Tailoring the therapeutic relationship or being an authentic chameleon. *Psychotherapy*, 30 (3), 404-407.

Lazarus, A. A. and Lazarus, C. N. (1991) Let us not forsake the individual nor ignore the data: A response to Bozarth. *Journal of Counseling and Development*, 69, 463-465.

Leedy, P. D. (1993) *Practical research: planning and design* (Fifth Edition). New York: Macmillan.

Levant, R. (1984) From person to system: two perspectives. In R. Levant and J. Shlien (eds) *Client-centered Therapy and the Person-Centered Approach: New Directions in Theory; Research and Practice*. New York: Praeger. pp. 243-260.

Lietaer, G. (1984). Unconditional positive regard: a controversial basic attitude in Client-Centered Therapy. In R. Levant and J. Shlien (eds) *Client-centered Therapy and the Person-Centered Approach: New directions in theory; research, and practice*. New York: Praeger. pp. 41-58.

Lietaer, G. (1993). Authenticity, congruence and authenticity. In D. Brazier (ed) *Beyond Carl Rogers*. London: Constable. pp. 17-46.

*The Living Bible* (1971) Ecclesiastes 4. Wheaton, IL: Coverdale House.

Luborsky, L., Crits-Christoph, P., Mintz, J. and Auerbach, A. (1988) *Who will Benefit from Psychotherapy? Predicting Therapeutic Outcomes*. New York: Basic Books.

Martin, D. (1983) *Counseling and Therapy Skills*. Monterey, CA: Brooks/Cole.

Martin, J. (1990) Individuals in client reactions to counseling and psychotherapy: a challenge for research. *Counseling Psychology Quarterly*, 3, 67-83.

Maslow, A. H. (1970) *Motivation and Personality*. (2nd ed.). New York: Harper and Row.

Mearns, D. and Thorne, B. (1988) *Person-Centred Counselling in Action*. London: Sage.

Mearns, D. (1994) *Developing Person-Centred Counselling*. London: Sage..

Merry, T. (1995) *Invitation to Person-Centred Psychology*. London: Whurr.

Merry, T. (1996) An analysis of ten demonstration interviews by Carl Rogers: implications for the training of client-centred counselors. In R. Hutterer, G. Pawlowsky, P. F. Schmid and R. Stipsits (eds) *Client-centered and experiential psychotherapy: a paradigm in motion*. New York: Peter Lang. pp. 273-283.

Mindell, A. (1992) *The Leader as Martial Artist: An Introduction to Deep Democracy*. San Francisco: Harper.

Mitchell, K., Bozarth, J. D. and Krauft, C. C. (1977) A reappraisal of the therapeutic effectiveness of accurate empathy, non-possessive warmth, and genuineness, In A. S. Gurman and A. M. Razin (eds) *Effective Psychotherapy: A Handbook of Research*. New York: Pergamon Press pp. 482-502.

Monroe, R. (1985) *Far Journeys*. New York: Doubleday Dell Publishing Group.

Moorhouse, D. (1996) *Psychic Warrior: Inside the CIA's Stargate Program*. New York: St. Martins Press.

Neville, B. (1996) Five kinds of empathy. In R. Hutterer, G. Pawlowsky, P. F. Schmid and R. Stipsits (eds) *Client-Centered and Experiential Psychotherapy: A Paradigm in Motion*. New York: Peter Lang. pp. 437-453.

Norcross, J. C. (1992, August) Are There Necessary and Sufficient Conditions for Therapeutic Change? *Paper presented at the 100th annual meeting of the American*

*Psychological Association, Washington, D.C.*

O'Hara, M. (1995, May/June) Why is this man laughing? *AHP Perspective,* 19, 30-31.

O'Hara, M. (1997) Relational empathy: beyond modernistic egocentrism to post-modern holistic contextualism. In A. C. Bohart and L. S. Greenburg (eds) *Empathy Reconsidered: new directions in psychotherapy.* Washington DC: American Psychological Association. pp. 295-319.

Orlinsky, D. E. and Howard, K. J. (1987) Process and outcome in psychotherapy. In S. L. Garfield and A. E. Bergin (eds) *Handbook of Psychotherapy and Behavioral Change: An Empirical Analysis.* New York: John Wiley and Sons. pp. 311-381.

Parloff, M. B., Waskow, I.E., and Wolfe, B. E., (1978) Research on therapist variables in relation to process and outcome. In S. L.Garfield and A. E. Bergin (eds) *Handbook of Psychotherapy and Behavior Change: An Empirical Analysis* (2nd ed.). New York: John Wiley and Sons pp. 233-282.

Patterson, C. H. (1964) Counselling and diagnosis. *Journal of Counseling Psychology,* 20, 17-31.

Patterson, C. H. (1969) Necessary and sufficient conditions for psychotherapy. *The Counseling Psychologist,* 1, 2, 8-26.

Patterson, C. H. (1984) Empathy, warmth, and genuineness in psychotherapy: a review of reviews. *Psychotherapy,* 21, (4), 431-438.

Patterson, C. H. (1985) *The Therapeutic Relationship: Foundations for an Eclectic Psychotherapy.* Monterey, CA: Brooks/Cole.

Patterson, C. H. (1986) *Theories of Counseling and Psychotherapy,* New York: Harper and Row.

Plas, J. M. (1996) *Person-Centered Leadership: An American Approach to Participatory Management.* London: Sage.

Prouty, G. (1994) *Theoretical Evolutions in Person-Centered/Experiential Therapy: applications to schizophrenic and retarded psychoses.* Westport, Conn.: Praeger.

Quinn, R. (1993) Confronting Carl Rogers: a developmental-interactional approach to person-centered therapy. *Journal of Humanistic Psychology,* 33 (1), 6-23.

Raskin, N. (1948) The development of nondirective therapy. *Journal of Consulting Psychology,* 12 (94), 92-110.

Raskin, N. (1988, May) What do we mean by person-centered therapy? *Paper presented at the meeting of the Second Association for the Development of the Person-Centered Approach, New York.*

Raskin, N. J. and Rogers, C. R. (1989) Person-centered therapy. In R. J. Corsini and D. Wedding (eds) *Current Psychotherapies.* Itasca: F. E. Peacock. pp. 155-194.

Rice, L. N., and Greenberg, L. S. (1990) Fundamental dimensions in experiential therapy: New directions in research. In G. Lietaer, J. Rombasuts and R. Van Balen (eds) *Client-Centered and Experiential Therapies in the Nineties.* Leuven: Leuven University Press. pp. 397-414.

Rogers, C. R. (1931) Measuring personality adjustment in children nine to thirteen years of age. *New York Teachers College.*

Rogers, C. R. (1939) *The Clinical Treatment of the Problem Child.* Boston: Houghton-Mifflin.

Rogers, C. R. (1940) The process of therapy. *Journal of Consulting Psychology,* 4, (5), 161-164.

Rogers, C. R. (1941) How is psychology used in clinical practice? In J. Gray (ed), *Psychology in Use.* New York: American Books. pp. 415-422.

Rogers, C. R. (1942) *Counseling and Psychotherapy.* Boston: Houghton-Mifflin.

Rogers, C. R. (1951) *Client-centered therapy.* Boston: Houghton-Mifflin.

Rogers, C. R. (1954) The case of Mrs. Oak. In C. R. Rogers and R. F. Dymond (eds)

*Psychotherapy and Personality Change*. Chicago: University of Chicago Press.

Rogers, C. R. (1956) *Client-Centered Therapy* (Third edition). Boston: Houghton-Mifflin.

Rogers, C. R. (1957) The necessary and sufficient conditions of therapeutic personality change. *Journal of Consulting Psychology*, 21, 95-103.

Rogers, C. R. (1959) A theory of therapy, personality, and interpersonal relationships as developed in the client-centered framework. In S. Koch (ed) *Psychology: A study of science: Vol. 3 Formulation of the person and the social context*. New York: McGraw Hill. pp. 184-256.

Rogers, C. R. (1961) A therapist's view of the good life: the fully functioning person. In C. R. Rogers, *On Becoming a Person*. Boston: Houghton Mifflin. pp. 183-196.

Rogers, C. R. (1963) The actualizing tendency in relation to 'motives' and to consciousness. In M. Jones (ed) *Nebraska Symposium on Motivation*. Lincoln: University of Nebraska Press.

Rogers, C. R. (1965) *Three approaches to psychotherapy I (Film)*. Psychological Films.

Rogers, C. R. (1970) *Carl Rogers on Encounter Groups*. New York: Harper and Row.

Rogers, C. R. (1975) Empathic: an unappreciated way of being. *The Counseling Psychologist*, 5, (2), 2-10.

Rogers, C. R. (1977) *Carl Rogers on Personal Power: Inner Strength and its Revolutionary Impact*. New York: Delacorte.

Rogers, C. R. (1980) *A Way of Being*. Boston: Houghton Mifflin.

Rogers, C. R. (1982) Reply to Rollo May's letter. *Journal of Humanistic Psychology*, 22, 85-89.

Rogers, C. R. (1986a) Rogers, Kohut, and Erickson. *Person-Centered Review*, 1(2), 125-140.

Rogers, C. R. (1986b) A client-centered/person-centered approach to therapy. In I. Kutash and A. Wolfe (eds) *Psychotherapists' Casebook*. Jossey-Bass. pp. 197-208.

Rogers, C. R. (1986c) Reflection of feelings. Person-Centered Review, 1, (2), 125-140

Rogers, C. R. (1987) Client-centered/person-centered? *Person-Centered Review*, 2, (1), 11-13.

Rogers, C. R. (1989a) Rollo May. In H. Kirschenbaum and V. Henderson (eds) *Carl Rogers: Dialogues*. Boston: Houghton-Mifflin. pp. 229-255.

Rogers, C. R. (1989b) A theory of therapy, personality, and interpersonal relationships, as developed in the Client-Centered Framework. In H. Kirschenbaum and V. Henderson (eds) *The Carl Rogers Reader*. Boston: Houghton-Mifflin. pp. 236-257.

Rogers, C. R. and Dymond, R. F. (eds) (1954) *Psychotherapy and Personality Change*. Chicago: University of Chicago Press.

Rogers, C. R., Gendlin, E. T., Kiesler, D. V., and Truax, C. B. (1967) *The Therapeutic Relationship and Its Impact: A Study of Psychotherapy with Schizophrenics*. Madison: University of Wisconsin Press.

Rogers, C. R., and Ryback, D. (1984). One alternative to nuclear planetary suicide. In R. F. Levant and J. M. Shlien (eds) *Client-Centered Therapy and the Person-Centered Approach: New Directions in Theory, Research, and Practice*. New York: Praeger. pp. 400-422

Rogers, C. R. and Sanford, R. (1984) Client-centered psychotherapy. In H. Kaplan and B. J. Sadock (eds) *Comprehensive Textbook of Psychiatry IV*. Baltimore: Williams and Wilkins. pp. 1374-1388.

Rogers, C. R. and Segal, R. H. (1955) *Psychotherapy in process: The Case of Miss Mun*. Pennsylvania State University Psychological Cinema Register.

Rogers, C. R. and Wallen, J. L. (1946) *Counseling With Returned Servicemen*. New York: McGraw Hill.

Rusalem, H. (1954) New insights on the role of occupational information in counseling.

*Journal of Counseling Psychology*, 1, 84-88.

Saltzman, C., Luetgert, M. J., Roth, C. H., Creaser, J. and Howard, L. (1976) Formation of a therapeutic relationship: experiences during the initial phase of psychotherapy's predictors of treatment duration and outcome. *Journal of Consulting and Clinical Psychology*, 44, 546-555.

Samler, J. (1964) Occupational exploration in counseling: a proposed reorientation. In H. Borow (ed) *Man in a World of Work*. Boston: Houghton Mifflin. pp. 411-433.

Schaff, A. W. (1992) *Beyond Therapy, Beyond Science*. San Francisco: Harper Collins Publishers.

Seeman, J. (1948) A study of client self-selection of tests in vocational counseling. *Educational and Psychological Measurement*. 8, 327-346.

Seeman, J. (1989) A reaction to 'Psychodiagnosis: a person-centered perspective'. *Person-Centered Review*, 4 (2), 152-156.

Seeman, J. and Raskin, N. J. (1953) Research perspectives in client centered therapy. In O. H. Mowrer (ed) *Psychotherapy: Therapy and Research*. New York: Ronald Press.

Seligman, M. E. P. (1995) The effectiveness of psychotherapy: The Consumer Reports Study. *American Psychologist*, 50, 963-964.

Sexton, T. L. and Whiston, S. C. (1994) The status of the counseling relationship: An empirical review, theoretical implications, and research directions. *The Counseling Psychologist*, 22 (1), 6-78.

Shlien, J. M. (1971) A client-centered approach to schizophrenia: first approximation. In C. R. Rogers and B. Stevens (eds) *Person to Person*. New York: Pocket Books. pp. 149-165.

Shlien, J. M. (1989) Boy's person-centered perspective on psychodiagnosis. *Person-Centered Review*, 4 (2), 157-162.

Shlien, J. M.(1990) *Personal communication*.

Shlien, J. M. (1998) Update on Gloria. *Paper presentation at the Twelfth Annual Association for the Person-Centered Approach meeting*, Wheaton, Massachusetts.

Shlien, J. M., Mosak, H. H., and Dreikhurs, R. (1962) Effect of time limits: a comparison of Client-Centered and Adlerian Psychology. *Journal of Counseling Psychology*, 9 (318), 15-22.

Shlien, J. M. and Zimring, F. M. (1970) Research directives and methods in client-centered therapy. In J. Hart and T. M. Tomlinson (eds) *New Directions in Client-Centered Therapy*. Boston: Houghton Mifflin.

Shostrom, E.L. (Producer) (1964) *Three approaches to psychotherapy*. Santa Ana, CA: Psychological films. (Film).

Silverman, W. H. (1997) Cookbooks, manuals, and paint-by the-numbers: Psychotherapy in the 90s. *Psychotherapy*. 33 (2), 207-214.

Smith, D.(1982) Trends in counseling and psychotherapy. *American Psychologist*, 13, 169-175.

Soloman, L. N. (1990) Carl Rogers' efforts for world peace. *Person-Centered Review*, 5 (1), 39-56.

Spahn, D. (1992) Observations on Healing and Person-Centered Therapy. *The Person-Centered Journal*, 1 (1), 33-37.

Strupp, H. H., Fox, R. E., and Lessler, K. (1969) *Patients View their Psychotherapy*. Baltimore: The Johns Hopkins Press.

Stubbs, J. P. (1992) Individual experiencing in person-centered community workshops: a cross-cultural study. *Unpublished doctoral dissertation, University of Georgia*.

Stubbs, J. P. and Bozarth, J. D. (1994) The dodo bird revisited: a qualitative study of psychotherapy efficacy research. *Journal of Applied and Preventive Psychology,* 3 ( 2), 109-120.

Stubbs, J. P. and Bozarth, J. D. (1996) The integrative statement of Carl Rogers. In R. Hutterer, G. Pawlowsky, P. Schmid and R. Stipsits (eds) *Client-centered and Experiential Psychotherapy: a Paradigm in Motion.* New York: Peter Lang. pp. 25-33.

Super, D. (1949) *Appraising Vocational Fitness by Means of Psychological Tests.* New York: Harper and Row.

Super, D. (1950) Testing and using test results in counseling. *Occupations.* 29, 95-97.

Super, D. (1951) Vocational adjustment: implementing a self concept. *Occupations*, 30, 8 8-92.

Super, D. (1957) The preliminary appraisal in vocational counseling. *The Personnel and Guidance Journal*, 36, 154-161.

Tausch, R. (1978) Facilitative dimensions in interpersonal relations: verifying the theoretical assumptions of Carl Rogers in school, family, education, client-centered therapy, and encounter groups. *College Student Journal,* 12, 2-11.

Tausch, R. (1982) Megavitamins. In R. Ballentine (ed) *Diet and Nutrition.* Honesdale, PA: Himalayan International. pp. 509-525.

Tausch, R. (1987a) Reappraisal and changing of emotions towards death and dying through imagination and person-centered group communication. *Unpublished paper.*

Tausch, R. (1987b) The connection of emotions with cognition-consequences for theoretical classification of person-centered psychotherapists. *Unpublished paper.*

Tausch, R. (1990) The supplementation of client-centered communication therapy with other valid therapeutic methods. In G. Lietaer and R. Van Balen (eds) *Client-Centered and Experiential Psychotherapy: Towards the Nineties.* Leuven: Katholieke Universiteit te Leuven. pp. 65-85.

Temaner, B. and Bozarth, J. (1984) Client-centered-person-centered psychotherapy: a statement of understanding. *Paper presented to the meeting of the Second International Forum on the Person-Centered Approach, Norwich, England.*

Thorne, B.(1991) *Person-Centred Counselling: Therapeutic and Spiritual Dimensions.* London: Whurr.

Teich, N. (1992) *Rogerian Perspectives: Collaborative Rhetoric for Oral and Written Communication.* Norwood, NJ: Ablex Publishing Corporation.

Tracey, T. J. (1977) Impact of intake procedures upon client attrition in a community mental health center. *Journal of Consulting and Clinical Psychologist,* 45. 192-195.

Truax, C. B. and Carkhuff, R. R. (1967) *Toward Effective Counseling and Psychotherapy: Training and Practice.* Chicago: Aldine.

Truax, C. B. (1969) *Personal communication.*

Truax, C. B. and Mitchell, K. M. (1971) Research on certain interpersonal skills in relation to process and outcome. In A. E. Bergin and S. L. Garfield (eds) *Handbook of Psychotherapy and Behavior Change.* New York: Wiley. pp. 299-344.

Van Balen, R. (1990) The therapeutic relationship according to Carl Rogers: Only a climate? A dialogue? or both? In G. Lietaer, J. Rombauts. and R. Van Balen (eds) *Client-Centered and Experiential Psychotherapy: Toward the Nineties.* Leuven: Katholieke Universiteit te Leuven. pp. 65-86.

Van Belle, H. A. (1980) *Basic Intent and Therapeutic Approach of Carl R. Rogers.* Amcaster, Ontario, Canada: Wedge Publishing.

Van Praagh, J. (1997) *Talking to Heaven: A Medium's Message of Life After Death.* New York: Dutton

Walsh, W. B. (1990) Putting assessment in context. *The Counseling Psychologist.* 18 (2), 262-265.

Watson, N. (1984) The empirical status of Rogers' hypothesis of the necessary and sufficient conditions of effective therapy. In R. Levant and J. Shlien (eds) *Client-*

*Centered Therapy and the Person-Centered Approach: New Directions in Therapy, Research and Practice*. New York: Praeger pp. 17-40.

Webster (1991) *Ninth New Collegiate Dictionary*. London: Collins.

Wexler, W. A.(1974) A cognitive theory of experiencing, self-actualization, and therapeutic process. In D. Wexler and L. Rice (eds) *Innovations in Client-Centered Therapy*. New York: John Wiley and Sons pp. 66-78.

Whitaker, C. A. and Malone, T. P. (1981) *The Roots of Psychotherapy*. New York: Brunner/ Mazel.

Wood, J. K. (1980) *Personal communication*, October 12, 1980.

Wood, J. K. (1982) Person-centered group therapy. In G. Gazda (ed) *Basic Approaches to Group Psychotherapy and Group Counseling*. Springfield, Ill: Charles E. Thomas pp. 93-106.

Wood, J. K. (1983) Communities for learning: a person-centered approach. *Paper presented at the First International Forum on the person-centered approach*, Quaxetec, Mexico.

Wyatt, G. (1998) The multifaceted nature of congruence within the therapeutic relationship. *Paper presented to the 12th International Forum in the Person-Centered Approach*, Johannesburg, South Africa.

Zimring, F. N. (1974) Theory and practice of client-centered therapy: a cognitive view. In D. Wexler and L. Rice (eds) *Innovations in Client-Centered Therapy*. New York: John Wiley and Sons.

# INDEX OF NAMES

# MAIN SUBJECT INDEX

# Also in this series

Person-Centred Approach
& Client-Centred Therapy
**Essential Readers**
Series editor Tony Merry

## Experiences in Relatedness: *Groupwork and the Person-Centred Approach*

edited by **Colin Lago** and **Mhairi MacMillan**
ISBN 1 898059 23 3   156 x 234   pp.182 + iv   £15.00

Edited by two of the UK's principal practitioners of the Person-Centred Approach, this book is an international collection of specially commissioned papers. Contributors include Ruth Sanford, Peggy Natiello (USA); John K. Wood (Brazil); Peter Figge (Germany); Irene Fairhurst, Tony Merry, John Barkham, Alan Coulson and Jane Hoffman (UK). This is the first substantial book within the person-centred tradition on group work since Carl Rogers' *Encounter Groups*. Topics include: the history of the development of small and large group work within the PCA; theoretical principles of person-centred groupwork; research and applications of PCA groupwork, working with issues of sexuality and sexism; the use of the group in training; and large groups and workshops in the PCA.

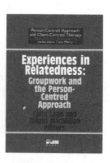

## Women Writing in the Person-Centred Approach

edited by **Irene Fairhurst**
ISBN 1 898059 26 8   156 x 234   pp. approx 200   £15.00

In *Women Writing in the Person-Centred Approach*, Irene Fairhurst has compiled an international anthology of person-centred writings by women. Contributors include Maria Villas-Boas Bowen, (Brazil); Barbara Temaner Brodley, Jo Cohen Hamilton, Peggy Natiello, Maureen O'Hara, Ruth Sanford, Suzanne Spector, Margaret Warner, Carol Wolter-Gustafson, (USA); Jane Bingham, Rose Cameron, Meg Hill, Mary Kilborn, Mhairi MacMillan, Anne Newell, Lesley Rose, Sarah Ingle, Sue Wilders, (UK). Irene Fairhurst writes:

'. . . in the field of counselling and psychotherapy, on person-centred training courses, women outnumber men by between seven and nine to one, yet in our literature the opposite is the case. In the volume *Client Centered and Experiential Psychotherapy in the Nineties* — the book of papers presented at the first conference on Client-Centred and Experiential Psychotherapy in 1988 — of the 52 authors of papers, 7 are women.'

*Women Writing in the Person-Centred Approach* both redresses that balance and presents the reader with a uniquely themed collection of work in the person-centred tradition. Irene continues:

'There is no thought that this book is representative of a stereotyped genre — it is not written specifically *for*women or *about*women. It is . . . a forum for women with something to say, to meet together and, for some, to find our voice.'

**Irene Fairhurst** is co-founder and past President of the British Association for the Person-Centred Approach. Her further involvement in the person-centred approach includes founding the Institute for Person-Centred Learning and working with Carl Rogers in Europe and the UK.